'Kim's knowledge and experience is evi<u></u>
assists us, parents of traumatised chil<u></u>
experiences and the implications of this <u></u>
how they live in it.

Kim offers us realistic and pragmatic <u></u>
children that are ground in the reality of our daily lives and our
children's worldview. She also reminds us of the impact on us as
parents and asks us to reflect and care for ourselves.

Highly recommended, an essential read for parents of children
who have experienced trauma, loss and separation.'

— Al Coates, adoptive parent, social worker, blogger at
Misadventures of an Adoptive Dad *and podcaster*

'Kim Golding has succeeded in encapsulating a whole range of issues
and challenges faced by those looking after children who have suffered
developmental trauma. Her book has excellent, clear descriptions
and diagrams explaining why our children feel and behave the way
they do, and what we, as therapeutic parents can do about it. The
use of practical examples and case studies enables therapeutic parents
to apply the P.A.C.E model effectively. A must-have addition for all
therapeutic parents' bookshelves!'

— Sarah Naish, adoptive parent, CEO National Association of Therapeutic
Parents and author of the Therapeutic Parenting *children's series*

by the same author

Foundations for Attachment Training Resource
The Six-Session Programme for Parents of Traumatized Children
Kim S. Golding
ISBN 978 1 78592 118 6
eISBN 978 1 78450 600 1

Creating Loving Attachments
Parenting with PACE to Nurture Confidence and Security in the Troubled Child
Kim S. Golding and Daniel A. Hughes
ISBN 978 1 84905 227 6
eISBN 978 0 85700 470 3

Nurturing Attachments
Supporting Children who are Fostered or Adopted
Kim S. Golding
ISBN 978 1 84310 614 2
eISBN 978 1 84642 750 3

Nurturing Attachments Training Resource
Running Parenting Groups for Adoptive Parents and Foster or Kinship Carers
Kim S. Golding
ISBN 978 1 84905 328 0

Observing Children with Attachment Difficulties in Preschool Settings
A Tool for Identifying and Supporting Emotional and Social Difficulties
Kim S. Golding, Jane Fain, Ann Frost, Sian Templeton and Eleanor Durrant
ISBN 978 1 84905 337 2
eISBN 978 0 85700 676 9

Observing Children with Attachment Difficulties in School
A Tool for Identifying and Supporting Emotional and
Social Difficulties in Children Aged 5–11
Kim S. Golding, Jane Fain, Ann Frost, Cathy Mills, Helen Worrall,
Netty Roberts, Eleanor Durrant and Sian Templeton
ISBN 978 1 84905 336 5
eISBN 978 0 85700 675 2

Using Stories to Build Bridges with Traumatized Children
Creative Ideas for Therapy, Life Story Work, Direct Work and Parenting
Kim S. Golding
ISBN 978 1 84905 540 6
eISBN 978 0 85700 961 6

Observing Adolescents with Attachment Difficulties in Educational Settings
A Tool for Identifying and Supporting Emotional and
Social Difficulties in Young People Aged 11–16
Kim S. Golding, Mary T. Turner, Helen Worrall, Jennifer Roberts and Ann E. Cadman
ISBN 978 1 84905 617 5
eISBN 978 1 78450 174 7

EVERYDAY PARENTING WITH SECURITY AND LOVE

Using PACE to Provide Foundations for Attachment

KIM S. GOLDING

Illustrated by ALEX BARRETT
Foreword by DAN HUGHES

Jessica Kingsley *Publishers*
London and Philadelphia

First published in 2017
by Jessica Kingsley Publishers
73 Collier Street
London N1 9BE, UK
and
400 Market Street, Suite 400
Philadelphia, PA 19106, USA

www.jkp.com

Library of Congress Cataloging in Publication Data
A CIP catalog record for this book is available from the Library of Congress

British Library Cataloguing in Publication Data
A CIP catalogue record for this book is available from the British Library

ISBN 978 1 78592 115 5
eISBN 978 1 78450 384 0

Printed and bound in the United States

This book is dedicated to the many parents, children and young people with whom I have worked and who have taught me so much about the impact of developmental trauma and the challenges this presents to both parents and young people. Thank you for sharing your stories, which have humanized my understanding and inspired the fictional stories presented in this book.

CONTENTS

PART 3. LOOKING AFTER SELF

FOREWORD

Dan Hughes

As we come to understand the complex process of human development, it is increasingly clear that for optimal development children need to forge strong relationships with their caregivers, and from there, meaningful and important relationships with other members of the family, as well as friends, teachers, mentors and many others over the course of their lifetime. Along with this understanding has come the awareness that for children to develop such relationships they need to have experiences that go beyond being given instructions, reinforcements and role models. They need to have experiences that are characteristic of a good relationship. Too often we stress that the child needs a relationship with their caregivers, teachers and counsellors without attending enough to what exactly defines those relationships as well as how to attain these qualities. In this important book, Dr Kim Golding provides us with the guidance needed to understand and develop relationships with children and youth who desperately need them in order to have success and joy in their lives.

Some of our best insights into what is a good parent–child relationship come from relationships that are characterized by trauma and deprivation. Children who have experienced abuse and neglect from their primary caregivers manifest pervasive problems, placing them at risk in all areas of their neurobiological, psychological, emotional, cognitive and social development. We have increasingly realized that their developmental problems are more to do with the failures and violations of trust in their relationships with those who are meant to provide them with good care than with the specific acts of abuse. When children experience relationships that are designed to provide safety but instead provide terror and shame, these children do not learn how to relate with others in ways that are necessary for their development. Their future ability to engage in healthy relationships is compromised, often in profound ways.

Dr Golding has provided us with a comprehensive understanding of parent–child relationships, how they develop and how they are repaired and maintained. She integrates the latest theories and research, ranging from the neurobiology of attachment and caregiving and psychological studies of attachment, to more general literature regarding emotional, social and cognitive development. While she focuses on providing healing and restorative relationships for children who have been violated in their early relationships with their caregivers, her principles and interventions are certain to be of value for all parents in their relationships with their children.

What characterizes such important relationships in the lives of children? Safety for a start, which is quickly joined in importance with reciprocal engagement between parent and child and the world, through joint interests and intentions. Children need to learn to regulate their strong, complex and often conflicting emotional states. Such learning is attained through parents co-regulating these states within their attuned relationships with their children. Children need to learn to make sense of their inner lives – their thoughts, feelings, perceptions, memories and wishes – as well as the inner lives of their parents. Such learning is attained through parents joining with them in this mental process of reflecting on and communicating about the meaning of what is happening within and between each of them. Children need to learn to be fully engaged in the present moment, while still being aware of the paths and goals that lead into the future. When walking in relationships with their parents, children are much less likely to lose their way.

I hope that this foreword provides a hint of what lies ahead in this book. It might be best to approach the book by trying to understand the experience of the child and of the parent raising their child, rather than focusing on learning specific interventions – though excellent ones are certainly provided. Joining Dr Golding in this journey of understanding and caring for children is likely to be the best way to learn how to successfully engage the children and their parents who we are trying to assist.

Dan Hughes, PhD

ACKNOWLEDGEMENTS

In writing this book I have drawn on many theories, ideas and models developed by a range of researchers and clinicians. I have tried to acknowledge these without making the book appear unduly academic. Apologies if you do not feel I have honoured your work fully.

I would like to give special thanks to Jon Baylin, Sandra Bloom, Mary Dozier, Peter Fonagy, Stephen Porges, Allan Schore, Dan Siegel, Colwyn Trevarthen and Ed Tronick whose writing and conference presentations I have drawn on so freely. Their work has made mine infinitely stronger. We must also not forget John Bowlby, Mary Ainsworth, Mary Main and colleagues who have provided us with such a rich understanding of attachment and its development in adversity.

This book is based on the Dyadic Developmental Psychotherapy and Practice (DDP) model developed by Dan Hughes. A special thanks to Dan who is always supportive and generous in helping me to develop my understanding and application of his insights. I would also like to thank Julie Hudson, whose careful thinking helps me to develop mine. Thanks especially for the discussion about connection and correction. While I have stuck with the term 'correction', your thoughts about this have helped me to explain it more carefully.

Discussion within the DDP community is another source of inspiration for my writing. With thanks to colleagues and friends for all your contributions. In this ever-growing community I can't name you all.

This book is dedicated to the families whom I have supported who have been touched by developmental trauma. I admire your courage and resilience, although you do not always recognize these, masked as they can be by your fears. I wish you could see what I see. Thank you for allowing me to come along with you on some of your journeys.

As ever, my thanks to my family, Chris, Alex and Lily, who cope with my preoccupation with writing. We always find time for our own journey together. A special thanks to Alex for joining me in my preoccupation this time, and helping with the illustrations.

Thanks to Steve, Sean, Emma and all the unseen people at Jessica Kingsley Publishers for continuing to support my work, and to Jessica herself for being so encouraging when I have met her.

INTRODUCTION

One of the hardest parenting jobs anyone can do is to parent a child who fears nurture and comfort. This can be expressed through self-reliance; the child pushes the parent away. Alternatively, the child might be coercively attention-needing, but without any sign of feeling soothed when the parent is available to her. Either way, the parent is left feeling rejected and with a pervasive sense of failure. Even the most resilient of parents can become worn down by this. Without good support, the parent can descend into depression and feel unable to continue caring for the child. Whether the parent has a birth child, or a child born to someone else, the parenting task can lose its joy and become a never-ending task borne out of duty, but with little sense of fulfilment.

This book has been written for parents of children and young people who are experiencing relationship difficulties, and those practitioners supporting these families. Often these difficulties are related to early attachment experience. An important role for parents is to be the attachment figures for their child; parents offer comfort as needed and provide a secure base from which a child can confidently explore. When this secure base is absent, or worse frightening, the child has to find a way of existing without safety and security. The child's development reflects this experience as the nervous system becomes wired for danger and loss. Once learnt, these ways of being do not change easily.

This type of experience is traumatic to young children and is a trauma which stays with them as they are growing up. This trauma has been described by psychologist Bessel van der Kolk (2005) as developmental trauma, and this is the term I will use throughout this book. This is a descriptive term that captures the early experience of the children. The trauma comes from the fear of parents, or the absence of safe caregiving, early in life. Trauma that comes from within the family will have a large impact on the development of the children. This can slow down developing maturity. It also interferes with the development of core capacities such as how to regulate emotions or manage impulses. Strong feelings can emerge but the children do not know how to manage these, or how to turn to parents and close others to help them with this. Similarly, the way children come to develop a sense of self – an understanding of who they are – can be negatively influenced by this early experience.

For biological parents it can be uncomfortable to think that difficulties have arisen from early attachment experience, but attachment difficulties can arise for many reasons. Parents' motivations are usually good and most are committed to being good parents for their children. Sometimes, however, external factors such as illness, or problems stemming from their own childhoods, mean that parents struggle to provide their children with the parenting experience that they need.

Parents who have become parents to an older child through adoption, fostering, kinship care or residential care may experience a less personal impact in exploring the early experience of their children. They are, however, still likely to be affected by an exploration of early experience and how it can impact on attachment and later relationships. Kinship carers especially can face additional complexity when parenting a relative's child.

Understanding a child's experience more deeply can be very painful. However, this is what this book is asking you to do – reflect on the children's early experiences, understand the challenges to parenting that they are now presenting and consider alternative ways of parenting the children that can help to overcome the challenges and increase their sense of safety and feelings of security.

The ideas presented within this book are helpful ways of parenting any child; they are particularly focused on helping children to develop security with their parents. When developing this security also means helping children overcome early fears and traumas, we can think about this parenting as being therapeutic.

These therapeutic parenting ideas are based on the DDP model. This is a model developed by clinical psychologist Dan Hughes (Hughes 2009, 2011). DDP stands for Dyadic Developmental Psychotherapy and Practice in recognition that it is both a model for therapy and a model for parenting. 'Dyadic' reminds us that the child will only feel secure when they can experience safety within a relationship. Developmental is helpful to remember that the experience of safety and security, or lack of it, at any age can impact on development. The DDP model provides us with some important principles for helping children to recover from early difficult experience, trauma, separation and loss.

There are many reasons why early attachment experience can be poor:

- Early physical difficulties in the child. These can begin before birth, with difficulties during pregnancy. Difficulties can also arise at or following birth; for example, prematurity. The infant might need to spend time in a special care unit, impacting on the early bonding experience between parent and child. The mother might be ill following the birth, further adding to this.

- Childhood illness. Illness in early childhood can lead to difficulties in developing security. Hospitalization can add to this, making it even more challenging. Alternatively, illness or hospitalization of a sibling or other family member can mean that the parents become less emotionally available to their young child. Death of a sibling can have an even bigger impact.

- Parental illness. Physical or mental illness can reduce a parent's capacity to be available, attuned and sensitively responsive to the child. A mother may have struggled with post-natal depression, long-standing mental or physical illness or have episodes of acute mental or physical illness. Hospitalization will be an added stressor, further compromising the child's security and, of course, death of a parent can be unavoidable but extremely traumatic.

- Family stress. Any chronic or acute stress on the family can lead to less emotional availability from the parents and thus insecurity for the child. Employment, poverty, relationship troubles between parents or with extended family members or illness/death within the extended family or with close friends can all be reasons why parents may struggle with parenting their children.

- Child characteristics. Children born with a learning or other genetic difficulty may have difficulty signalling their needs clearly to the parents. This makes it harder for the parents to emotionally attune with them, understand what they need and meet these needs. This can be further complicated when parents are struggling with feelings of grief and loss for the child they expected to have. Similarly, children born with fussy, hard-to-soothe temperaments can place additional demands on the parents, which can make parenting stressful.

- Parents who have their own early history of trauma or experience of poor parenting will not know how to be available and responsive to their child. Parenting styles can end up being repeated between generations, or parents can overcompensate, trying so hard not to be like their parents that they become insensitive in other ways.

- Sadly for some children, the experience of the parent goes beyond insensitive to being frightening (abuse) or absent (neglect). Both of these can have a profound impact on the child's ability to feel safe and secure within the family. This includes experience of parents who are frightening because of domestic violence, alcohol or drug abuse.

- Experience of separation and loss. Often compounded by abuse and neglect and multiple placements within the care system, this can leave a child emotionally distressed and with defensive patterns in relating to caregivers. This can make it challenging for later parents. Children looked after and adopted are a highly vulnerable group who can be developmentally traumatized by their early experience and who struggle to trust and feel secure in their current families.

All of these experiences can lead a child to develop complex and defensive ways of relating to others. These relationship difficulties can then be hard to overcome, even when the parent is now in a better position to offer sensitive care or another parent has stepped in to provide the care the child needs.

This book has been written to complement the Foundations for Attachment Programme (Golding 2014), a six-session or three-day programme for those parenting children who have relationship difficulties. This book can be read alone, or alongside attending the programme.

Foundations for Attachment introduces four significant challenges of parenting children whose capacity to emotionally connect with parents has been compromised. These are outlined here:

1. *The child experiencing blocked trust.* The child develops around core experiences of being loved conditionally, of not feeling good enough. Feelings of mistrust in the intentions of the parents develop into blocked trust as the child's development becomes organized around this lack of trust. The term 'blocked trust' has been coined by Jon Baylin and Dan Hughes and can be explored more fully in their book (Baylin and Hughes 2016).

2. *The child fearing intersubjective connection within reciprocal relationships.* Infants are born ready to enter relationships which are reciprocal: each member of the relationship is open to influencing and being influenced. Psychologist Colwyn Trevarthen (2001) calls this aspect of relationship intersubjective. When being open to influence is painful, young children quickly learn not to remain open. Instead they become controlling of the other. This is a defensive response within which they try to influence without being influenced in turn.

3. *The child experiencing high levels of shame.* Shame is a very normal emotional experience, felt when a relationship becomes misattuned. This means that there is a rupture, or break, in the connection between the child and parent. This can be caused by the child or by the parent. A sensitive parent will quickly repair such a relationship experience and the shame is regulated. Children left in unregulated shame have a different experience. Without an attuned, sensitive parent making it all right, the shame becomes bigger and more toxic. Children develop defences against such big feelings of shame, which can make life difficult for themselves and for others. Over time these defences make it difficult for the parent to offer attuned care which can regulate the shame.

4. *The child miscuing his attachment needs through a pattern of expressed and hidden needs.* When attachment figures are not able to offer a secure base to their children, they learn to compensate for this insensitivity. Children learn complicated ways of relating which provide some sense of safety in a world that is inherently unsafe. They express what they anticipate is acceptable and hide what they have experienced as unacceptable to their parents.

These four challenges combine into a toxic mix of increasingly difficult behaviour fuelled by the children's emotional experiences of not being good enough and a lack of trust that others will help or care for them. Children need support from others to calm this emotional experience but they also resist the connections that could help them. What they need most they are least open to.

Within this book you will:

*   gain a deeper understanding of these four challenges and with this understanding explore ways of building emotional connections with children. This can increase trust in reciprocal and attachment relationships leading to increased attachment security and reduced levels of shame

*   understand how to provide support for behaviour alongside building these connections. This has been termed 'connection with correction' by Dan Hughes (2009)

*   reflect on your own self-care and consider ways that you can take better care of yourself

*   understand the significance of exploring your own attachment history when caring for children with attachment difficulties

*   explore the dangers of blocked care when caring for children with blocked trust and understand the importance of looking after yourself in order to prevent or recover from blocked care.

The book is organized around the Foundations for Attachment model (see Figure I.1).

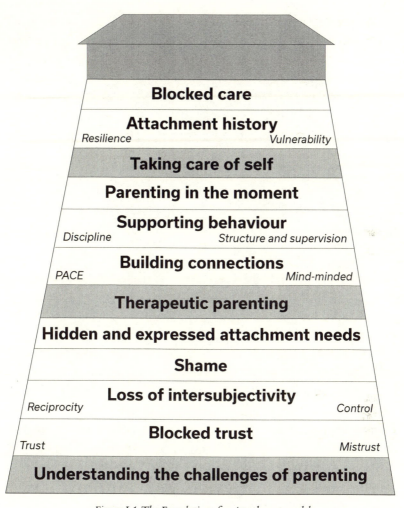

Figure I.1 The Foundations for Attachment model

Following this model, the book is divided into three parts.

PART 1: UNDERSTANDING CHALLENGES OF PARENTING

In this part the challenges often associated with parenting children with attachment difficulties will be introduced. This is linked to attachment theory, an understanding of the theory of intersubjectivity and the impact of trauma on development.

Alongside this exploration of theory, thought will be given to the implications of parenting children who experience these difficulties.

At the end of this part a chapter is included about the development of the nervous system and the brain for those interested in exploring the biology of why children become so defensive and therefore less open to social engagement with others who could help them.

PART 2: THERAPEUTIC PARENTING

This part explores DDP-informed therapeutic parenting. This is based on the Dyadic Developmental Practice model developed by Dan Hughes, which pays special attention to the parenting attitude of PACE (playfulness, acceptance, curiosity and empathy). PACE-led parenting requires some important strengths within the parent.

Emotional regulation is an important part of therapeutic parenting. Remaining emotionally regulated, even when the child is behaving in a way that increases stress, will lead to less defensiveness in parenting. This in turn allows the parent to stay open & engaged with the child so that she can connect emotionally with the parent.

Connection with children's emotional experience is an important part of helping them to develop trust and security with parents. Alongside emotional regulation, this requires the capacity to mentalize and to be mind-minded. This describes the parents' ability to make sense of the internal experience of the child; e.g. what the child is thinking and feeling. These abilities allow the parent to understand without judging the internal experience of the child.

Emotional regulation and mind-mindedness will help parents to adopt an attitude of PACE and to maintain this, or return to it, when under stress. As parents connect with their children through this attitude, their ability to emotionally regulate and to make sense of their child will strengthen, making PACE easier to maintain over time.

Alongside this, children also need behavioural support. We will explore how to maintain the connection that PACE brings, while also providing structure, supervision and behavioural limits. The child will then experience the security of being understood alongside the safety that comes from clear boundaries and parental discipline.

Within this part I include some frequently asked questions about PACE and the use of this approach within parenting.

PART 3: LOOKING AFTER SELF

In this final part the focus moves away from the parenting of the child to the parents looking after themselves. Self-care is important for any parent, although not always prioritized as they try to meet all the day-to-day needs and demands of parenting. When parents realize the complexity of caring for children with attachment difficulties, it becomes clear that taking care of themselves is a high priority if they are to develop the resilience to continue parenting the child successfully.

A part of self-care involves understanding the impact of attachment and relational history on parenting. Whether this experience has been challenging or supportive, parents will have developed both resilience and vulnerabilities from their previous experience. This can invade the present and affect current parenting of the child. In particular, past relationship experience can make it hard to stay present, leading to more defensive parenting. This reduces the security that the child is experiencing. When past is separated from present the parent will be able to stay open & engaged with the child.

Even for the most resilient of parents the long-term nature of helping children recover from developmental traumas can take its toll. Parents are at risk of blocked care (Hughes and Baylin 2012). This part also explores how to recognize blocked care and ways to unblock this care.

THE CHILDREN

Throughout the book the ideas and thoughts expressed are illustrated by the experience of children and their parents. While these are fictional they are inspired by families I have known and supported. Let me introduce you to the children and their parents.

Karen and Teagan: Karen and Teagan were born to Dawn and Philip, who are sensitive, responsive parents. Both Dawn and Philip had some difficulties during childhood, but were able to develop security, which they can now hand on to their children. Dawn's parents separated when she was five years old. While this was a troubling time she had a close relationship with her maternal grandmother, and as the difficulties between her parents resolved, Dawn was able to have good relationships with both of them. Philip had a secure childhood. His mother did have an episode of post-natal depression when his younger sister was born, but both Philip and his mother were well supported by Philip's father. Karen and her younger sister Teagan have therefore been offered the early environment that they need for a secure attachment and this stands them in good stead as they grow and develop into well-adjusted children. Karen is a quiet but confident child, while her sister Teagan is more exuberant.

Ian: Ian was born to single mum, Rachel. Abandoned by her boyfriend when he found out she was pregnant, Rachel is supported by her mother. This is an uneasy relationship, full of unspoken recriminations about the state she has found herself in. Rachel had a difficult pregnancy and birth and Ian was born prematurely. Rachel provides an insensitive, insecure early environment as she tries to deal with her own stresses. Ian has developed an avoidant attachment pattern. This leads to difficulties for Rachel and her new partner Jane as Ian grows and develops into a withdrawn, anxious child.

Lottie: Lottie was born into a chaotic, unpredictable household. Her young parents led a transient lifestyle. Lottie would be left with grandparents each time they became homeless and had to find yet another place to live. Lottie's mother is white British and her father is from Afghanistan. Both parents have been subjected to racial abuse – one reason for the frequent relocation. They both cared for their daughter but struggled to recognize or meet her needs. They were experimenting with some low drug use during her earliest years and this then gradually increased. Lottie went to live with her maternal grandparents when it was discovered that she was being physically abused by her parents. Lottie lived with these grandparents from the age of five to seven. At this time her grandfather died and her grandmother, herself in poor health, decided she could no longer care for Lottie. Lottie moved into a short-term foster placement, a busy household which increased her insecurity and attention-needing behaviours.

The foster parents decided that they could not manage this level of challenging behaviour and Lottie had two further foster placements before moving into a long-term placement with Belinda when she was ten years old. Lottie's early experience of unpredictable parenting coupled with instability and separation has led to an ambivalent attachment pattern. She has developed into a loud, needy child whose anxiety is often displayed through more challenging behaviour. This has settled somewhat since she has experienced Belinda's sensitive and available care.

Harry and James: Harry lived with his birth parents for three years before moving to foster care and then being adopted together with his younger brother James. Harry's mother was young and had lived in residential care as an adolescent. She became pregnant while absconding from the home and now lives with Harry's father, who is considerably older than she is. Both parents have mixed heritage; Harry's mother has a British mother and a largely absent Dutch father, while Harry's father has a mixture of African and British heritage. Neither family offers a stable upbringing to their children. Drugs, alcohol and domestic violence are constant companions in the lives of Harry's birth parents. They both find it difficult to keep Harry in mind, and when they do connect with him it is harsh, critical and non-nurturing. They offer conditional parenting, needing Harry to be quiet and undemanding. Harry has learnt that he is a source of trouble to his birth parents, and this internalized experience feeds his developing sense of self. Harry has a disorganized controlling attachment style. When his brother James was born the boys were moved to foster care. They lived in the foster home for 18 months before being adopted by Marian and Robert. Sadly, Marian and Robert separated when Harry was eight years old, and Robert moved abroad. Since then Marian has been bringing the boys up alone. Harry continues to be highly coercive and challenging in his interactions and these alternate with self-reliant behaviours as he attempts to control those around him. James is a quiet, compliant child often overshadowed by his brother Harry.

Within this book you will also meet some minor characters:

Andrew and Joseph: These boys are school friends but with very different experiences of being parented on the day they fall out with each other at school.

Benjamin: Mum helps Benjamin when he also has a particularly difficult day at school.

Harmony: Harmony's toddler-like tantrums give her adoptive mother some cause for concern.

NOTES ON TERMINOLOGY

Throughout the book the generic term 'parent' is used to describe the range of caregivers who parent children with attachment and trauma difficulties. This is in recognition that they all take on a parenting role for the children they are caring for.

To avoid clumsiness, I have alternated gender for both parent and child throughout the book.

— Part 1 —

UNDERSTANDING THE CHALLENGES OF PARENTING

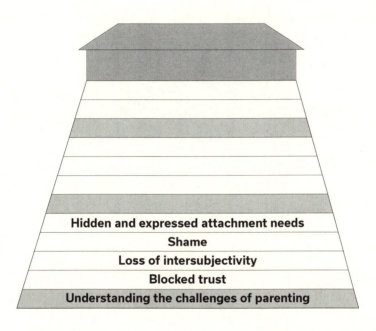

Hidden and expressed attachment needs

Shame

Loss of intersubjectivity

Blocked trust

Understanding the challenges of parenting

In this first section, we will explore four key experiences of children with developmental trauma. These are the development of blocked trust, loss of intersubjectivity, feelings of shame and learning patterns of hiding and expressing different attachment and exploration needs. The consequences for these children are a lack of trust in others, especially close caregivers, a fear of close relationships and doubts about their own sense of worth or lovability. I have called these 'challenges of parenting' because the way that the children adapt to living with these difficulties can present a major challenge to the parents who are trying to nurture and care for them.

Chapter 1

CHALLENGE ONE
BLOCKED TRUST

The first challenge is the tendency for children to develop blocked trust. This is the term that Jon Baylin and Dan Hughes (2016) have used to explain the impact of early experience on children's capacity to trust that their parents love them unconditionally. Jon and Dan explore how an inability to trust that their parents love them, and therefore to develop confidence in their own lovability, gets built into the development of the brain. When this happens, the nervous system is prepared for danger rather than for safety. A lack of responsive care leads to anticipation that a lack of such care will continue and the child adapts accordingly. As we will explore, this can lead to children experiencing even normal parenting as a sign that they are about to be hurt or abandoned.

To understand this, it is helpful to think about what happens when an infant is born into a secure relationship with a parent or parents. Infants are very immature when they are born and are reliant on their parents to know how they are feeling and what they are needing. An attuned and sensitive parent can recognize the signals that tell her what her infant's experience is, and can respond empathically and responsively sufficiently often that the infant develops feelings of security.

This can be a challenge, as sometimes a parent will guess wrongly, trying to feed an infant who has a tummy ache or playing with an infant who is hungry, for example. A sensitive parent will quickly realize that what she is doing is not helpful and will adjust this until the infant is soothed and content again.

This ability to tune into the infant and to meet the infant's needs is at the foundation of the development of safety and security for the child. Parents provide consistent, predictable and reliable nurturing care; they are determined to find out what the infant needs and to meet this need, and are willing to make things right again when the connection goes wrong (repair the relationship). This allows the infant to experience trust in his parents. As we will discover, this feeling of trust is very closely related to the development of an experience of being unconditionally loved. This means that the infant is learning that whatever happens his parents will love him and take care of him; even when things go wrong or are difficult the parents will make it right in the end.

This is Karen's experience. Her parents are loving and caring. Karen experiences parents who can understand what she needs and meet this need much of the time. This is a bit challenged during toddlerhood as they adjust to Karen's developing autonomy and her need to test out the limits in her life. When they do get frustrated or cross with her, however, they are able to take responsibility for this and they always ensure that Karen knows she is loved even at these difficult times.

A psychologist working in the 1960s called Erik Erikson explored this very early experience (Erikson 1963). He noticed how children went through different stages of development. The first of these stages, which occurs during infancy, he described as the crisis of trust versus mistrust. What he meant by this is that infants need a particular experience of being parented if they are to develop trust in their parents' love for them, and therefore a sense of being lovable. This relies on an experience of feeling safe with parents – safety leads to feelings of trust, and therefore hope that all will be well.

Karen has a developing nervous system that is adapted to her safe and benign environment. She is open & engaged with her parents much of the time, and when she does become distressed and more defensive she is able to let her parents guide her back into this more comfortable state. Karen has deep feelings of trust in her parents, combined with a sense of self developed around the feeling of being unconditionally loved.

Infants whose experience is of unresponsive and insensitive parents do not develop these feelings of trust. Danger is experienced when parents are unable to recognize what their infant needs and cannot respond to help the child feel soothed and content. For a very young and immature child this experience is frightening. It is especially frightening because an infant is completely dependent on his parents for getting what he needs. It is even more frightening when parents act in scary or unpredictable ways. Illness or expressions of anger within the home, unpredictable behaviours and simply not being there when needed can all add to the experience an infant is getting that the world is a dangerous place and that he will not be taken care of. While infants cannot think about or make sense of this at this age, the experience of mistrust leads to feeling conditionally loved. It is as if the infant is responsible for his behaviour, and only if he behaves well will all be right in his world. Parenting therefore communicates to the infant that he is loved conditionally – I will love you 'only if'.

Ian, Lottie and Harry do not have the secure early experience that Karen received. Ian and Lottie experience their parents as frequently unavailable to them. Ian feels the psychological absence of his mother leading to deep-seated fears that his needs will not be met. He also picks up the tense, sometimes argumentative atmosphere created as his grandmother tries to help. Lottie experiences a high level of unpredictability. She is never sure whether her parents will respond to her as she needs, and frequent separations from them only add to this uncertainty. Harry simply finds life frightening. He only experiences rough handling of his needs and is surrounded by an environment that is highly stressful and at times terrifying.

None of these children experience themselves as easily lovable and all are growing up with an experience of conditional love. Ian learns that love is dependent on him managing his emotional experience by himself, while Lottie learns to make a fuss to display her emotional experience and that love might come if she makes enough noise to be noticed. Harry has no early sense of being loved or cared for. The nervous systems of these children are adapting to these difficult early environments. These are becoming sensitized to the insecurity and danger that they are being bathed in and biologically they are being prepared to deal with this. Each of the children is quick to move into a defensive state. As infants this can be limited and at times disorganized but as they mature they will be ready to fight, flee or withdraw at a moment's notice. They will learn to suppress social engagement in favour of these more reactive states and they will suppress the social pain that results when their biological need for social relationships is not met by early caregivers.

Infant behaviour is relatively simple and focused on eliciting care and learning about the world. The infant is not considered to be responsible for his behaviour and therefore does not need discipline. Parenting such as Karen receives therefore communicates to the infant that she is loved unconditionally as there are no conditions on the relationship or on the behaviour. The parent communicates I will love you 'no matter what'. This is the foundation needed for secure attachment.

If a child like Karen has experienced trust in infancy she will be able to benefit from a secure and loving home. When she experiences worry or distress she will expect that others will be there to help her. She anticipates being loved unconditionally and has trust in her own lovability. As secure children grow older this very early experience stays with them and impacts on the later relationships that they experience.

Toddlers learn to be mobile and they can move further away from their parents to explore the world around them. Now children can start to get into mischief. The parents will have to put in some conditions on their behaviour – 'if you do this...then...'; 'when you do this...then...' The secure child will experience this within the context of a relationship that remains unconditional. The parent communicates that I will still love you no matter what, and I will make things okay when I put limits on your behaviour. In this way the parents ensure that their children are kept safe and are taught how to behave, matched to the values of the community they are living within. The children experience safety in this new aspect to their relationship with their parents because they continue to have the experience of being unconditionally loved. The children trust in the good intentions of their parents.

Karen, at 20 months, is busy expanding her exploration of the world around her. She is confidently walking and is keen to reach out to explore anything within reach. Her parents have put much out of her way, but they are still on guard ready to guide her away from potential dangers. Karen has a particular fascination for the fire. It is protected by a fireguard and Karen is drawn to this. Karen is getting used to the word 'no' and to restrictions on her environment as her parents ensure that she moves away from this potential danger. Sometimes Karen has a tantrum as she experiences this limitation on her desire to explore. The power of her toddler rage can frighten her, but always her parents are on hand to soothe and comfort. Karen is learning that there are some things she cannot do; that she can get very strong feelings about this but that her parents always make this okay for her in the end. The feelings reduce because of the parents' regulating presence, even while they place restrictions on her. Karen is loved, cherished and kept safe.

Mistrust arises when an infant is treated as if responsible for his behaviour. Parenting communicates to the infant that he is loved conditionally. I will love you 'only if'. For the growing child the provision of boundaries and restrictions, alongside irritation, frustration or anger from the parents, especially in the absence of empathy or warmth, only serves to reinforce this conditionality. The child learns to associate boundaries with his developing sense of self as a bad child.

At 20 months of age Ian is boisterous but less comfortable sharing his experience with his mother. He too is exploring the world, but this is more tentative than Karen. He will pick things up and look at them, sometimes approaching his mother and then stopping, as if uncertain whether to go to her or not. Sometimes she takes things from him, the dog's toys for example, before he can put them into his mouth. Ian protests but this is with no expectation that his mother will help him. When he is very frustrated major tantrums can burst from him. His mother, unsure how to deal with these and uncomfortable herself with such big feelings, picks him up and puts him in his cot until the tantrum subsides. Ian experiences his mother's availability only when he is emotionally contained; he develops a sense of emotional expression as being bad and works harder to suppress this difficult experience. He is developing a sense of self as bad, and a need to conceal his emotions in order to ensure that he is loved.

In contrast, Lottie is learning that the world is out there to be grasped. She runs around busily engaging with anything in reach. She especially loves to chase the pet rabbit when he is free from his pen. When her mother tries to stop her she has an instant and intense tantrum. Her mother tries to distract her but she will not be soothed and continues to express her distress. In the end, she is allowed to go to the rabbit as her mother pleads with her to be gentle. These outbursts continue at intervals throughout the day. She is offered a sandwich for lunch, but it is the wrong filling. They go to the park and Lottie is frustrated that she has to sit in her buggy. Her mother continues to alternate with getting cross and placating her. Often she just holds her hands up in frustration; she cannot please her small daughter. Lottie is developing a sense of self as bad, and a need to ensure that she gets what she wants in life, not able to trust that others will be there for her when needed.

Harry is having the hardest experience. At 20 months he is barely walking and he spends much of his time sitting staring into space. When he does move he frequently finds himself under his mother's feet and she complains to him as a consequence. When his father is around his mother becomes more anxious, trying to ensure that Harry stays out of the way and does not make a fuss. She often smacks him, keen to ensure that he stays quiet and does not irritate his father. When he does encroach into his father's space he is often picked up roughly and thrown from the room. Harry already knows that he is a bad child and is learning to disappear as he attempts to keep out of his parents' way.

If infants have experienced fear and mistrust in infancy they are less likely to benefit from secure, loving homes. Based on previous experience, as demonstrated by Ian, Lottie and Harry, they expect to be taken care of conditionally. You will love me 'only if', rather than 'no matter what'.

These experiences remain with children.

Ian's mother recovers from depression, finds a new partner who embraces her and her child and she becomes more available to Ian. He does not understand these changes. Ian continues to try to manage his feelings by himself. His mother experiences this as a rejection of her and is hurt by these behaviours. She withdraws too, and avoidance continues to be a feature of their relationship.

Lottie moves to foster care but takes her attention-needing and demanding behaviours with her. These help her to be noticed, but this comes at a cost as one placement moves into another. It will be much later before Lottie finds some stability with Belinda and can begin to experiment with a different way of being.

As Harry matures, within his adoptive home, he develops into a highly controlling child. He cannot believe in his lovability. He is free from the fear that was ever present with his birth parents but he continues to act based on the assumptions that he will not get what he needs and that others will hurt him. He can be coercive and challenging, but also self-reliant as he takes what he needs apparently unconcerned about anyone else. His parents are hurt and dismayed by these behaviours and unsure how to gain some control and offer their child what they know he needs.

As Ian, Lottie and Harry demonstrate, when developmentally traumatized or emotionally troubled children are being cared for by benign and loving parents they feel mistrustful of this. They anticipate that they will be hurt or that these relationships will be lost to them when their own badness is discovered. They have little capacity to trust in others or to believe in themselves.

Children who have experienced mistrust therefore become blocked in their trust of the parenting they are offered, even when this parenting changes for the better. Boundaries and discipline are not experienced as kind and loving support for their behaviour. Instead they are perceived as confirmation of their sense of badness, a sign that the parents will hurt or abandon them one day. The child's sense of insecurity and fear is increased by the very ordinary parenting that he is experiencing.

Children have to suppress the need for comfort and companionship to survive their earliest experiences when needs are not met (neglect) and when they are hurt by their caregivers (abuse). This is the big sacrifice when adapting to a harsher world where comfort and companionship are in short supply. Through blocked trust the child finds ways to learn to do without these things. This requires the brain to organize around the need for self-defence and at the same time to suppress the need for social engagement. The way the brain functions leads the child to become defensive and to avoid engaging socially with the people around him. This brain organization is occurring to help the child to survive in a world which is harsh and non-nurturing; reliance is on self rather than trust in the caregiver. If you would like to learn more about the brain and nervous system you can find this in Chapter 5 (that chapter can be skipped if lots of detail about biology is of less interest to you).

Children therefore learn not to trust that comfort and companionship will be safely given to them by their caregiver, because their initial cues to elicit these were met with pain, fear or silence. They learn to suppress these innate, instinctive needs which are common to all humans when born. This means that they suppress feeling the social emotions. These are emotions which help the child to connect with parents and to reconnect with them at times of difficulties.

Joy is a social emotion. When a child is connected to a parent who is playful, fun to be with, and is appreciating the child, joy is experienced. This joy is amplified for child and parent because of the connection between them. Good feelings arise from these connections and the child is motivated to continue to seek these interactions.

When a child is separated from his parent, especially at a time when he needs connection to feel safe and comfortable, another social emotion is felt. This is social pain, the pain of separation. This pain motivates the child to find the parent again, to call out for her, to seek her. Once found, the parent provides comfort and the pain reduces.

Karen, aged five, is out at the park with her parents and younger sibling Teagan. The children love feeding the ducks. Teagan has thrown all her food into the water and is distressed to find that the food is now gone. A toddler tantrum ensues and her parents become focused on helping her manage this distress. Karen, unconcerned, continues to throw her food. She moves around the lake finding different ducks to feed not noticing that she is moving away from her parents. Her food gone she looks up and is dismayed to find that her parents are not in sight. Only a few minutes have passed and unbeknown to Karen her father has kept an eye on her. Unsure which direction to walk and unaware that her father is nearby Karen calls loudly and then cries. In no time Dad is there; he picks her up and holds her to him as her fear subsides and her sobs reduce. Soon she is back with the family group ready to enjoy the playground that is next on offer to both girls.

When relational experiences have been frightening and painful the joy of companionship and comfort of reunion do not occur. Experiencing a need for companionship and for comfort is a source of anxiety for Ian, Lottie and Harry. Needing, but anticipating that the need won't be met, is an uncomfortable state to be in. Ian and Lottie work hard to receive moments of companionship and comfort. They have adapted their behaviour so that these moments are likely to occur either by suppressing emotional discomfort for Ian or expressing a perpetual state of discomfort, as Lottie does.

When there is no joy of companionship or comfort of reunion, as is the case for Harry, more drastic development is needed. The need for comfort and joy has to be avoided to find some sense of safety in the world. Harry feels safer being asocial. He develops into a state of chronic defensiveness; defending against both the real and anticipated pain found in social engagement. Much-needed and enduring emotional bonds with caregivers are sacrificed along the way. Children like Harry learn to suppress their relational needs, keeping the parent at a safe distance by becoming self-sufficient.

Thus when Harry is separated from Marian at the duck pond he is unconcerned. He continues chasing the ducks that are waddling around him. Marian, distracted by James momentarily, loses sight of him. She anxiously scans the area around the lake, her anxiety rising as she cannot see him. She takes hold of James's hand and moves towards the area where most ducks are. Finally, she catches sight of him chasing a duck into the lake. She is powerless to intervene as he gets closer to the water. Fortunately, one of the adults close by notices Harry and pulls him away from the edge. Harry looks at the stranger unconcerned and turns away to find another duck. Marian reaches him and urges Harry not to move so far away. She also berates him for chasing the ducks. Harry just laughs and turns around to find more fun. Marian is left wondering why she thought a trip to the park was a good idea!

FEAR OF ABANDONMENT

The experience of blocked trust and conditional love is closely associated with the fear of abandonment. Children who cannot trust have core anxieties about not being good enough, and therefore anticipate that they will lose their parents one day. This is a fear that can especially resonate with children who have experienced separation and loss of parents, sometimes multiple times.

The fear of abandonment may also resonate from ancestral memories. For example, anthropologists and evolutionary biologists have explored the practice of baby abandonment. This was relatively common both in Western history and also in some modern tribal communities where resources are scarce. This has been explored by Daniela Sieff (2005) in her book about emotional trauma. In particular, her interview with Sarah Blaffer Hrdy provides an evolutionary and anthropological perspective on why the experience of conditional love can so easily trigger fears of loss and abandonment.

Blaffer Hrdy suggests that the modern mother–infant relationship has been shaped by our ancient history. Modern Western societies are privileged by having enough resources; mothers no longer have to make decisions about whether to rear or abandon a baby. In less affluent communities such decisions are still being made, providing us with an insight into historical parenting practices. For example, mothers of the !Kung of the Kalahari desert, Botswana, will abandon an infant in the bush if they are still nursing a child when the infant is born. They are not able to provide for both children and therefore they choose to continue to support the child in whom they have already invested. It is likely that such practices were commonplace historically, as mothers chose to parent in a way that ensured that some descendants would survive. Lack of resources, little social support, or pairing with a new husband following the death of the child's father are all reasons given for a mother sacrificing a child.

Even in recent times in Western cultures some hangovers from these practices can still be seen. The practice of foundling hospitals of previous centuries led to thousands of infants being left, with two-thirds dying before their first birthdays. In the 1800s in London, many infant deaths were reported to be due to accidental smothering, a condition described as overlaying, and in numbers much larger than this relatively rare accident should suggest. Even the folk legends of changeling children point to a culturally sanctioned way of abandoning babies in the forests. The ancient need to invest in healthy children may be why mothers of pre-term twins were found to unconsciously direct more attention to the healthier twin when observed eight months after the twins' birth. (Mann 1980 in Blaffer Hrdy and Sieff 2015).

We can speculate, based on these observations, that children have evolved to be hypersensitive to signs of a lack of commitment, especially from their mother. Deep-rooted fears of abandonment are triggered when the child senses any signs that he is not worth being cared for: '… human infants, so helpless at birth, and so dependent on others for years afterwards, have evolved to be exceptionally sensitive to signs of emotional distancing, and to do whatever is needed to avoid abandonment' (Blaffer Hrdy and Sieff 2015, p.202). For children who have experienced a lack of love, and conditionality early in life, even ordinary boundaries and discipline might provide such indicators. The experience of blocked trust and fear of abandonment may have cultural roots in the practice of baby abandonment. Ancestral memories can be very long.

BLOCKED TRUST AND COMFORT, JOY AND CURIOSITY

Blocked trust can help children to survive in a harsh world; it is an adaptation to help them to manage when care is frightening, bewildering or absent. It comes at a great cost, however, a cost that is still there even when the parent is now able to offer care and comfort. This is a cost that continues to be paid even when children have moved to live with different parents who can be more nurturing in their care. The children behave as if nothing has changed. They do not easily open themselves up to the parent; the risk that things will still be the same as previously experienced is too high.

Dan Hughes has helped us to understand that within blocked trust there are three great losses for the children. These are the capacity for comfort, curiosity and joy within relationships. I remember hearing Dan talk at a conference in 2014. It made so much sense of what I was seeing in the children I was working with when he told us that blocked trust is: 'When young children block the pain of rejection and the capacity to delight in order to survive in a world without comfort and joy' (Baylin and Hughes 2014). He went on to explore how curiosity and the need for comfort and joy – essential parts of being human – are lost in developmental trauma. Finding these again is an enormous challenge when biologically, as well as behaviourally, the children are prepared for a world where they anticipate danger in relationships rather than safety.

Comfort

Children who have experienced a lack of the care they need early in life anticipate that they will not be comforted when they need this. If you don't expect comfort, then it is safer not to feel emotional distress. If you don't need then it won't be so hard to be comfortless. This is one of the reasons that children display such controlling behaviours. Being in control can help them to suppress emotional distress and the need for others. Control reduces the need for comfort. A great sadness, and a challenge in caring for children with developmental trauma, is that they are afraid to appear vulnerable. Vulnerability exposes their need for parents. They may demand and cling while also pushing away; they may be self-reliant, acting as if they have no need of you, but either way they stay in control. This feels safer than being exposed as vulnerable, even though in vulnerability they could elicit and receive care and comfort in a way that would allow them to be soothed.

Joy

Alongside finding it difficult to receive comfort these children also have reduced capacity to be in a relationship that is joyful. The children are highly tuned in to signs of unavailability or potential hurt. They are exquisitely sensitive, perceiving this in parental actions that are actually benign. Danger is seen everywhere and the children remain hyper-alert and vigilant. They are being governed by a defensive nervous system. This means that they are ready at any moment to defend against danger – the fight or flight response – but they are not at the same time able to relax and enjoy the moment. It is not possible to be mobilized for danger and for safety at the same time. It is extremely hard therefore for these children to relax and to be able to enjoy and have fun with their parents. They need to experience a high level of safety over a long length of time before their hypervigilant nervous system can take some time off. The switch from defensive control to relaxed social engagement does not happen easily.

Curiosity

In building trust for the child the parent is also helping the child to discover the wonder of curiosity. It is hard to imagine how curiosity can be lost to children. The drive to know about the world around us is so powerful and is at its most evident in childhood. Children seek to understand and explore. Trauma rips through this curiosity. This is because to manage trauma we have to be alert to the dangers we imagine are ever present. Just try to relax and read a book when you have heard an unusual sound somewhere in the house and you will get a small insight into what this is like. Once we are watching or listening for the next danger we cannot also be attending to the things right in front of us. The beauty of a sunset is lost for us when we imagine that danger is approaching from across the horizon. Curiosity absorbs us in the small things around us; trauma focuses us away from this onto the bigger dangers we imagine to be ever present.

When children experience blocked trust they become focused on perceived dangers from within the relationships that surround them. This is the great sadness of blocked trust. The relationships that could guide them out of this – to help them discover comfort, curiosity and joy – are also the relationships that they perceive as their greatest danger. The children learn to manage without the relationships and in the process lose the chance of comfort, curiosity and joy. Thus the children develop the controlling behaviours that are such a trademark of trauma. They cannot trust in the parents' good intentions and so they resist their authority. They cannot believe in unconditional support and love and so they are not open to parental influence. Developmentally traumatized children trust in themselves rather than others and this is the source of their controlling behaviours. The children are taking charge of their own safety; it feels so much safer to be in charge than to be open to the influence of others. We will explore this further in the next chapter.

THE CHALLENGE OF PARENTING CHILDREN EXPERIENCING BLOCKED TRUST

When the parenting environment changes, children with blocked trust anticipate the same difficulties as they experienced previously. The parents want to demonstrate their unconditional love, and the capacity they now have to care for and cherish the child. Whether a new parent, or a renewed parent, the children cannot believe in this. It is safer to continue to be alert for the danger that was present in the past and is therefore anticipated in their future.

There is a further twist in this tale of trauma. Remember, when we explored infancy we noticed how in the first year of life the parent has a unique time when they can unconditionally care for their child without the need for discipline. A baby does no wrong and the parents' job and joy is to care for and protect him unconditionally. As the infant matures to toddlerhood the parent also has to bring in some discipline. Teaching the child what is safe and acceptable behaviour. Unconditional love continues but there are now some conditions on behaviour. Behavioural support sits alongside unconditional love. Children who have experienced unconditional love in infancy can manage this addition to the parenting that they experience. This is because they trust in the parents' good intentions. I know you love me unconditionally therefore you must be doing this in my best interest too. Of course, children push against these boundaries as they test the limits, and they display their great distress when life does not go as they want it to, but underlying this is trust. The children trust that however testing or distressed they get the parent will make it all right in the end. This is the gift of unconditional love.

With an older child who has not had the experience of unconditional love in infancy there is a problem. The parent cannot bring discipline in on top of a secure emotional connection already built with the child. Instead, the parent needs to build security through emotional connection at the same time as she is putting restrictions on behaviour. These children are already doubting their lovability, and anticipating that care comes with conditions. Discipline and boundaries are not viewed as frustrating restrictions on their behaviour done in their best interest. Instead, they are seen as evidence that the relationship continues to be conditional, and thus opportunities for emotional connection are not taken while restrictions are fought against. The conditions are experienced as: 'If I am not good enough then I will be hurt and/or abandoned.' The child, however, cannot be 'good enough'. He will experience frustration, anxiety, anger and the range of emotions that are so normal for all of us. These will burst out of him. He will need behavioural support to manage this range of emotional experience, just like any young child. The behavioural support, however, is a sign of conditionality. All children need behavioural support, but from within unconditional relationships. Behavioural support when relationships are expected to be conditional signals for the child that hurt and loss are on their way. Anxiety builds and safety and security are lost to the child. This is the challenge of parenting these children who developed blocked trust in infancy. The building of trust and offering of an unconditional relationship cannot be developed first, acting as a foundation for the provision of behavioural support. These have to be developed together rather than sequentially.

Beyond infancy children cannot manage without boundaries and discipline; they have not yet learnt to behave safely in the social or the physical world. So, we tell them that they are loved unconditionally while we let them know that their behaviour is not okay. Developmentally traumatized children cannot experience this distinction. Their past has taught them that they are not worthy of unconditional love; these restrictions on their behaviour therefore become proof that this is still true. If their behaviour is bad, it is because they are bad.

The challenge of parenting children who are blocked in their capacity to trust is how to offer them the connection and understanding through which unconditional love is communicated while also empathically providing discipline and boundaries.

PARENTING CHILDREN WITH BLOCKED TRUST

Parenting needs to help children to recover from blocked trust. This is done through continually demonstrating and making explicit that the child is unconditionally loved. To do this, the parent needs to attune to the internal experience of the child, find empathy for this experience and help the child to know that his feelings are understood.

This can be tricky for several reasons. As we will explore later, it is not always easy to know what a child is feeling or thinking, especially when he has learnt to hide it from others. Parents learn to be mind readers, making guesses about how the child might be feeling. Next parents need to accept this experience, to remember that feelings are neither right nor wrong, they just are.

It is worth pausing and thinking about this as it is a critical part of understanding how to parent these children. We all have an inner life, which we are more or less in touch with. Our inner life is full of feelings, thoughts and beliefs. Children need help to notice and make sense of their inner life. Importantly, they need to know that it is okay to have even difficult and negative feelings and thoughts. We have all had strong, angry feelings at times, and may have a passing thought: 'I could kill you right now.' Of course, we have no intention of acting on this thought, it is just a sign of how strongly we are feeling. We keep the thought to ourselves, take care of our strong feelings and then go on to manage the relationship with the person who has made us angry. Children are much less able to do this. They have the strong feeling and express the thought. Thus they might shout angrily: 'I am going to kill you!' They need us to help them manage this strong emotion and not to become judgemental about what they are saying. Accept the statement as a symbol of the strong feeling and connect with this emotional experience. A parent might say to the child: 'You are feeling so angry right now. I expect you are angry because… If that is how you are feeling I am not surprised that you are so cross.' Notice that the parent is not saying to the child that the feelings and thoughts are right, nor that they are wrong. This is just how it feels right now. This acceptance and understanding, which is conveyed with empathy, will soothe the child. The angry feelings will reduce in a way that would not happen if the parent tries to tell him that he should not talk about killing people. This is connection with the internal experience of the child. This connection is what helps the child to feel safer and, over time, to start to trust in the parents' good intentions and to believe that he is acceptable to them – that maybe he is loved unconditionally.

This acceptance does not excuse behaviour. If the child has hit the parent in this anger the hitting remains wrong. Once the parent has connected with the feelings, she can then support the behaviour so that the child learns to deal with strong feelings and thoughts without acting on them. This is what discipline literally means; it is an act of teaching someone, giving them knowledge. In our discipline, we are teaching children how to behave. We will explore this further later in this book.

Of course, parents also have their own internal experience, their own thoughts and feelings which can be triggered by the child's behaviour. When a parent hears her child telling her that he will kill her, she will feel angry with him. The parent might worry that she is failing the child or believe that if she can't stop the child saying these things then he might actually do this at some time in the future. A parent's own internal experience, which again is neither right nor wrong but just is, might provoke a less helpful response to the child. When a parent has her own defensive reactions to her child she is less able to accept his internal experience. This is normal and understandable.

The parent may feel frustrated that she has not been able to stay open to accepting her child's feelings. She is only human, and her own feelings can make it hard to continue with acceptance for the child. Fortunately, she does not need to be too hard on herself. She has what I like to refer to as a 'get out of jail free' card. In other words, she can notice that she is being defensive, have compassion and acceptance for herself, and then work to make it right again. This is relationship repair. The parent lets the child know that she was cross and that she is sorry that she showed him this. She conveys that her relationship with him is important and therefore she will make the relationship okay again. Hitting is not right, but feeling angry is acceptable. The child learns that none of this is because he is a bad child, and that parents always make things right again. He really is loved 'no matter what'. Grudgingly, the child may then be able to accept the consequence for his behaviour, knowing that he is acceptable to his parents, that his behaviour will be supported and that he is worthy of his parents' love.

RECOVERING CAPACITY FOR COMFORT, CURIOSITY AND JOY

When children start to feel safer and to build trust in the parents, their nervous systems also change and start to organize around this newly found sense of safety. They can become less alert for danger and therefore more open to social engagement. They become open & engaged with the parents, open to their comfort, and also open to curiosity. In addition, the child can be joyfully engaged with his parents.

Let's slow down again and think about each of these in turn.

Comfort

Children need their parents to help them to recover the capacity for sadness. Feeling sad is such a vulnerable feeling, but when a child is able to experience sadness she also becomes open to comfort. Karen is sad and distressed when she loses sight of her parents at the park. She is highly vulnerable and feels this to the full. She is comfortable expressing her distress and anticipates that somehow her parents will find her and make this all okay again. Her distress quickly reduces as her expectations are realized. Karen is open to comfort because she trusts that sadness is acceptable to her parents. She will express it to the full, confident in her parents' ability to comfort and soothe.

If a child anticipates pain instead of comfort he will try to remain disconnected from the feelings of sadness, and in turn disconnected from the person who might be the source of comfort for him, but who he fears is more likely to be the source of pain.

When parenting a developmentally traumatized child the parent needs to awaken the pain of disconnection in order to awaken the need for comfort. Allow the child to express his fear and discomfort so that he can be soothed.

Sadness is the hardest emotion to experience for traumatized children. They are afraid to feel sad, because they anticipate no comfort. They therefore resist the parents' empathy, fearing the emotional experience that this empathy will awaken. They try to hide from their own emotional experience of fear and sadness – emotions that make them feel so vulnerable. Often these feelings get covered in a blanket of anger and rage – emotions that make the child feel less vulnerable and help to keep the sadness buried within.

The parents need to help the children to experience empathy, demonstrating their availability to help them with the emotional experience that this evokes. The child feels safe to be sad and to need comfort; the child is able to cry in the parents' presence and becomes open to the comfort that follows.

Curiosity

Children need their parents to help them to recover the capacity for curiosity. Ian demonstrates little curiosity in the world. If we observe Ian at the park with his mother, he is likely to be less engaged with the experience. He might feed the ducks, even appearing to enjoy this, but the extra sparkle that a curious exploration of the world brings is missing. Notice Ian next to Karen, and his experience is likely to be less rich as he remains vigilant to his mother's mood. Responding to this is a more important consideration for Ian, and thus a carefree exploration of feeding the ducks doesn't happen.

As these children begin to experience some safety and security with their parents they become able to relax in their own curiosity. Now the parents can remain open & engaged with the children, using their own curiosity to awaken the curiosity of the children. Within these relationships the children experience it as safe to be curious and to share in a state of wonder about the world, themselves and others. If this is a new experience for the child, he may behave much as a toddler does with his awakening experience of the world around him. Children look to their parents to help them make sense of this. Remember the endless 'whys' of toddlerhood. It is hard to discover the world for yourself if you haven't discovered this in your relationship with another first. If a child is starting to behave in a way that seems developmentally young, and is looking to the parent to do more with him than is expected for his age, this is a good sign. The child is becoming open to the relationship and is starting to use this relationship as he might have done earlier if the parent had been available to him at that time.

Joy

Finally, children need their parents to help them recover the capacity for relational joy. It follows that when children resist relationships they cannot also experience joy within these relationships. Parents need to help children to shine in the delight of the other and to mirror their joy in being with them. You always know when you have a joyful connection with another because each of your feelings is amplified by the experience of the feelings of the other. Just remember a time when you have ended up in helpless laughter over something that is not really that funny. It just happened to have tickled one of you, who shares his amusement. You become amused in turn and the amusement becomes amplified into helpless laughter. This is the power of the relationship. The sense of fun and happiness is relational.

This is very different from the kind of 'manic happiness' that children can display. This is a defence against sadness but it is not relational. Remember Harry chasing the ducks? He is not experiencing a happy time with Marian, neither is he distressed when he cannot see her. Harry is working hard not to feel something more vulnerable and is acting as if he is happy and having fun. Chasing the ducks is therefore a welcome distraction and a way of feeling some control in a world where lack of control feels dangerous. Harry is acting cheerfully but in truth joy is not an emotion he recognizes. He doesn't get an amplified feeling of joy in visiting the ducks because he is not able to experience this visit relationally. He is not open & engaged with the experience or with Marian. His is defensive behaviour leading to more disconnection rather than connection.

Parents need to help these children to experience relational happiness, to discover safety in the fun moments. Small moments and low-key activities can offer opportunities to dip into these feelings. The child will manage these because they are light and momentary. As he gets used to experiencing fun and joy, the small moments can become bigger and more extended.

LIVING WITH A TIGER, OPOSSUM OR CHAMELEON

Baylin and Hughes (2016) describe the differences in the way that children can respond to the experience of blocked trust; not all children respond the same way and they have helpfully expressed this with comparison to different animals – analogies which I am borrowing from them in this section.

The first type of child is a *tiger*. Harry is a tiger. Parents always know when they are trying to nurture a tiger, as the child is obvious about how mistrust feels, responding with anger and aggression. If the parent is drawn into these cycles of negative, aggressive reactions, both are left experiencing mistrust. Taming the tiger means supporting the child who has strong feelings of anger. The child is accepted; this is how he is feeling. As anger is accepted the child has less need to display anger through aggressive behaviours.

Anger and vulnerability will alternate as the child explores being more open to the parent and the possibility of comfort. These will be small moments, and then a retreat back to anger as the child fears the vulnerability being expressed. If the parent can stay open and accepting of both when her child is vulnerable and when he is angry, the child will be able to spend more time in vulnerability and less in anger.

The *opossum*, however, will keep a very low profile. As Ian matures he becomes more like an opossum. Unlike the tigers, these children will try to appear small and silent as they attempt to stay out of sight and out of mind. They do not want to draw attention to themselves. The parent reaches out but finds the child not there. The parents feel rejected and a sense of failure as they try to reach these shut away children. They find it hard to stay engaged with the children and end up caring out of necessity as they are receiving so little back. This too can end in a cycle of mutual mistrust.

Again, acceptance is the key. The parent remains close to the child, accepting his need to withdraw from the relationship. Gentle presence provides the child with an experience of the parent remaining open even when the child needs to stay closed and shut off. The parent is then also present when the child makes tentative moves to be more open. The parent remains steady as the child moves backwards and forwards between being open and being shut down. As the child experiences acceptance for both these parts, trust will build and the child will be withdrawn less often.

The *chameleon* is the third animal. James, Harry's brother, is more of a chameleon. We have not noticed James very much so far, as our focus has been on Harry. This is typical for this type of child. Chameleons are expert at blending in and these children have this ability also. They will constantly assess the mood of those around them and try to adapt their behaviour to this mood. These children suppress their own needs as they attempt to accommodate the needs and moods of the adults. They are superficially social, but without any substance to the connections they are forming. Marian experiences this with James, but compared with the challenge of parenting Harry she is less aware of it. She is glad that James will respond to her and experiences more satisfaction in her parenting of James than her parenting of Harry. These children can be lost in families where other children are taking up so much of the emotional energy.

Parents of chameleons can describe a fakeness about these children which makes any connections they have with them feel manipulative and unreal. As with tigers and opossums, parents need to stay present and steady whatever the chameleon is expressing. Their openness to their children and the acceptance that these children need to present this 'fitting-in' self just now will build trust. Children may tentatively test out how acceptable their authentic self is. As parents accept the children in all their parts, the chameleon tendencies will reduce.

OPEN & ENGAGED PARENTING

When environments change, the child is likely to remain defensive and less open to social engagement. New learning does not happen easily. If a child anticipates that he is going to be hurt, rejected or ignored he will behave defensively. If the parent can help him to feel safe, over time he will move across to the open & engaged state. When we are in a relationship we tend to move into the same state as the other person. If a child is defensive, it can pull the parent into matching this and becoming defensive in turn. If, however, the parent can remain open & engaged at these times, a level of safety will build up; mistrust becomes trust, and the child will be able to match the parent and become open & engaged in turn.

Such experience can reset the sensitivity of the stress system so that children are less likely to react to innocuous events as if they are dangerous. However, this is not an easy or quick process. The children are hyper-focused on threat or potential threat, and much less able to attend to signs of safety. Facial recognition provides a good example of this. Studies have shown that children who have experienced abuse will detect anger in faces and voices faster than children who have not experienced abuse. They also cannot withdraw this attention to notice other things (Pollak 2003, cited in Baylin and Hughes 2016). Thus, children will miss signs of safety in their environment because of this hyper-focus to signs of threat – a phenomenon that Baylin and Hughes (2016) have called 'safety blindness'. The task of the parents is to hang on in there, calming the children's defensive reactions through their open & engaged state and thus providing the regulatory support needed. As they are doing this, they will be cracking open the door on the children's blocked attachment system and the children will learn to anticipate safety and care from their current parents.

CONCLUSION

In this chapter we have explored the first challenge of parenting. The challenge presented when children are experiencing blocked trust. This experience emerges from an early environment that has not given them the best relationship experience. The child has developed an experience of himself as not good enough, not worthy of love. He finds that the love of others is conditional rather than unconditional. When children live in social environments, such as their families, which feel dangerous they become alert to any potential signs of this danger.

Biologically we have a social monitoring system that is used to judge whether our relationships are safe or dangerous. For these children, this system becomes sensitized to this early experience. This can be likened to a smoke detector set to be very sensitive and consequently triggered even when there is no possibility of fire. The children become hyper-alert to signs that people around them are going to hurt or ignore them. When these fears are triggered the children become less open & engaged, not able to relax and enjoy the relationship. Instead, they are ready to defend themselves. In this defensive state the children are not open & engaged to the influence of others.

Deep cultural memories of danger are triggered as the children experience big fears about not being good enough, not being strong enough. They anticipate abandonment and learn to behave in ways to ward off this impending loss.

Much of this behaviour is organized around a need to be in control. Children become less open to the influence of others. This in turn shuts down the capacity for comfort, curiosity and joy. Only with emotional connection from parents will the children begin to experience the safety needed to unblock the trust. Only then can they engage deeply in relationships with the emotional wellbeing that this brings.

Chapter 2

CHALLENGE TWO
FEAR OF
INTERSUBJECTIVITY

We now move on to the second parenting challenge. This explores how children develop a fear of relationships with close caregivers. This is because, within developmental trauma, the children lack a feeling of safety stemming from their earliest experience of being parented. This might be because the parenting is frightening to them, because there is no one there when they most need care or because they are experiencing lots of change to who is parenting them. This is especially difficult for young children because infants are immature and totally dependent on others. They need emotional connection in order to survive. When this connection comes with an experience of loss, pain and fear they learn to fear connection. As soon as children are able to do without connection they will find ways to exist disconnected from others. We see this most clearly in the controlling behaviours that even very young children can develop. They use the close relationships around them but with a resistance to being influenced by the caregiver. This means they cannot enjoy reciprocal relationships. An intersubjective relationship within which each person is open to the influence of the other becomes a source of fear. How children learn to avoid such intersubjective relationships is the focus of this chapter.

WHAT ARE INTERSUBJECTIVE RELATIONSHIPS?

Let's return to the start of life for Karen. Just a few hours ago, Dawn gave birth. Karen is now lying in her mother's arms as both recover.

Karen is quietly alert as she takes her first looks at her mother's face. Dawn looks down and is enchanted by this tiny being whom she has carried for so many months but is seeing for the first time. Their eyes lock and each becomes absorbed with the other. All else is forgotten as Dawn enters into this deeply emotional experience. She no longer hears the noises on the hospital ward; she is not aware of the dragging pain where stitches were needed; she is not thinking about her partner who sits quietly by watching this pair – he knows his time will come. Dawn and Karen have entered into an intersubjective relationship. This is a close connection within which each is open to the influence of the other. As Dawn experiences Karen's attention on her she is drawn to this tiny being in a way that is totally captivating. She is influenced by her new daughter's connection to her and she responds by offering this connection back. Karen in turn, so tiny, so immature, is having an experience which provides the foundation for much of her development. She is discovering that it is safe to connect to her mother; even more, she is discovering that she can influence her mother. Even at a few hours of age Karen is already experiencing the safety of seeking for her mother and her mother responding to her. As she grows older these first experiences will stand her in good stead. She will continue to respond to the safety and connection that her parents offer to her. She will discover that they are influenced by her, responding to the cues she gives and making things right for her. With increased mobility, she will learn about boundaries and discipline. She will be frustrated, cross, demanding, but always there is this connection to return to. Always there is the safety of knowing that she is loved and that her parents will strive to make things okay in the end.

Karen is also influenced by her parents. In infancy, these are simple interactions. Her parents call to her and she turns to them. They smile, and she smiles back. As she matures she learns to turn to her parents when she needs soothing. She begins to behave in ways that her parents approve of. She is gentle with the dog, she pulls her boots off when she comes in from the garden. She discovers their joy in her as she explores the world. Karen discovers a world that is bigger, brighter, more fun and less scary when she is sharing it with her parents.

Karen also discovers an internal world of feelings, thoughts, worries and desires, which makes sense to her because her parents make sense of it with her. As she grows older she discovers that she can also make sense of this inner world in others. She learns to understand the behaviours of her parents, and others around her, because she can understand that they have feelings, thoughts, worries and desires themselves. Others become predictable to her. Karen is learning about herself, others and the world from within these connected relationships. She has the safety and fun of intersubjective relationships within which she can influence others and is open to their influence.

THEORY OF INTERSUBJECTIVITY

Psychologist Colwyn Trevarthen observed infants and children, like Karen and her parents, interacting with each other (Trevarthen 2001). He filmed their interactions, slowing these films down so that he could see the moment-by-moment connection between them. He observed how there was a relationship dance going on as each responded to the other in synchronized movements. He discovered how important these connections were for the healthy development of the children. He added to our understanding of relationships between parents and children and how much these intersubjective connections provide a foundation for so much of the child's development.

Trevarthen has helped us to understand that an intersubjective relationship is a contingent and responsive relationship. Each response within the relationship can only occur because of the previous action of the other. The contingency between the partners in the relationship means that there is a connection between them. Trevarthen called this connection intersubjective. It is subjective because the individual is having a personal experience. The 'inter' represents the sharing of personal experiences with each other. Within intersubjective relationships we go on a journey of discovery as each partner learns what is unique and special about the other, and they share this understanding together. Intersubjective relationships are connections within which each impacts on the other. The relationship is immediate, present and each response follows on from and is connected to the action of the other.

As we explored with Dawn and Karen, this intersubjective relationship begins with an absorbed relationship between child and parent. Their focus is on each other and not the outside world. Trevarthen called this *primary intersubjectivity*. This is an attuned relationship within which the infant and parent discover each other and in the process discover more about themselves.

Let us have another look at Dawn and Karen during infancy. Karen is a sturdy, cheerful infant. She has just been fed and is now having a kick on her changing mat before a new nappy is put on. Dawn catches Karen's eye and pokes her tongue out at her. Karen is captivated. She watches intently and moves her own mouth in response. She discovers her own tongue and nearly pokes it out. Dawn delights in Karen's attempt at this simple imitation and puts her own tongue out again. Dawn responds almost poking her tongue out, and so they go on. Karen then breaks this intense concentration between them as she wriggles and squirms. Dawn, not yet ready to end this delightful interaction, picks up a toy and shows it to Karen. This is of no interest. Karen looks intently at her mum and does the best and strongest poking out of her tongue she has so far managed. 'Forget the toy Mum, I want to still play that other game!' Dawn laughs, discards the toy, and pokes her own tongue out again.

Dawn and Karen are enjoying a primary intersubjective connection. Their attention is on each other and not on the outside world. Within this relationship Karen is experiencing safety in being influenced by her mother. She notices what her mother is doing and responds. Karen is discovering that she can be part of a reciprocal relationship.

Within this interaction Karen is making a further huge discovery. She is discovering that she can influence her mum. When Dawn tries to divert her attention to the toy Karen quite clearly says: 'No!' and her mum responds. Karen is learning that she has autonomy. She can act independently and can exert some influence over her mother. Psychologists link this to the idea of self-efficacy, the experience of being effective.

This also impacts on Karen's developing sense of self. She is learning that she is a person who can be successful in her interactions, because Dawn is responding to her as someone who is successful. Karen is learning who she is through the responses of her mother.

The final influence of this simple interaction is Karen's developing capacity to manage her emotional responses, her emotional regulation. The interaction between them evokes an emotional response in Karen; in this case, probably one of enjoyment, maybe even excitement. These feelings in Karen are mirrored back to her by Dawn. She might even comment, 'You are enjoying this. This is fun, isn't it?' Karen doesn't understand the words yet, but she is getting a sense of her emotional responses to the situation, making sense and being understood by another.

We all have a window of tolerance for our emotional responses. Within this window, emotions are manageable. If we go above the window, emotion becomes overwhelming; under the window and we become switched off to it. Emotional regulation means keeping our emotions within our window of tolerance. As Karen and Dawn are illustrating, an infant does this with the help of her parent. Karen feels excitement, a sense of fun. Her emotional response to this is arousing to her. Dawn's quiet enjoyment of Karen means that this affect doesn't become too arousing and she can continue to enjoy the interaction. Dawn contains Karen's emotion, and as she matures Karen will learn to do this for herself.

When Dawn picked up the toy she was attempting to provide Karen with a different relationship experience. This is an experience within which the parent and child remain intersubjectively connected while together they look outward on the world. Trevarthen describes this as *secondary intersubjectivity*. On this occasion Karen lets her mum know that she is not yet ready for this. She wants to remain within the primary intersubjective relationship.

On another occasion, Karen will be happy to make this shift of attention. Karen is now seven months old. She and Dawn are sitting on a rug in their garden. Dawn gently blows a few bubbles in front of Karen. As they float up Karen is captivated. She smiles at them and Dawn smiles in return. Karen reaches out and touches one of the bubbles, it pops and Karen looks startled. Dawn smiles and comments, 'Did you pop the bubble?' Karen understands that it is not alarming and smiles in turn. She reaches out to another bubble and when it pops she laughs. Dawn laughs too, delighted in her daughter's response. The next popped bubble seems even more amusing as Karen giggles away. Dawn responds to her daughter's giggles and laughs even more. Notice how they are both attending to the bubbles, but they are also in a relationship together as they do this. This is secondary intersubjectivity. Notice too how both of them have emotional responses to the bubbles. Initially Karen is startled; her emotional experience is a little negative. This is immediately contained by Dawn – emotional regulation. This allows Karen to experience a more positive emotional response, which grows in intensity as her mother enjoys it with her. Their enjoyment of the bubbles increases because they are experiencing this together.

This example shows how a child can learn about the world as the child and parent together focus their attention outwards. The child is being helped to make sense of what is happening through the meaning the parent gives to it. With the adult's help, the child's capacity to think and understand is developing. In this way, through these intersubjective connections, children learn that the world, themselves and other people make sense. This in turn allows children to reflect on, process and learn from their experiences.

These primary and secondary intersubjective experiences are essential for the healthy development of a child. When children experience safety within intersubjectivity this becomes a part of the relationships that the children go on to develop. In other words, they are able to connect with other people.

There are several things that need to be present if a relationship is intersubjective. These can only occur for children when they are comfortable in these connected relationships:

Joint attention – both partners in the relationship are attending to the same thing at the same time. They each bring their own unique perspective to this, leading to a different joint experience of the event. Dawn and Karen are both attending to the bubbles. The attention that Karen has on the bubbles is extended because she is enjoying this experience with her mother. If Dawn had left Karen with a bubble machine it is likely that her enjoyment of the bubbles would have quickly waned. It is their joint experience that maintains the enjoyment. At the same time, Karen is learning to extend her attention to events around her. Children need these joint experiences in order to learn to regulate their own attention. Without this support children's attention to things can be more fleeting and they are more distractible.

Matched affect – within contingent relationships both partners share the emotional experience. For example, Dawn and Karen share a sense of joy and fun. The positive emotional state of each is magnified as each shares the same affective experience. At one point Karen is a bit alarmed; the bubbles have the potential to cause her some distress. Dawn, however, is on hand to help her. She matches the affective experience associated with the distress but stays regulated by not getting distressed herself. If both were startled, Karen would not be helped. In this case, however, Karen is soothed and her enjoyment can continue. Children need these experiences in order to learn to regulate their emotional states. Without this, children will continue to have affective responses to events, to be startled, distressed, worried, angry or even excited, without knowing how to manage these. They dysregulate but have no means to get back to a state of regulation.

Complementary intention – the final element of an intersubjective relationship is that both partners have an intention that is complementary to the other's intention; both are on the same page of the book. Dawn wants to entertain Karen with the bubbles, while Karen is happy to be entertained. They are in tune with each other. If Dawn was intent in engaging Karen with the bubbles while Karen was feeling hungry and wanting food, complementary intention would be missing and the interaction would not be intersubjective. Children need these experiences in order to learn to engage in co-operative behaviour. The give and take of relationships is learnt in these early intersubjective experiences.

These reciprocal influences feel safe and secure, thus adding to the attachment security also being provided by the parent. We will be exploring the attachment relationship later but it is helpful to notice here that intersubjectivity and attachment are different but complementary relationship experiences. Attachment to the caregiver has the potential to increase the child's safety and security, while intersubjectivity helps the child to learn how to engage in reciprocal relationships. Notice how the attachment relationship is a hierarchical relationship: 'I look to you to keep me safe and well; I do not need to keep you safe and well.' In this sense, it is one way. The parent is the wise other who can offer security and safety, while the child is the less mature partner in the relationship needing this security. The intersubjective relationship, however, is non-hierarchical – parent and child are equal in their influence of each other: 'I influence you, I'm open to influence from you.' Children need both relationship experiences to thrive.

WHEN INTERSUBJECTIVITY IS LACKING

Dawn and Karen are quickly able to establish an intersubjective experience and this provides them with a positive beginning to their relationship. This is a foundation within which Dawn can grow in confidence as a parent while Karen can experience relationship security and efficacy. I have focused on Dawn to illustrate this, but don't mean to ignore the importance of fathers. Karen's father, Philip, can also contribute to these early experiences, offering an additional intersubjective connection when he too is spending time with his new daughter.

This is not the case for Rachel and her son Ian. Rachel's pregnancy was not straightforward. Ian was born prematurely and had to spend several weeks in the special care baby unit. When Rachel goes to see her son in the unit she is feeling anxious. All the noise and equipment worries her, and the efficiency of the staff is intimidating. Rachel holds Ian tentatively, worrying that she might hurt him. She is vigilant to what is happening around her, noticing where the nurses are and anticipating that they will approach and tell her she is doing something wrong. Being alert for this she misses her son's first tentative looks towards her. His gaze is not captured by her gaze and their first possibilities for sharing an experience are lost.

Rachel changes and feeds Ian. This too is a tense time as she worries and expects criticism. Ian feels tense in her arms as he focuses on sucking the bottle, but without seeking out his mother's face. Rachel is holding Ian but she is thinking about how soon he can go back to the incubator. He is awake but seemingly unaware of her. She looks down at him, marvelling at the head of brown hair he has, but is then distracted as another alarm goes off. The easy, absorbed connection we witnessed with Dawn and Karen is missing for Rachel and Ian. The safe and secure foundation within which they can discover each other and begin to feel effective in their relationship is just not there. Both are becoming tense and anxious in each other's company. Rachel returns Ian back to the care of the nurses feeling thoroughly ineffective as a mother.

When Rachel and Ian go home things do not improve. Rachel's mood is still low, despite the medication she has been given, and she continues to be anxious around Ian. She tries to do everything she has been taught, ensuring that he is clean, changed and fed during the day, but she experiences no joy in these tasks. She is always relieved to put him back in his cot. When he cries she can feel herself tensing up, worried that she won't be able to soothe him. Ian is a fussy, grizzly baby who seems to get more tense as she tries to settle him. She is beginning to feel uncomfortable holding him, and at times will just sit in the chair watching him cry in his cot. She knows she should be attending to him but she is struggling to get up and go to him.

She feels useless, and is aware of feeling that Ian doesn't like her, although part of her also knows that this is silly. When her mother comes round it is even worse. Her mother is trying to help her, but the ease Rachel sees between grandmother and grandson only makes her feel worse. There is also the unspoken tension between mother and daughter at the lack of a father in Ian's life. Primary intersubjective connections are few and far between for Rachel and Ian.

As Ian grows older these first experiences do not provide a foundation of safety and connection on which his later development can build. Ian is not feeling effective within the relationship. Rachel tries hard, and wants this to be better, but when Ian gives out cues she does not notice and respond to them. Rachel finds it hard to help Ian to feel soothed when he is unsettled, or to share in his delight as he explores the world around him. Deep within Ian there is a sense of love being conditional, that his tired, grumpy self is not acceptable to his mother. Ian is learning to live in fear and mistrust rather than hope and trust.

As Ian becomes more mobile, Rachel tries to put in some boundaries and discipline with the guidance of her health visitor. Her depression has lifted, but she still remains anxious parenting Ian. When Ian is exploring, she ensures that he is safe, but the tantrums he displays can last a long time. Each tantrum reminds Rachel that she is a poor parent, and she continues to doubt his love for her. She finds it hard to connect with him as she waits anxiously for the next outburst. Ian, in turn, is learning to manage without his mother's soothing presence. When he feels unsettled or distressed he does not turn to her, and his tantrum usually ends in his own exhaustion and sleep. Ian doesn't understand how to get his mother's approval and so he just acts on his own impulses. The cat has learnt to stay out of his way and Rachel has put locks on the fridge to stop him helping himself when he is hungry.

Ian is an active toddler who likes to be out in the garden. However, his play is unfocused as he lacks the shared experiences that would open the world up to him. Moments of secondary intersubjectivity are scarce. Ian gets frustrated easily and then screams and protests. Rachel struggles to manage this little bundle of rage and ends up getting cross with him. Ian is not learning that his emotional world makes sense to his mum, and is struggling to regulate this emotional experience. Ian is not learning about himself, others and the world around him from within a connected relationship. He lacks the safety and fun of intersubjective relationships within which he can influence others and is open to their influence.

Ian is an example of a child who has not had enough intersubjective experience early in his life. Rachel's mental health has improved and she is trying hard with Ian, but without this foundation it is difficult for both of them.

When a child experiences parenting which does not respond to emotional needs – in other words, when these needs are neglected – this child does not feel special or lovable. Through neglect the parent has not recognized or acknowledged the internal world of the child. Without this experience the child finds it difficult to make sense of this internal experience. Seeking connection and not receiving it is a painful experience for a small child. It can feel dangerous. Infants are highly vulnerable because they are so immature. Not getting the right parenting experiences will increase the sense of vulnerability. While he cannot consciously understand this yet, a child like Ian is learning that seeking connection is painful and feels dangerous. There are large parts of Ian's experience that are not held in mind by his mother. This is translated into a sense of not being good enough, not being lovable, and this in turn generates a largely unconscious fear of being abandoned. Anxiety is high for children like Ian.

All of this reminds me of an experience such as putting your hand into a fire. It is such a painful experience that you do not try it again. Rachel is now ready to offer Ian a different experience, but he has learnt to manage by staying disconnected from her. As if he has touched fire, he does not reach out to touch again. Ian cannot learn that things are different and that Rachel can offer him experiences she was unable to offer before. This is painful for Rachel. She experiences this as rejection from her son. She too withdraws from the relationship as she struggles to feel good as a parent. Ian's need to be self-sufficient increases, and his sense of his emotional experience being unacceptable to his mother is confirmed.

Lottie's experience is different. Her parents are captivated by her when she is born. They enjoy their time in hospital; with little else to concern them they can welcome this newcomer into their lives. When they arrive home this becomes harder. They have so many problems to deal with, not least the urgent need to move again. Not accepted within the local community because they are prickly and difficult, they frequently get into angry exchanges with neighbours. They are quick to interpret this as racism, unable to notice their own contribution to these difficulties. With all of this going on it is hard for them to hold on to the special moments they experienced with Lottie when she was born. At moments of less stress they will still attend to her, and find some moments of enjoyment. These are sporadic, however, and often her needs are neglected as they try to manage their chaotic lifestyle. As Lottie becomes older and more demanding, this becomes more difficult. At times it seems as if Lottie has joined the neighbours' condemnation of them as she becomes more demanding of their attention. Their anger at the injustice they perceive around them becomes mixed up with their attempts to manage their maturing infant.

WHEN INTERSUBJECTIVITY IS FRIGHTENING

Ian is insecure because his mother was unable to respond to his needs when he was an infant. Unavailability can be damaging to young children because they experience a lack of nurture when they need it most. They do not get the intersubjective experiences they need. Lottie, too, did not get enough early intersubjective experience, but for her this was unpredictable rather than unavailable. She has learnt to seek out parental availability by behaving coercively, forcing her parents to be available as she is uncertain that they will be there if she doesn't.

Harry has had a more frightening experience of being parented. For him, intersubjective experiences have been terrifying. He has learnt not to seek connection because of this terror. Let's take a glimpse into Harry's earliest experiences.

Harry is lying in his cot. He is hungry, wet and uncomfortable. He has been crying but no one has come. Now he just lies on his back staring at the ceiling. The sun through the blinds is casting a pattern and this briefly draws his attention, but he is soon aware of the pain and discomfort within him and he whimpers. He then falls silent again and stares into space. He can hear noises in the house, raised voices and screaming. A gnawing anxiety joins the feeling of hunger in his tummy. He starts to cry again. Suddenly the door bursts open and his father is there. He shouts at him to shut up, picks him up roughly and shoves him at his mother. 'Here, you deal with him. He is your brat. And shut him up for f***'s sake.' His mother sits down and shoves a bottle in his mouth. Harry sucks at the bottle but avoids his mother's face; only a few months old, he has already learnt not to look. The blank or angry faces around him are too frightening. Not looking feels much safer.

A child, such as Harry, who experiences parents who are angry, fearful or rejecting when he tries to connect with them is not given healthy intersubjective experiences. When parents' thoughts and feelings towards a child are hostile and contemptuous the child gets an experience of persecution. These children experience themselves as unacceptable to parents. They feel a sense of terror or shame associated with this experience. This is an even bigger fire to have been burnt by. These children will learn to avoid connection not just because they fear abandonment, but also because they experience themselves as victims of the parents' own anger, fear and hostility.

When young children learn to manage without the connected relationship experience that moments of intersubjectivity bring they develop in ways that help them to manage without this. Children are strong and resilient. They will adapt to worlds where their needs are not being met, but this adaptation will come at a cost. They learn to avoid intersubjective experience. In disconnecting from such experiences they are also ensuring that they are not open to the influences of others. In finding such influences painful they avoid them so as not to be hurt. This means that connection starts to frighten them and they find ways to avoid it.

The children will, however, seek to maintain their influence over others. This feels safer, at the least because it makes others more predictable. The children try to be in charge, and parents often behave in predictable ways to this. These are the controlling behaviours which are so familiar and challenging in this population of children.

Children who are comfortable with intersubjective relationships will engage in reciprocal relationships. They are able to stay open to influence as well as to influence in turn. Their autonomy develops from this foundation. In other words, these children are growing up and developing independence, while staying connected with others.

Children who fear intersubjective relationships will not engage in reciprocal relationships. They try to exert influence without staying open to influence. Their autonomy also develops but independence comes from controlling others rather than being connected with them. In other words, autonomy without reciprocity equates to controlling behaviours. This need to control tends to spread out into other relationships. The children are socially defensive rather than socially engaged, and the cost is that they lose the experience of mutual influence with others.

PARENTING CHILDREN WHO FEAR INTERSUBJECTIVE CONNECTIONS

Parenting children who are not open to connection within the relationship has a negative impact on the parents. Offering an open & engaged relationship that seeks to connect to the other is part of what healthy parenting is all about. When this is not responded to this can have a painful impact on the parent. A child like Ian might respond with rejection and hostility and this is experienced as hurtful. Alternatively, a child like Lottie might be very clingy but whatever the parent does she will not soothe or be comforted. This triggers a sense of uselessness in the parent. In these situations, the parent can be left with a range of worries, fears or beliefs: 'Am I a bad parent?' 'Maybe I can't do this' or for foster and adoptive parents: 'Maybe this is the wrong placement?' 'Maybe we are the wrong family.'

Thus the lack of intersubjectivity impacts on the parents' beliefs about themselves. They start to feel a sense of failure as parents. They feel unsafe with the child. The parents now withdraw from the intersubjective relationship also. They try to manage the children without connecting with them. They too become more controlling as they close down the pain of offering reciprocity and receiving hurt or inadequacy in return. We see both child and parent turning their backs on intersubjective relationships and turning away from each other in the process.

This is what happens to Rachel. As her little boy can't forget the pain of his early months he responds to Rachel as if she is still not able to meet his emotional needs. He has learnt to be self-reliant and he is not going to give this up easily. His resilience is built around his ability to stay in charge. Unfortunately, this resilience is brittle and ineffective; problems are being stored for the future. In particular, it is likely that Ian will struggle with future relationships, finding it difficult to respond to teachers, not understanding the give and take of friendships. For the present though, he cannot face the hurt of rejection again and so he resists connection at all cost. Rachel is struggling too. Recovered from her early difficulties she has developed some resilience of her own. She wants to try and change things in her relationship with Ian and works hard to follow the advice of those supporting her. Her resilience is also fragile, and she struggles with complex feelings about herself as a parent. She knows she has let down her son early on and is struggling with her own feelings of guilt and shame at not giving him what he needs. When Ian is rejecting of her she finds it difficult to remember that this is his way of coping. It is hard for her to stay patient, to gently guide him into being with her in a more connected way. Instead, she becomes defensive, responding to Ian as if he is deliberately hurting her. She feels cross with him and she tries to make him respond differently. She also becomes overly focused on his behaviour, providing rewards and punishments in order to lead him into behaviours that will make her feel more effective as a parent. This unfortunately just reinforces Ian's sense of his mother's love being conditional and strengthens his own need to stay in control within their interactions.

Lottie's parents remain chaotic and unpredictable. Moments of feeling effective as parents are generally lost in the general ineffectiveness they experience with their lives. As Lottie moves into foster care she continues to anticipate similar experiences of chaos and unpredictability. Her foster carers find themselves being drawn into this chaotic world. They try to avoid this by providing a high level of structure and routine. When Lottie does not respond easily to this they look to the behavioural strategies that have worked well for them when parenting their own children. They provide consequences to the challenges that Lottie presents and rewards for the rarer moments of success. Lottie takes the rewards without connecting these to her behaviour, and experiences the consequences as further signs of the unpredictability of parents. Without connecting this to her behaviour she perceives the parents as alternating between being nice to her and being mean to her – a reminder of the unpredictability of her experience with her birth parents.

Behavioural parenting without intersubjective connections becomes a battle of wills as each tries to control the other. The parent feels useless and ineffectual but communicates this to the child in a way that makes her feel naughty and not good enough. The child is making sense of her own experiences from within the relationship with her parent. If the parent is communicating to her that her behaviour means that she is a bad child, then the child will internalize this view of herself. This increases her insecurity and challenging behaviour is more likely to occur again. The parent too is making sense of his experiences from within the relationship. The child is not responding to him with improved behaviour. This communicates to him a sense of failure as a parent and the pair become even more disconnected.

In these situations, the child needs a parent to make sense of her internal emotional experience more than she needs behavioural controls. As long as sufficient structure and supervision are in place to keep her safe and behaving within acceptable limits, the parent can focus on communicating to the child that he understands her fears and worries. This starts to provide a tentative connection from which safe intersubjectivity can grow. The parent needs to demonstrate to the child that the fire is now cold and it is safe to put her hand into it. It is safe to look into her parent's eyes, to witness the understanding and empathy there and to open up to the nurture and comfort that are now on offer.

It is hard for parents to take these steps without someone offering them the same support as they need to provide to their child. They too need someone to accept and empathize with their strong feelings of failure and regret. To know that these make sense to someone else who is not judging them for it is very healing. The intersubjective connections they can safely make with others will help them to remain open & engaged with their child, and to move back to this at times when this is inevitably lost. It is this type of support that can lead to resilience. This helps the parents to continue trying despite their fears and doubts. If the parents can find ways to stay connected to the children, then they can help the children to become more open to relationships. As intersubjectivity becomes possible, the children experience a relationship within which they can heal. Both parent and child can experience a relationship that feels both loving and successful.

CONCLUSION

Within this chapter we have met the second parenting challenge. This is the difficulty of parenting a child who fears the connections we are offering to her. Children are born ready for these connections, innately ready for an intersubjective relationship. When they seek but there is no response, or the wrong response, to their open and trusting initiations they experience fear. They quickly learn not to be open and trusting. They develop in ways that defend them from the pain of needing connection but not getting this. They avoid eye contact and learn to behave in ways that allow them to cope when safe parents are not available.

This early learning stays with the children as they grow and mature. They remain vigilant to fear and hurt and this means that they are not open to change and difference. They do not recognize the open and available parent who is now ready to offer them what they need. The children continue to respond defensively as this feels the safest way.

This becomes even more difficult when the parent provides normal and necessary limits and restrictions. The children, not safe with parents, view these as more signs that they are not good enough and not loved unconditionally. They resist the discipline as they have resisted connection. Self-reliance and coercion increase as the children try to manage their own safety rather than being able to relax in their parents' good intentions.

Chapter 3

CHALLENGE THREE UNDERSTANDING SHAME

Closely linked to blocked trust and fear of intersubjective experiences are children's experiences of shame. The fears that we have been exploring in the first two chapters are explicitly fears about relationships. Underlying these fears is a more personal fear, that of not being good enough. In order to make sense of this fear we need to understand the emotion of shame and what happens when children are not helped to manage shameful experiences. This can lead to a range of challenging behaviours which make these children difficult to live with. As we try and manage these behaviours we can unwittingly reinforce the shame that created them in the first place. This is the third parenting challenge: understanding and supporting children experiencing shame.

WHAT IS SHAME?

Shame is a very normal emotion that all of us have experienced. It is those times when we feel horrible about ourselves and we just wish the ground would open up and swallow us. It is in shame that we want to be hidden from view. We feel exposed and want to hide away from everyone. This is a rather different experience from guilt. Both of these emotions have their roots in feeling we have done something bad, which has or is likely to impact on others. Shame makes us feel bad about ourselves, hence the desire to hide. Guilt, however, makes us feel bad for the other; we experience remorse and want to reach out and make it right again. Notice how shame is inwardly directed: 'I am a bad person.' Guilt is outwardly directed: 'I am a good person but I made a mistake and I want to make amends.'

When children have experienced developmental trauma they have had many shaming experiences. They are also likely to have been left to manage these alone without the support that would help them to regulate this intense emotion. They are therefore likely to get stuck in dysregulated shame – strong negative feelings which overwhelm them. It is this experience that leads to a range of challenging behaviours.

When we respond to these behaviours we can also reinforce the sense of shame. When we provide punishments, when we berate children for their behaviour, when we ask the children to behave better, we are hoping that they will experience guilt, feel remorse and work with us to improve. A child stuck in shame cannot do this; these responses reinforce how bad he is feeling. Children in shame do not have a hole to crawl into and so they often attack us instead. Only when we can connect with the children and regulate the shame will it reduce. Now the children can experience guilt and remorse. With this shift the children benefit from consequences; these at their best help the children to make amends and repair relationships. This further strengthens their connections with others and increases their positive feelings about themselves.

It is helpful to explore how children develop such shame-filled identities, noticing how the early parenting that they experience contributes to this. When infants are born they experience a few simple emotions. We see them experiencing interest in things happening close to them; sadness, anger and joy are also evident in relation to different experiences. These emotions form the foundation for the later development of more complex emotions; embarrassment and pride, for example, are clearly experienced by pre-schoolers but not infants. Shame is another one of these later developing emotions. It develops at the same time that the infant matures into toddlerhood and becomes mobile. With this extra freedom to explore the world the toddler becomes a mischief-maker. Parents need to provide some boundaries to keep the toddler safe and to begin to help the toddler to behave in socially acceptable ways.

This is done through sequences of attunement, breaks and repair. For example, Dawn and Karen are walking up the road to the park. Karen at two years old is interested and excited about the world around her. They pass a field of sheep and Karen and Dawn watch the new lambs gambolling. They are sharing this experience intersubjectively and their enjoyment of the lambs increases because of this. Dawn and Karen are in a state of attunement; both are connected in an emotional experience of interest and enjoyment. At this very moment, Karen's interest is grabbed by a cat on the other side of the lane. She breaks away from her mum and runs across, just as a motorbike can be heard approaching. Dawn shouts out and grabs hold of Karen, pulling her safely back out of the bike's path. Karen is frightened by the abrupt change in mood. The happy, curious, emotional connection between them is broken, as Dawn focuses on keeping Karen safe and ensuring that she learns the lesson of not running across roads. Karen is upset by this broken connection and cries. Now it is time for reconnection. As Dawn comforts Karen her distress is soothed and they re-enter a state of attunement. Soon the mini-crisis is over and they continue their walk to the park.

Attunement between Dawn and Karen signals the emotional connection between them. The break in attunement represents a disconnection, and it is this that is experienced as shame. For a short time, Karen experiences her world as having gone wrong and she senses that this is because of her own badness. Dawn is on hand to help her manage this difficult emotional experience. As she soothes her daughter the experience of shame is regulated, it grows smaller; she did make a mistake but she is not bad. Dawn is also ensuring that the relationship rupture that has occurred between them is repaired. She communicates that the relationship is still okay, that she still loves her daughter and that she will support her even when things go wrong. Karen is experiencing that she is loved unconditionally. She will get into mischief, she will get things wrong, and over time she will mature and learn to behave in ways which are acceptable to those around her. Through all this learning experience she will also have the confidence that she is loved, and the relationship will always be stronger than any particular behavioural episode. She is loved no matter what.

The attunement–break–repair experiences are therefore an important part of the parenting children need in order to experience being loved unconditionally while also having limits put on their behaviour.

This experience of being able to regulate shame allows guilt to emerge. Without feelings of guilt a person cannot experience the remorse needed to make amends. Shame locks a child into self-loathing. When shame is regulated the children experience guilt, allowing them to regulate their behaviour in a way that is helpful for them and meets the approval of others.

Karen has had many experiences of being admonished for being rough with their cat. One day she reaches out and pulls the cat's tail, but then she remembers. She has a momentary feeling of guilt and this motivates her to do something different. She reaches out and gently strokes the cat instead. Karen is learning how to be around their pet and the cat is discovering that it is safe to be with Karen.

When children experience poor attunement and the parent does not repair the relationship following difficult breaks between them, the children become trapped in feelings of shame without being able to regulate this emotion. Harry is now two years old and things have not improved. He is walking, but not yet talking. Ignored for much of the time, he wanders around. His eyes are drawn to the television, which is always on in the corner. He stands there transfixed for a while before wandering into the kitchen. He notices a dog biscuit forgotten in the corner. He looks around and checks that Boss, the Staffordshire bull terrier, is nowhere in sight. He has already been bitten by him and does not want another encounter. With no sign of him, Harry picks up the biscuit and shoves it in his mouth. When his mother comes in, Harry turns away, but trips over the pile of laundry. His mother grabs him and pushes him to one side, saying, 'Look what you've done now! Can't you look where you're going!' Harry stands frozen for a while and then moves back to the television. When his mother passes near to him he flinches slightly but doesn't look round. Harry has no experience of attunement with his mother. In fact, she appears to have no interest in what his experience is. She does not recognize when he is hungry, and she does not help him to explore the world around him. Relationship ruptures happen repeatedly as Harry experiences himself as a nuisance, in the way and not good enough. Harry is experiencing shame, which left unsupported is becoming bigger.

The experience of shame that builds up into toxic, unregulated shame influences the children's developing sense of identity and they develop a sense of not being good enough. As these children grow older they remain self-focused. They cannot experience guilt and therefore are unable to feel the remorse that would motivate them to make amends. Instead, they remain focused on their own sense of badness. They fear abandonment because they do not feel lovable; love is only conditional. I will love you 'if' rather than 'no matter what'.

Lottie and Ian have less extreme experiences of shame and misattunement and therefore their experience of shame is less toxic compared with Harry. However, they too can be quick to experience shame in certain conditions.

Ian has most experience of poor attunement and lack of repair at times when he has displayed his big emotions. His sense of shame therefore develops around this aspect of himself. As he matures, Ian strives to be a good child by suppressing his emotions, trying to conform to what he perceives his mother wants from him. His need to be a good child, acceptable to his mother, becomes centred on his need to hide negative emotional experience from her. His experience of shame drives him to reinforce the parts of himself that are self-sufficient. He feels good when he is achieving; he becomes focused on the cognitive – what he knows and can learn in the world. The cost is to the emotional parts of himself that are undernourished as a consequence.

Lottie's experience is more confusing. It is hard to figure out the rules, what is acceptable or unacceptable to her parents. Attunement and repair are random and unpredictable. She develops the sense that she is in some ways unacceptable to her parents, but effective in using emotional expression to maintain their focus on her. Her sense of self develops around a sense of being naughty. She experiences shame and has no confidence that she can figure out how to behave in a way that reduces this. Lottie abandons reason in favour of emotion. She is less concerned about figuring out how to be a good child than in seeking what she needs but does not expect will come readily to her. She accepts her role as 'the naughty child', as this gives her confidence that others will be there for her. Any attention becomes better than no attention; negative attention means that she is not forgotten.

THE SHIELD AGAINST SHAME

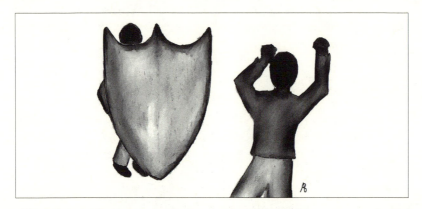

Living with this level of shame is intolerable. The only way the children can manage this is to project the feelings of badness onto others. It is never them but always the other person. In other words, the children develop a shield which defends them against the high level of shame that they are experiencing (see Figure 3.1). They appear as if they don't care, that they can't take responsibility for their own behaviour and that they are indifferent to the hurt of others. This is the shield doing its job. Behind the shield the children are caring deeply; they feel self-loathing and they fear that others will see this in them too. The shield helps them to ignore these feelings. Unless this is understood, the response of others to the behaviours that make up the shield just serve to increase the shame. A vicious circle of shame, shield and more shame is set up. Without support from understanding others this is a circle that is hard to break.

It is easy to spot the shield in action. The children tend to display a range of very typical behaviours which together provide the defence they are striving for. Thus the children will lie. They deny responsibility: 'It wasn't me' or 'I didn't do it.' This can be extremely frustrating, especially when it is obvious that the child is at fault. The parent will get pulled into an argument as she tries to point out the obvious. The child just digs his heels in and refuses to shift his position. A step up from this is to blame others. Now the child not only denies responsibility but shifts this onto another person. 'It is your fault, if you hadn't...' or 'It was his fault. He made me do it.' There is a third behaviour in this triad aimed at shifting the focus away from the child and onto others. This is to minimize. The child protests that it is no big deal anyway, what is everyone making a fuss about? Together these behaviours try to protect the child from the sense of shame he is experiencing, but often this is to no avail. Despite his best efforts, the child just experiences a growing sense of his own poor worth. He explodes with rage and anger as he tries so hard to get away from these difficult beliefs. Often this anger is directed outwards as the child shouts, threatens and verbally abuses the other person. He might trash the room as he vents his anger. He might become violent towards those near to him. Sometimes the anger is directed inwards. The child shouts his hate for himself, he trashes his own belongings, he becomes violent towards himself. In these states the children are not open to support or help. The parents are left hanging, waiting for the volcano to subside. All they can do is keep the child and themselves safe until the anger is spent. Only then will the shield drop a fraction and the parent can move in to soothe and comfort.

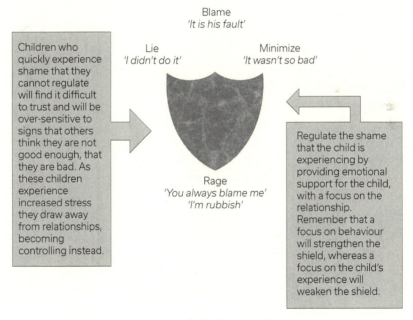

Figure 3.1 The shield against shame

Now is not the time for recriminations, for consequences or for trying to make sense of what has happened. Instead, the parent needs to demonstrate her unconditional love for the child as she shows by her presence that she cares enough to support the child even at these most difficult times. There will be time later to explore what happened, to help the child to repair the damage done. For now, it is enough to demonstrate that the parent is there, supporting the child even at the darkest of moments.

This is difficult; living through these storms is possibly the hardest time to stay present for the child. Children in shame can evoke very strong feelings in those around them. It is at these times that parents are most vulnerable to their own feelings of shame as they experience the sense of failure that comes from watching a child self-destruct. When children appear unable to take responsibility it can evoke big fears about the future for them. When children rage, parental sense of failure deepens. Parents too can develop a shield and when both shields are up, only escalating behaviours are likely. It is at these times that parents need their own support. This is a journey parents can't do alone. In the third part of this book we will explore these reactions further and consider how parents can take care of themselves so that they have the resilience needed for the child.

PARENTING CHILDREN LIVING IN SHAME

Children in shame probably test our traditional ways of parenting more than any other challenge. Behavioural management strategies, aimed at children reducing these behaviours, demonstrating remorse and making amends, just serve to increase the sense of shame and the shield is reinforced. However, this clashes with the need for parents to do something to show that they are working towards improving the child's behaviour. It is very easy for parents to get caught up in the criticisms of those witnessing the difficulties: 'I would never have treated my parent like that', 'This child needs a firm hand', 'You are being too soft on the child.' They can pile on top of this their own recriminations: 'I am a useless parent', 'Why did I ever think I could parent this child?', 'Someone else would do better.' Shame intensifies and parents can end up becoming more punitive as a consequence. They take the traditional parenting methods and apply them in ever more extreme forms. They are not being deliberately cruel and they do have good motivations. They want the child to behave, not only because it will reflect better on them but also because they know the child will ultimately be happier too. However, good intentions without understanding the shame and fear of the child will not provide the behavioural support needed.

These children need parents who help them to regulate the shame they are experiencing. As the shame reduces and becomes less toxic, the children become open to kinder behavioural support. This helps them to take responsibility for their behaviour, to experience remorse and to make amends. The children learn that things can go wrong but this is recoverable. They are good people and relationships are stronger than the worst that they can do. They are worthy of unconditional love and support. They now want to find a way forward and to work with the parent to make things right again.

As we will explore in the next part of this book, regulation and behavioural support need to start with connection with the child's internal experiences. The parent understands and accepts the fear, shame and complex range of emotional experiences that can be connected to behaviours. This is communicated to the child via the empathy that the parent experiences alongside understanding. The key to this acceptance and empathy is curiosity. If the parent can hold on to her curiosity, to wonder about the experiences of her child, she will understand her child more deeply, and acceptance and empathy will follow. A parent can't be both curious and defensive at the same time. As we move into defensive behaviours, curiosity will reduce. Holding on to curiosity, or moving back to curiosity when it is lost, is central to providing the connection that these children need.

As the children experience the parent truly understanding their anxieties, worries and fears, the behaviours will start to reduce. If the parent can reach a place where she genuinely accepts and has empathy for the child's experience, the child will become open to behavioural support. Now the child can experience remorse. Making amends becomes a collaborative process as the parent supports the child in figuring out what to do. Connection with behavioural support allows children to experience an attuned relationship. They learn that relationships can always be repaired, and that they are loved unconditionally.

CONCLUSION

This chapter has explored the third challenge of parenting children who are experiencing shame. When children are not experiencing the attunement and repair that regulate shame and make it manageable, they are left stuck in increasing feelings of shame. This impacts on the development of identity, with children forming a sense of self as bad. When they are in situations that lead to disapproval from others, this sense of shame is triggered and the children raise a shield to defend against it. Lying, blaming and minimizing defend against the sense of self as bad, and when these fail the child rages. Parenting these children relies on parents being able to connect with the emotional experience of the child, helping the child to regulate the shame being experienced. Only with such connection can the child let the parent help him to make amends. The child's fears reduce as he discovers that he can be unconditionally loved despite the behaviours he sometimes displays.

Following this chapter, the story of Andrew and Joseph illustrates the experience of shame and how it differs from guilt, linked to the parenting the children are experiencing.

ANDREW AND JOSEPH FALL OUT. A STORY OF SHAME AND GUILT

It has been a fraught day in school. The children in Year 5 are all getting tired as the end of term approaches and on top of this the rain has kept them inside. Andrew and Joseph have been provoking each other all day. The teacher Mrs Jones and teaching assistant Miss Smith have tried to keep them apart but during the last break time, while the staff are dealing with other children, a fight breaks out between them. Both children are removed from the classroom to wait for their parents to collect them.

At home time, Mrs Jones records the incident in the home–school book, as agreed with Andrew's parents. She takes Andrew out to meet his mother. She briefly tells her that Andrew has had a hard day today and expresses the hope that tomorrow will be better.

In the meantime, Miss Smith escorts Joseph out to his mother. She lets her know of the fight between the children, and again expresses the hope that tomorrow will be better.

Andrew and his mother walk home together. Judging that it isn't the right time to talk about school instead his mum engages Andrew in a favourite game, making up words based on the car licence plates that they pass. Andrew is soon laughing as he makes up strange and funny words. They arrive home and Andrew has a drink and snack. He wants to watch television but his mum suggests they figure out what was difficult at school today first. Andrew protests but his mother gently talks to him:

Mum: It sounds like today has been hard. Maybe we can figure out what went wrong.

Andrew: (Andrew hides under the cushion, but listens)

Mum: I wonder if you were worried about something at school today?

Andrew: No. I was just tired. (Andrew comes out from the cushion and looks at his mum)

Mum: Ah, it's hard to manage school when you are tired, isn't it? It sounds like maybe you were feeling cross too?

Andrew: I was cross with Joseph; he was being really annoying.

Mum: That sounds difficult. You guys usually get on so well. I wonder why it was hard today?

Andrew: He was being a pain. He got more spellings right than me, and he kept reminding me. I told him to shut up, but he wouldn't.

Mum: That does sound irritating; no wonder you got angry with him. You tried so hard to learn your spellings this week. Were you upset that you got some wrong?

Andrew: Yes, I wanted to get them all right like last week. Joseph had his name on the board and I didn't. He wouldn't let me forget it.

Mum: I can understand that you felt cross with Joseph if he was teasing you like that. I wonder why he did that. It doesn't sound like Joseph.

Andrew: He was really pleased he got his spellings right.

Mum: I expect he was. He finds spellings harder than you, doesn't he?

Andrew: Yes, and I was cross when he got more than me. (Andrew looks embarrassed) I told him he was thick and he must have cheated.

Mum: Ah, you were cross and so you said those mean things to him?

Andrew: Yes, I was really cross. And then we started fighting. I guess it was my fault, wasn't it?

Mum: It does sound like it. I guess Joseph was upset and then he got mad.

Andrew: Yes, and then we fought. Do you think he will stay mad with me?

Mum: He might for a while. I wonder what might help?

Andrew: Do you think I can phone him? What if he won't come to the phone?

Mum: Yes, it might be hard for him to talk to you just now. I wonder what else you could do.

Andrew: I know, I could give him one of my trading cards. I know which one he needs. When Dad gets home do you think you could take it round to him?

Mum: I tell you what, I need to take Bracken out for his walk later. You can help me and we can post it through their letterbox if we go that way around. You will have to miss television tonight, but it would be a help to me with Bracken, and Joseph would know you are sorry tonight.

Andrew: (Looking a bit doubtful) Okay, I guess.

In the meantime, Joseph and his mum have left the school. Mum asks Joseph why he was fighting. Joseph looks down at the ground and doesn't answer.

Mum: I am really not happy, Joseph. I don't like to be met by the teacher telling me you have been fighting. What on earth got into you? I thought you and Andrew were friends.

Joseph: I hate him. I'm never going to be his friend again.

Mum: What has got into you today?

Joseph doesn't answer as they get into the car. As they drive home his mum tries to find out what went wrong.

Joseph: It was Andrew; I didn't do anything. I hate him.

Mum: It usually takes two to fight, something must have happened.

Joseph: He called me thick.

Mum: Well that doesn't sound like Andrew. What did you do to make him say that?

Joseph: (Shouting) *I didn't do anything!*

They arrive home and Joseph jumps out of the car and runs up to his bedroom. His mum reflects that maybe she hasn't handled this very well. She decides to leave him while she makes tea and then she will have another chat with him.

Chapter 4

CHALLENGE FOUR UNDERSTANDING HIDDEN AND EXPRESSED ATTACHMENT NEEDS

In this chapter, we are going to consider attachment theory and explore children with insecure and difficult attachments. Attachment difficulties are commonly found in children who have developmental traumas. This is not surprising as the very nature of this type of trauma is that children cannot feel safe with their attachment figures. It is the parents who offer the children security, but in this case it is also the parents who are the source of trauma, whether through neglect, illness, abuse, separation or loss. For a young child who is highly immature, this lack of safety and security is a significant problem. All the parenting challenges we have explored have relationship difficulties at their heart. This is equally true when we explore problems with early attachments.

ATTACHMENT THEORY

Attachment theory was originally conceived by John Bowlby (1988, 1998), a child psychiatrist with an interest in many disciplines, which touched on child development including psychology, psychoanalysis and anthropology. His unique contribution to our understanding of child development was how he integrated these multiple disciplines into the theory of attachment. Interestingly, he also drew on his own personal experience when exploring this. The loss of his nanny at three years old was an experience that stayed with him. As his nanny had been his most significant early attachment figure, it is perhaps unsurprising that he became especially interested in the impact on children of maternal deprivation.

Bowlby suggested that children develop attachment bonds with their caregivers. Whether mother, father, relative or even paid nanny, whoever is providing nurture and protection for the child is the attachment figure. This relationship is essential for the young child to provide a sense of security and to offer comfort when experiencing distress. The attachment figure therefore acts as a secure base for the child. Alongside this nurture they can also help the child to explore the world. Children are drawn to their attachment figures as a source of security and as a facilitator of exploration. They will seek closeness with this person when feeling distressed or uncomfortable, they will protest if separated from them, and they will use this familiar adult as a base as they explore the world around them.

Karen in her early years has three attachment figures: her mother Dawn, her father Philip and her maternal grandmother, who takes care of her when Dawn and Philip are at work. Each of these people can provide Karen with nurture and comfort. Dawn is her primary attachment figure. It is she who gets up in the night when Karen is unsettled. She also spends most time with Karen. Philip is a very close second as attachment figure. He is able to settle and soothe her when she is unsettled, and is also her chief playmate. Bath time when Daddy is home from work is a special time for the two of them. Nana is a secondary attachment figure, able to act as main source of support when parents are unavailable so that Karen continues to feel secure and protected.

This is a typical picture for white, British families and probably familiar across the Western world. Just as in heterosexual couples, in same sex couples it is usual for one parent to be the principle source of comfort and the other to be the principle provider of play, with these roles being reversible of course. In other cultures there will be differences as to who acts as attachment figures, with larger family groups in some cultures, and more use of paid help in others. The need for close people to provide safety and security is, however, universal; the differences arise in who provides this safety and security.

This early attachment experience leads to the development of what Bowlby called an internal working model. The experience the child has impacts on the development of the brain. In early child development a lot is happening which gives the child a remembered sense of how the world works. She learns, for example, that she can't walk through objects, that bath water can be splashed, that cookers can get hot, and so on. All this gives her information that she uses daily to navigate through the world. She does not need to learn this afresh each time. You might consider this as the development of a series of memory templates that can guide day-to-day experiences. Without memory, life would be a very confusing experience. Attachment figures provide the young child with a template of how relationships work; this is the internal working model. Children learn what to expect and what not to expect, and they adapt their behaviour to these developing expectations. Through experience of parents, people become familiar to children. The earliest experience with close others will guide the children with future relationships. They anticipate what they have already experienced. Sometimes this expectation is realized and the internal working model is strengthened. Sometimes, however, the child might have a new relationship that is very different. In this case, the internal working model will be revised, although the original model always remains. It is a case of adding to, rather than replacing.

This attachment experience is pivotal for helping children learn about themselves in relationship with others. Children's sense of self, their identity, develops in a way that is influenced by the relationships around them. For example, a child will only learn that she is lovable if she has someone loving her. In a similar way a child may learn that she is a nuisance because of the reactions of those closest to her. Children can only know themselves from their experience with others. Attachment relationships provide the experience that leads to the children's earliest development.

In Karen's case she is learning that others are kind, nurturing and available when needed. Alongside this, Karen experiences herself as lovable, of interest to others and worth caring for. Lottie and Ian have a more insecure template; they are experiencing others as less or unpredictably available and that they have to manage their behaviour in a way that ensures they receive nurture and comfort. They experience themselves as less lovable and doubt their interest or worth to others. Harry will be having a very different experience from Karen, Lottie or Ian. He is learning that others are unkind, hostile and not available when needed. His identity is being formed by this. He experiences himself as not lovable, unlikely to be of interest to others and only to be cared for under sufferance.

Karen is developing in a climate of unconditional love; Ian and Lottie are developing in a climate where love is conditional but they can figure out ways to behave to achieve some love and nurture. Harry is developing to manage in a climate where love is unavailable and he needs to figure out how to attend to his own needs with little expectation that others will be there for him.

Mary Ainsworth (Ainsworth *et al.* 1978), Mary Main (Main and Solomon 1986) and others worked with John Bowlby and followed in his footsteps to explore the way that patterns of attachment develop depending on the experience of parenting. They identified sensitive parenting as leading to secure patterns; this is the experience that Karen is having. Insensitive parenting leads to insecure patterns, demonstrated by Ian and Lottie. The insecure patterns are made more complex dependent on the level of fear associated with the attachment experience. Harry's early experience has a high level of fear associated with it. This moves organization of attachment style towards disorganization. The more frightening or bewildering the experience, the more disorganized the behaviour is likely to be. In other words, behaviour becomes more erratic, bewildering or switched off to what is going on around him. Harry, for example, might need his mother to comfort him, but will also anticipate that she will shout at him. The need for her conflicts with the fear of what might happen. Very young, Harry does not know what to do and his behaviour will reflect this. He might stand and shake his hands, he might approach and then withdraw as the conflict plays out or he might switch off. Psychologists call this latter dissociation as he cuts off from the immediate experience, which is too overwhelming. This type of cutting off can help in the short term, but is damaging long term as he is not being helped to manage the strong emotion he is experiencing. As Harry grows older he is likely to develop different ways of dealing with a world that feels unsafe, through patterns of controlling behaviour. The conflict is dealt with by taking control through extreme coercion of others and/or patterns of compliance, caregiving and self-reliance.

As disorganized children adopt a range of these types of behaviours they become less and less able to enter into relationships. They learn to manage without emotional connection with others, as connection becomes a source of fear. Notice how the development of the controlling patterns represents the loss of the ability to feel soothed and comforted by the parent. As we explored when we thought about intersubjective relationships, children like Harry are learning to influence while staying closed to the influence of others.

SENSITIVE AND INSENSITIVE PARENTING

Karen, Ian, Lottie and Harry are growing up with parents who have very different capacities to be sensitive to their children. Mary Ainsworth helped us to understand the differences between sensitive and insensitive parents. This is determined by the differing abilities to notice what need a child is signalling and to respond to these signals. The child gives a cue to the parent about what she is experiencing at that moment. The parent's job is to read this cue, interpret it, and then meet the need the child is expressing. Sensitive parents like Dawn and Philip can do this pretty well. They won't always get it right. Sometimes they are distracted or simply misread what Karen is signalling, but they get it right enough of the time to help Karen to feel safe and secure with them.

There are three things parents like Dawn and Philip need to do to sensitively respond to their daughter. They need to notice that their daughter is signalling a need, they have to figure out what this need is, accept that this is what their daughter is experiencing, and then they need to step in and meet this need so that it reduces.

Neither Ian's nor Harry's mother can do this when they are young. For Ian, his mother is lost in her own post-natal depression. She often doesn't notice what Ian needs. She therefore cannot accept and meet this need a lot of the time. Harry's mother is able to notice her son, but is also preoccupied by her partner. She is aware that she needs to protect them both from his violence, and is therefore alert to how Harry's behaviour might trigger this. Her anxiety overrides her ability to be sensitive and responsive. She may notice Harry's needs, but her motivation is to keep him quiet at all costs. When she cannot do this she becomes more anxious. She may then respond angrily to Harry, as he is the immediate source of her failure; in the background, however, is the fear of her partner. She cannot be angry towards him and thus these feelings also become directed towards Harry. Ian is experiencing an unavailable parent and is experiencing himself as ineffective in getting his needs met. Harry, however, is experiencing a parent who is available but this is frightening. When he is effective in signalling his needs, this feels more dangerous. Ian stops signalling his needs because it leads to failure, while Harry stops because it leads to fear.

Lottie has a different experience. At times, when stress has reduced a bit her parents can be available, noticing what Lottie needs and meeting this need. At other times they might look to Lottie to meet their own needs. Their need for nurture and comfort is high, and they might pick Lottie up and cuddle her as a way of meeting this need. Lottie might respond to this cuddle, or she might be more interested in getting down and continuing her exploration of the world. Her parents can feel rejected by her when she cannot give them what they need. They will express their irritation at these times. However, when they become preoccupied with each other and the difficulties around them they turn their attention away from Lottie; now they need her to be quiet and uncomplaining. They become irritated with her when she does not comply with this need of theirs. Life is very confusing for Lottie, and she will give up trying to make sense of this, finding her own way to ensure that she gets the attention she needs.

PATTERNS OF ATTACHMENT

In this section, we will explore the different patterns of attachment in more depth, in particular thinking about how these can affect how children display their needs to their parents. Figure 4.1 provides a map of these different attachment patterns that you can refer to as we discuss each one.

Organized secure attachment	Insecure ambivalent attachment	Insecure avoidant attachment	Disorganized controlling attachment
Straightforward in eliciting care or support for exploration	Feels safe maximizing displays of emotion. Miscues by eliciting care at expense of exploration. Resists being soothed or comforted	Feels safe minimizing displays of emotion. Miscues by appearing to explore when needs care	Frightened within relationships Unable to organize behaviour to feel safe. Controls relationships for fragile sense of safety using self-reliant and coercive behaviours

Figure 4.1 Patterns of attachment

To understand these attachment patterns it can help to think about how attachment and exploration needs are experienced by children. Young children have two innate drives which motivate their behaviour in relation to their attachment figures. These are the attachment system and the exploration system. When children are feeling some degree of discomfort or distress their attachment system will be activated. In others words, children are motivated biologically to seek out their attachment figures when they need nurture and comfort. This might be because they are hungry, tired or worried by something. At these times their interest in playing and exploring the world reduces. The exploratory system is deactivated. Once they have been soothed and their needs for nurture have been met, the attachment system will deactivate and the exploratory system will activate. The children are ready to play and explore once more. They are now open to their parents joining them in this exploration. You might find it helpful to think of this as a see-saw. On one end is the attachment system and on the other is the exploratory system. As the see-saw moves up and down the two systems are high and then low, but they cannot both be in the same state at the same time. It is the way that parents respond to these different systems being activated that determines how children's attachment patterns develop.

Secure attachment pattern

In this pattern children like Karen have experienced good enough sensitive parenting. The parent has recognized and responded to the signals the child has displayed enough of the time. The well-oiled see-saw is free to move up and down. When the child needs comfort and protection the attachment needs are activated and the see-saw moves so that the attachment system is higher. As these needs are met the child feels soothed and the see-saw moves again, now the exploratory system is higher. As the attachment needs have been met the exploration needs can increase, with the associated drive to learn about the world. In this way the secure child moves smoothly between seeking comfort and seeking exploration, supported by the attuned, sensitive caregiver. This in turn leads to the development of an internal working model of self and others. The child develops a sense of self as effective, worthwhile and lovable, and others as loving, supportive and protective. This model builds resilience, helping the child to be successful in later relationships and to manage adversity when it arises. The child is able to notice what she is experiencing and to signal the need in a straightforward way related to this. She moves into a different experience as her needs are met.

When we move away from the secure attachment patterns life gets more confusing. Young children such as Ian and Lottie organize their behaviour in order to create some feelings of security based on their experience of their parents.

Children like Harry are not able to do this because none of the adaptations that they could use are successful and the parents still remain frightening. These children disorganize, displaying behaviour that expresses the conflict they are in: 'My parent should be my haven of safety but is actually the source of my fear. I do not know what to do.' As the children grow older, and if things don't change, they will continue to display these behaviours, with the disorganization becoming more centred around a need to control.

Even if parenting does change, these patterns of relating can be surprisingly resistant to change. The children seem unable to recognize and believe in the more sensitive parenting that they are now being offered and continue to behave as if this parenting is insensitive. Unfortunately, as we will explore, the parents can end up being pulled into the insensitive parenting that the children are foreseeing.

Securely attached children can signal their needs in a straight-forward way. They cue their parents as to what their needs are and the parent is then able to respond. This is very different in children with insecure and disorganized attachments. American psychologist Mary Dozier has helped us to understand how these children develop complex patterns of hidden and expressed needs. In this way they miscue their parents about what they need (Dozier *et al.* 2003). A bit like going into Alice's wonderland, the parents are left in a world where what you see is not always what you get.

As we explore the range of attachment patterns that insecure children develop it is important to note that children will often display a mixture of these patterns, responding both to the different parenting they experience from the range of attachment figures they are relating to and to differences in this parenting over time. The children who have disorganizing experience early in life tend to show the most marked variation as they alternate between coercive, attention-needing behaviours and strongly self-reliant behaviours. This can be confusing in itself, but is even more perplexing when parents are faced with a child who is very attention-needing but then rejecting of them when they try to respond. The mixed messages the children are persistently giving can be very bewildering to the parents, who are trying to stay consistent, responsive and sensitive to their children.

Ambivalent-resistant attachment patterns of relating

This attachment pattern is a response to parenting which is inconsistent and unpredictable. As Lottie's experience illustrates, parents will be available to their children at times and unavailable at other times. Whether they are available or not appears to relate to how the parents are feeling and is not linked to any signals the child is giving. When children can't trust in availability they try to make sure of it through displays of coercive behaviours. They constantly signal that they need their parent, and are not soothed when the parent does try to respond. Because the child is always in a high state of need it is harder for the parent to move from available to unavailable. Lottie's high level of attention-needing behaviour is difficult to ignore. Her parents might feel irritated or frustrated with her but they can't ignore her!

To return to the see-saw analogy, children with an ambivalent-resistant pattern are like a see-saw stuck in one position, with attachment needs permanently activated (see Figure 4.2). The child maximizes the expression of attachment need in order to maintain the availability of the parent. The cost of this is that it reduces exploration. If children are busy making sure that their parents are noticing and attending to them they cannot relax and engage in play and exploration.

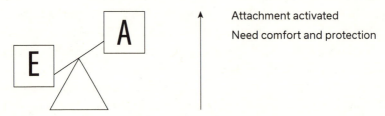

Figure 4.2 See-saw metaphor: ambivalent-resistant attachment pattern of relating

These children express their continuing need for comfort and protection. They are saying, 'You are unpredictable, I can't trust in your availability. I need you to attend to me all the time.' They then maintain the parents' attention by a pattern of push and pull. The children pull the parents into attending to them, at which point they push them away only to pull them in once more when the parents try to withdraw. This coercion of the parents is hard to escape as the children are never soothed or satisfied. In order to keep expressing this need they have to hide their exploration needs: 'I will not show my need to separate and explore. I will pull you in and push you away to keep you noticing me.' The parents are miscued about the children's experience because the children are expressing their needs on the basis of their expectations of the parents rather than on how they feel internally. They are saying, 'Stay with me, notice me, attend to me,' but they hide, 'Okay, I can do this. I'm comfortable enough to be apart from you at the moment.'

This continues to be problematic when these children are cared for by parents who are able to be sensitive. At times when Lottie's parents are more settled, they discover that they are unable to soothe their young daughter. This increases their anxiety, and feelings of frustration grow. Their own childhood experiences, which lacked available parents, make them particularly vulnerable to this. Similar to their daughter, they doubt their own lovability. As Lottie's demands and rejection of their attempts to soothe her grow, their level of anger towards her also grows. Lottie reminds them of their own experience of insecurity and conditional love. Their reactive responses to their daughter reinforce her attention neediness and the pattern is confirmed. Eventually their frustration grows to the point that they are physically abusive towards their daughter.

Lottie arrives in care bringing the only pattern of attachment that she knows with her. Her foster parents try to meet Lottie's expressed need. This is the only need that they see. They try to demonstrate their availability: 'I will reassure you that I am available. I will be here when you really need me.' This does not soothe Lottie and eventually her foster parents also feel frustration that they can't meet the need. They become irritated with her. The foster parent can also become unpredictable to the child. Because they have a less troubled past experience than the birth parents they are able to manage this frustration without it escalating to physical abuse, but the child still finds that this provokes anxiety. Lottie's expectation that parents will be inconsistent and unpredictable is confirmed and the pattern is reinforced. Her increasingly challenging behaviour is difficult to manage, and some foster parents reluctantly decide that they cannot continue to offer a home to her. It is only when Lottie moves to live with Belinda that she finds some stability within which the possibility of change arises.

As Belinda is able to manage the degree of challenge that Lottie presents over a longer period of time, Lottie is able to experience a parenting that is different from her previous experiences. Belinda can provide a high level of structure and consistent routines, helping Lottie to begin to trust in the predictability of the parenting. Belinda is also able to co-regulate the emotion that Lottie is expressing but not managing. Much as a parent does with a typical toddler, the parents of older children with ambivalent-resistant patterns need to use their calm presence to help reduce the emotional turmoil that the child is experiencing. The parent communicates: 'I will stay with you, I will support you and I will protect you when you are having these strong feelings.' In this way the expressed needs are being met and the oscillating coercive behaviours can reduce.

Parents also need to be mindful of the hidden needs that the child is not displaying. Mary Dozier suggests that they gently challenge the hidden needs (Dozier 2003). The child needs help to be apart and to feel secure that the parent will be there when needed. Belinda is sensitive to this; she finds ways to help Lottie manage some gentle challenges to her consistent presence, while also communicating that she will be here when Lottie really needs her. Lottie slowly starts to feel more secure, although this security is fragile, as we will see later. At times of increased stress when Belinda is finding it harder to maintain this sensitive but challenging parenting, Lottie quickly returns to her previous anxious-ambivalent attachment style.

Avoidant attachment pattern of relating

This attachment pattern is a response to parenting which is unavailable at the times of highest emotional need. This was Ian's experience when Rachel was experiencing depression and the stress of managing a small child as a single parent, and without her mother's wholehearted approval. When children are feeling most distressed and emotionally uncomfortable, parents in the position that Rachel was in are highly likely to withdraw from them. The parent signals that the child's distress is not accepted by her. Children find this very disturbing; learning that your parents are not available when needed most feels highly unsafe. The children learn to deal with this by not displaying their need of their parent when emotionally aroused. They act as if they are okay in order to maintain their parents' availability. Thus the children look as if they are confident exploring and playing, but this is a front. These children remain alert to their parents' presence while they act as if this is not important to them. Children with an avoidant attachment pattern have the see-saw stuck in the opposite position to the children with ambivalent-resistant patterns (see Figure 4.3).

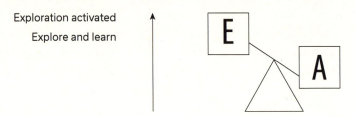

Exploration activated
Explore and learn

Figure 4.3 See-saw metaphor: avoidant attachment pattern of relating

These children therefore display a lack of need. They miscue the parent by acting as if they want to explore at times when they actually need comfort. The children anticipate that any displays of need will lead the parents to withdraw and become unavailable when they are most needed. They are saying, 'I will do it by myself. I fear my need of you. I will push you away.' The hidden needs remain well out of view: 'I will not show my need for comfort and soothing.'

Rachel's depression improves and she finds some stability in her life as she makes a new partnership with Jane. Resolving her sexuality is also a huge relief for her, and Jane is more than happy to become a parent to Ian. Rachel and Jane bring renewed confidence and determination to their parenting of Ian.

However, this parenting task does continue to be difficult. If the parents do not understand that the children are miscuing them they can unwittingly reinforce this attachment pattern. The child signals 'I'm fine' and so the parent tries to meet this expressed need by letting the child manage on her own. The child's expectation that the parents will not be there when needed is confirmed and this pattern is reinforced. Rachel and Jane initially struggle to find a way to help Ian discover the difference in their ability to parent him now and to help him feel more secure with this parenting.

Rachel and Jane will discover that children with avoidant patterns can be helped over time if they gently challenge the hidden needs. They guess when the child is experiencing emotional arousal that is not displayed and then provide the comfort and safety that they predict the child needs. These guesses are based on the context: 'I would expect you to feel emotionally wobbled by that and therefore I am going to respond to you as if you feel wobbled.' The risk of getting these guesses wrong is less than the risk of reinforcing the child to continue to miscue the parents. Gradually the children can begin to trust that their emotional needs will not overwhelm the parents. Parents also need to co-regulate the emotion that the children are hiding but not managing. As with parents of children presenting with ambivalent patterns, these children also struggle to regulate their emotions. This can be more perplexing, however, when these emotions are being experienced so firmly out of view.

These children do need the calm, soothing presence of their parent despite the act they are putting on. In this way, parents can help the children to feel comfortable needing and being helped by them. Generally, children will learn to express minor physical hurts first. They will test out their newly developed but fragile confidence in their parents when the danger does not feel too great. Thus Ian makes a great fuss over a small knock when he walks into the table. Rachel and Jane can see that he has not hurt himself, but he is acting as if he has been mortally wounded. However, the day that he falls from his bike and breaks his arm he hardly makes a fuss at all. The doctors comment on how brave he is while Rachel and Jane are saddened to see how easily Ian can still hide his distress from them. More emotional worries not connected to anything physical are hidden from view for the longest time. Ian has many fears that he does not demonstrate to his mums. When Rachel goes away for a school reunion weekend Ian is more fractious but he does not disclose his big worry that his mother may not come home again. Children do not start to express these types of worries until they have developed a lot more confidence in their parents.

Disorganized controlling patterns of relating

As already explored, children with disorganized controlling patterns of relating are more complex. This is the attachment pattern or style of relating that develops when attachment needs are triggered but the child has experienced the parent as frightening. This might be because the parent is frightening to the child. Harry's father shouts at and hits Harry. He has no sense of safety with his dad and thus he has developed the disorganized controlling pattern of relating. Generally, this is expressed through being quiet and compliant in his father's presence. Experiencing a parent as frightened is equally dysregulating for a child. Harry's mother is frightened much of the time. When her partner isn't around she can relax a bit and Harry experiences her as more available. At other times her fear is tangible, especially when parenting Harry, who can upset her partner at any moment. Harry experiences this as frightening because of the fear, tension and unavailability of his mother.

Infants like Harry experience difficulty organizing their behaviour at times of stress. It is as if the see-saw collapses underneath them. As they grow older, children with these patterns of relating under stress learn to control relationships to force predictability. Controlling relationships develop instead of reciprocal relationships; the child wants to influence the other without being open to influence from the other. He is now standing on top of the see-saw ready to take on the world.

Therefore, when attachment and connection feel dangerous, this prior experience influences how a child responds. Miscuing occurs through complex patterns of hidden and expressed needs. The secure base is frightening, the world is scary and the children express their needs by trying to take charge. They are saying, 'I will not rely on you. Relying on you is dangerous. I must be in control.' As Marian and Robert witness when they adopt Harry, his early experience moves in with him. He controls them through a combination of highly self-reliant, rejecting and coercive ways, communicated through angry, oppositional and defiant behaviours. Harry is hiding away both his need to explore the world and his need for comfort and nurture, except on his own terms.

Robert finds this especially difficult. His own father was a very controlling man, and Harry's behaviour takes him uncomfortably back to this. He becomes more authoritarian himself as he tries to reduce his own stress and increase his sense of control. Marian dislikes the changes she sees in her husband, and possibly becomes more lenient towards Harry as a consequence. They are no longer parenting from the same book. This clearly impacts on their marriage as the tension between them grows. Maybe they would have separated anyway, they will never know for sure, but the challenges that Harry presents to them are very likely to be a contributory factor.

Marian has to learn how to be available, responsive and gently challenging. It is a challenge for parents to meet the hidden needs of controlling children while also trying to deal with the impact of the expressed needs. These children need safety and low stress environments but behave in ways that reduce safety and increase stress.

Parents of disorganized controlling children like Harry are challenging hard-won beliefs: 'Parents can't keep you safe', 'Parents are dangerous', 'I am so bad, nothing you can do or say will change this', 'I should take care of you, and not expect you to take care of me.'

THE IMPACT OF CARING FOR CHILDREN WHO REMAIN INSECURE

Whether parents have made changes in their lives, recovered from illness or children have been moved to live with different parents through foster care, kinship care or adoption, the children will find this is very different from their previous experience. Their attachment patterns of relating are adaptations to help them manage with the parenting they have experienced. In these new environments, these adaptations that have helped them to survive are suddenly maladaptive. We hope that they can change these patterns to better adapt to the more sensitive parenting that is now on offer. This is a big ask, however. Attachment patterns are not just ways of behaving; they are linked to a nervous system that has developed for the environment they were initially raised in. They are biological as well as behavioural. Children do not adapt to new environments quickly. They find these unsettling and they initially anticipate what they have experienced previously and behave as if nothing has changed. Parents find themselves being treated as if they are the insensitive or frightening parent of the past. If you think about attachment as a parent and child dancing together then we might consider that the children are leading the dance.

Mary Dozier (2003) studied what happened to attachment patterns of relating when toddlers moved into their foster and adoptive homes. She found that when the children were leading the attachment dance then the parents could unwittingly respond in kind. Therefore, some parents would behave as if the children did not need them when the children demonstrated avoidant attachment patterns or they would became frustrated, and sometimes angry, when the children demonstrated ambivalent-resistant attachment patterns and would not be comforted by them. It appears that parents can respond to the miscuing of the children and try to meet the needs that are being expressed but overlook the pattern of hidden needs that the children are not displaying.

Children need parents who can accurately interpret the child's need for nurturance despite the miscues the child is giving. This means that the parents need to find ways to connect with the hidden experience of the child as well as the expressed needs.

CONCLUSION

The miscuing of attachment needs can be very bewildering for those caring for children with attachment difficulties. Hidden needs are hard to notice precisely because they are hidden. It is easy to be pulled in to meeting the expressed needs without providing the gentle challenge that the children need. Without this, however, the children will never discover that being parented can be different; old experiences do not need to be repeated. Understanding attachment theory, and the way that children develop patterns of attachment which are replicated within later relationships, is important if parents are going to be able to find ways of helping the children to feel safe and secure within their care.

Chapter 5

BRAIN, BIOLOGY AND THE DEFENSIVE CHILD

If you want to understand the biology of why children develop ways of being which reflect their blocked trust, fear of relationship, shame and need to miscue their attachment needs then this chapter will help. Biology isn't for everyone so feel free to skip this chapter if this level of detail is not for you.

IMPACT ON THE DEVELOPMENT OF THE NERVOUS SYSTEM

We have explored how the very early experience of an infant can have a profound impact on the development of the child and his ability to trust in later relationships. This development is founded in current experience, but perhaps influenced by many hundreds of years of parenting experience leading to the development of cultural memories about safety and danger.

We will now explore another aspect of the way that this develops by thinking about how the experiences young children have influences the way that their brain and the rest of their nervous system develop. The important message is that children's early experiences will lead them to respond to later parenting, sensitized by the earlier environment. If they experienced a lot of frightening things, their nervous system will be prepared for these same experiences later in life, even when they are no longer happening. They will respond as if they are still being hurt, even when they aren't.

Our brain is part of our nervous system and is influenced by what is happening in our bodies. At birth the brain is relatively unsophisticated but this immature organ is ready to develop in response to the social world that the child is born into. In other words, the biology of the child is impacted on by the experiences the child is having. The brain matures influenced by the social world a child is living in because it is linked to the rest of the nervous system. This runs throughout the body bringing messages from the outside world to the brain and receiving messages from the brain in response. The brain connects to the body via the spinal cord (this is called the central nervous system). This receives messages from the rest of the body via the peripheral nervous system. This is made up of parasympathetic and sympathetic branches of the autonomic division of the peripheral nervous system. The parasympathetic branch is like a brake; it slows us down and allows us to relax or to withdraw. The sympathetic branch is like an accelerator; it revs us up and gets us ready to be active – to fight, flee or play and explore. These branches respond to messages from the brain, which direct it in terms of how safe or dangerous things are feeling.

This is where the amygdala, the brain's alarm system, comes in. This receives messages from outside through our senses, processes these very rapidly and then sends a message to the autonomic nervous system about how to respond. The amygdala can become sensitized to early experience that feels dangerous. It then becomes highly sensitive to possible signs of danger, causing the nervous system to respond to this; the smoke detector is set too sensitively. This is why children who were born into more dangerous worlds can react to safer worlds as if they are still dangerous. A simple example is a child who was hit by his father who now responds to his foster father looking a little annoyed with him as if he is about to be hit. In fact, even neutral expressions on parents' faces can be interpreted as dangerous by children who have had very difficult early experiences, because of the way the brain and nervous system have developed.

Psychologist Stephen Porges has developed polyvagal theory to explore how the nervous system develops (Porges 2011). The vagal system describes the nerves that carry the messages within the nervous system. This theory can also help us to understand how the experience of fear and danger early on will directly impact on the way the nervous system develops. As we have been exploring, this then influences how children respond to later and perhaps more benign environments.

Porges suggests that our modern nervous system is a complex product of our evolutionary history. We have ancient systems and modern, more evolved systems, which have developed in response to the changing worlds we have evolved in. The more ancient systems, concerned with fight or flight and shutting down or 'playing dead', helped our ancestors cope with highly dangerous and less sophisticated environments. The modern system has developed our ability to be socially engaged, helping us to become the social species living in complex social worlds that we now inhabit. Important for our understanding of developmentally traumatized children, our nervous system remains a complex mix of the ancient system, ready for defence, and the more modern system, ready for social engagement. We cannot do both of these at the same time, but will be either defensive or socially engaged from moment to moment.

This helps us to understand how we respond to the experience of safety and danger. When we are feeling safe we are helped by our modern nervous system, whereas when we are experiencing danger our more ancient defensive system takes over. The choice of which system will operate depends on our monitoring system. As we have already seen, one of the jobs of our amygdala, within the brain, is to be alert for signs of danger and to switch from the safe to the defensive system to help us to cope. When we are experiencing safety our nervous system works in a way that helps us to engage socially with people around us. Our sympathetic nervous system operates in a way that mobilizes us to play and explore. Similarly, our parasympathetic nervous system can allow us to immobilize, to relax, hug with the ones we love and to generally be quiet and relaxed. At signs of danger, however, there is a switch and we reduce our social engagement and behave defensively instead. Now our sympathetic nervous system will mobilize to cope with the danger that is anticipated. We might freeze momentarily while we assess the situation and prepare to act. As we remain defensive we will then move into a fight or flight response. We try to flee from the danger or take more direct action. However, if the danger feels high and our possibilities are low, we can't run and fighting would be dangerous, then we become immobilized instead of mobilized. We shut down, dissociating or cutting off from what is going on around us. This is protective in the short term, but can come at a cost if it continues for any length of time. It is the equivalent in humans of an animal's playing dead response.

Think of the rabbit being chased by the fox: at first the rabbit freezes, still, but totally alert to the first signs that a fox is nearby.

The rabbit detects where the fox is coming from and now runs in the opposite direction; fight is not an option for the rabbit! Unfortunately for the rabbit, the fox is faster and catches up. When all seems lost the rabbit plays his last card. He pretends to be dead. Physiologically everything slows down so that his heartbeat is almost imperceptible, he barely breathes, his muscles lose their tone and become floppy. The fox, satisfied that this rabbit is dead, can put it to one side while he seeks further prey. The rabbit then shakes himself, and mobilizes again. He runs off, living to flee another day! This is a high-risk strategy whereby if the biological systems shut down too much the animal actually dies. Immobilizing to danger is a last line of defence.

A response that we see in humans, not unlike the playing dead of the rabbit, is dissociation. This is a very normal response that is not always associated with danger. Think, for an example, of a time when you have been driving but have become switched off to what is going on around you. You suddenly become alert to the road again but are surprised to find that you have safely navigated the last two roundabouts without being consciously aware of it! This normal response can also be used more dramatically in experiences that are far from normal. Children who have experienced sexual abuse often describe something similar. Fight or flight are not options and so these children dissociate. They are no longer consciously present to the experience. Sometimes the children will describe this experience as being on the ceiling looking down at themselves, or living in a shadow of themselves rather than in their body. This is extreme dissociation to manage an extreme circumstance. When they have had these early experiences, children will respond to sudden hints of danger in the same way. We might notice brief dissociative lapses; the child feels no longer with us for a short moment. Alternatively, a child might shut down for longer, for example a child curls up at the side of the room, not asleep but also seemingly not aware of what is happening around him.

Earlier I suggested that the way we detect whether there is danger is like having a smoke detector in our brains, providing a warning when necessary. Just like a smoke detector, it can be set at different levels of sensitivity. An over-sensitive smoke detector will sound an alarm even when there is no fire. In a similar way our amygdala, supported by the hippocampus, can be set to be more or less sensitive. When a child has experienced a high level of fear early in life the amygdala becomes overly sensitive. The child becomes hyper-alert to signs of danger, triggering the amygdala to sound the alarm and the nervous system to respond defensively. The social engagement system becomes deactivated in favour of the social defence system. When we are responding defensively to people it reduces our capacity to be open & engaged with the relationships around us. Defensive behaviours are generally seen to be socially unacceptable, others disapprove of a child who is running or fighting. The child's sense of badness can be increased if his behaviours are not understood. This in turn can reinforce the experience of mistrusting others, which of course will continue reinforcing the sensitized nervous system.

Figure 5.1 shows the defence and social engagement systems within the brain, adapted from a diagram Stephen Porges presented at a conference (Porges 2014). Porges used this to explain why social connection is part of our biology, 'a biological imperative' as he described it. His theory also helps us to understand how our capacity to self-regulate – to soothe ourselves when we are feeling emotionally aroused – develops out of regulation that is embedded within relationships. In other words, connection is part of being human, which stems from early relationship experience and develops a child's capacity for later successful relationship experience.

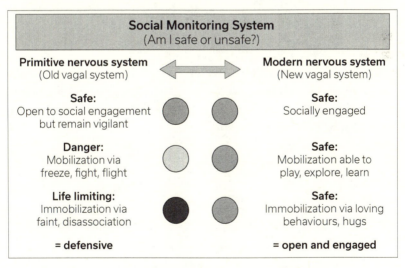

Figure 5.1 Summary of the defence and social engagement systems
(Adapted from Porges 2014)

Thus when a child is feeling in danger, physically or emotionally, he is more likely to be in the state suggested on the left of the traffic lights. If he thinks he is going to be hurt, rejected or ignored he will behave defensively. If the parent can help him to feel safe, he will move across to the state suggested on the right of the traffic lights; he will be open & engaged with his parent. The snag is that when we are in a relationship we tend to move into the same state as the other person. If a child is defensive, it can pull the parent into matching this and becoming defensive in turn. If, however, the parent can remain open & engaged at these times, the good news is that the child will then move to match the parent and become open & engaged as well. How to do this will be explored in the next part of this book.

The brain-based development of blocked trust

We have considered how the whole nervous system will respond to either safety or danger. It is defensive responding that we see in a mistrustful child. Baylin and Hughes have explored this further (2016). They describe what is happening in the brain of a child when blocked trust has developed, and suggest that five brain systems are affected. These are core brain systems that are responsive to the quality of care that a child receives.

1. *Self-defence.* At times, everyone needs to defend themselves, whether against physical or emotional threat. Our self-defence system allows us to do this, switching on at times of need and then switching off when the danger is over.

2. *Social engagement system.* This is the system that is strengthened by good care. It helps us to stay socially engaged with others, even when these interactions are a bit tense. This facilitates social bonding and taking care of each other.

3. *Social switching system.* This system helps us to move between social engagement and self-defence. When we do this will depend on circumstances influenced by the current state of safety and threat appraised during interactions. We have a watchtower in our brain looking out for danger and moving the switch as needed. This reminds me of meerkats: one or two meerkats remain on high ground, constantly on the lookout, alert for any danger that might approach. As these lookouts see the snake approaching they will sound the alarm. The whole pack immediately takes notice and responds to the danger, abandoning what they are doing and seeking safety underground.

4. *Social pain.* From early in life children will experience the pain of social separation. This is a necessary part of the development of a call and response dyadic relationship between an infant and his parent. The infant signals distress (the call) and the parent responds to reduce the distress. A neuroscientist called Nim Tottenham has described this as social buffering. This means that the parent is on hand to help the child feel safe again, and this in turn allows the child to emotionally regulate (Tottenham 2014, cited in Baylin and Hughes 2016). Responding to the distress calls provides much-needed soothing and regulation. As the parent provides this regulatory support it allows the child to mature and develop his own capacity for emotional regulation. Without this support the child remains emotionally immature, still needing support from others but also avoiding this support because of the way distress calls were previously responded to. The child has adapted to life with poor capacity for emotional regulation.

5. *The stress system.* How a child will respond to stress, therefore, is determined early in life dependent on the quality of care received. It is this that will set the balance between defence and engagement in relation to experience and thus determine how well the stress system is supporting the ability to respond to the challenge of increased stress. This is done by mobilizing physical, cognitive and emotional resources to deal with it. We all need some activation of our stress system. When this is activated we get a release of the hormone cortisol, which helps us to deal with both good and bad challenges. Without this we could not do many of the fun things in life – dancing, playing football, even taking the dogs for a strenuous walk. It is also this response to stress and moderate levels of cortisol that helps us to learn and remember new things. Problems only arise when the stress system is activated at more extreme levels.

In infancy, these systems develop in a subcortical, bottom-up fashion, with top-down support coming from the parent. In other words, the infant only has the lower levels of the brain active – the emotional parts rather than the thinking parts. The child is reliant on the parent's more mature thinking brain to support the still developing, immature infant brain. This is social buffering. It provides the child with the experience of safety in closeness to the parent. When a young child is well supported by the parent there is a release of a hormone called oxytocin, the social bonding hormone. The presence of oxytocin reduces the brain's sensitivity to danger. The child is better able to deal with stress, can turn for support to others (social engagement system) and the self-defence system can stand down quicker as a response.

As the infant matures into toddlerhood and beyond, the upper parts of the brain start to develop. These early emotional brain systems connect to the developing higher brain regions, which develops the child's ability to think. By 18 months of age, with good care, the toddler has his own executive system for the social brain. He still needs co-regulation with a parent to help this function but he is beginning to learn to think and this reduces the need to respond defensively. The child is comfortable with social engagement; he will seek interactions with others and will importantly turn to these when he is feeling an increase in stress. He has capacity to engage with others and to sustain this engagement even when interactions are tense. These interactions also support the child's continuing development. The child is being helped to become increasingly self-aware through his introspection and ability to reflect. He understands who he is in relation to others. This in turn helps the development of empathy as the ability to think about self and others increases.

Thus, good quality care of an infant will support the shift from bottom-up to top-down functioning in the brain. Initially, the infant can only use his brain from bottom-up and relies on the parents' top-down brain functioning for support. With maturity, the child's top down brain functioning is developing, allowing the development of the social engagement system. The child is learning to regulate and to reflect, which supports learning from new experiences. As social engagement occurs, instead of defensive reactions, trust is developed and the child can attune to inner experiences through the development of empathy.

Poor care, however, will leave the child's brain in a less developed, connected state. This brain is adapted for more dangerous environments where reacting rather than thinking is needed (see Figure 5.2). This is reflected in the child's stress system, which is tuned up high to respond to stress early and quickly. The social switching system has a very low threshold and so turns to defence early. As the child experiences the world as dangerous and himself as bad, the self-defence system in the brain is favoured over the social engagement system. This allows the child to become vigilant to the external world rather than reflecting on his inner life. Being quick to act is more important than thinking when life is dangerous. This also provides an advantage for a child who has learnt to see himself as bad and others as unsupportive or even dangerous. It allows him to react in the world rather than think about self. This protects him from the dual dangers of a dangerous world, which he is reacting to, and an inner life of terror and shame, which he is avoiding thinking about. The stress system becomes chronically activated, easily triggered and hard to turn off. This allows social pain to be blocked. If the child does not feel the pain of social disconnection, of no one being there when needed, he is protected from the fear of this pain with no way to stop it. If he does not feel pain he does not need comfort – a useful block when comfort is unavailable. Tragically, however, this setting of the brain is not conducive to new learning. The brain is organized to manage in a dangerous world. This blocking of new learning becomes a big disadvantage when the environment changes. When parents recover their ability to care sensitively for the child, or when the child moves to a new parenting environment, the brain cannot catch up. The child continues to respond to the earlier experience unaware that these defences are no longer needed.

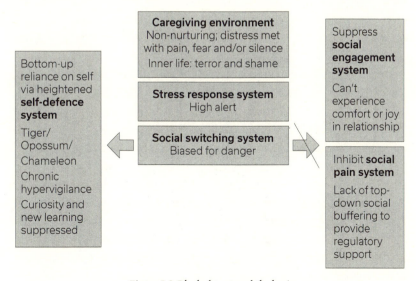

Figure 5.2 Blocked trust and the brain

From this description of blocked trust, we can see how children can develop styles of relating that are angry, controlling and highly intrusive towards the safe care that the parent is offering – the fight or flight of the sympathetic nervous system. The child is oppositional, ready to fight and defend himself. Alternatively, the child develops the ability to shut off from what is happening around him – the dissociation of the parasympathetic nervous system. The child is present but disconnected from those around him. In neither state is the child open to social support.

CONCLUSION

In this chapter we have explored how developmentally traumatized children develop nervous systems that have developed to be good at defence. When we are biologically wired for defence we are much less able to be socially engaged in reciprocal relationships with others. Early experience can, therefore, provide children with an environment within which they adjust to the danger of not being protected or cared for well enough, and they learn to cope with loss of parents. This adaptation provides some protection for them, allowing them to survive, but it comes at a cost. They develop blocked trust alongside an emerging sense of self within which they see themselves as not worthy of love and care. They live in the shame of not being good enough. This means that they cannot anticipate that others will be able to love or care for them unconditionally. They learn to fear connection within relationships because of the pain that seeking but not receiving connection brings. In order to get their needs met they miscue their parents about what they need, adapting to what they expect of parents rather than what they feel internally. Their attachment security is compromised and they work hard to feel safe in a world where safety and security do not come easily.

This is the tragedy of developmental trauma; in order to survive the children have to lose something that is at the heart of our humanity – our capacity to socially connect with others. In staying in charge of relationships, reciprocity is sacrificed. Children can influence but are not open to influence. Children are more comfortable with disconnection from others than with feeling socially connected.

— Part 2 —

THERAPEUTIC PARENTING

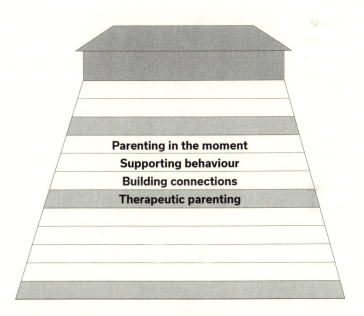

Parenting in the moment
Supporting behaviour
Building connections
Therapeutic parenting

In this part the focus is on parenting. This will consider how to parent the children in a way that allows them to recover from trauma, emotional difficulty and the associated fears linked to this. When parents emotionally connect with their children they are helping the children to discover that parents are safe and that they can be loved unconditionally. The children are able to move from mistrust to trust. Now the children can cope with the behavioural support that is important to provide the boundaries and limits they need. In the last chapter of this part this parenting approach is summarized within a model called 'parenting in the moment'.

Chapter 6

BUILDING CONNECTIONS

I have now reviewed the four key challenges for children and parents where there has been experience of developmental trauma and emotionally insensitive parenting. Children are left with difficulties in trusting in relationships. They develop a shame-based sense of self and learn complex ways of relating to others that miscue their needs, leading to patterns of hidden and expressed needs. In this chapter, the focus will be on the parenting that can help children with this range of difficulties. This pays particular attention to building emotional connections with the children.

DIFFICULTIES WITH TRADITIONAL PARENTING

Parenting children with experience of developmental trauma is especially challenging because the parents are trying to provide nurture, behavioural support, guidance and teaching to children who do not trust them or in their good intentions. As we have seen, the trauma that these children have experienced has led to the development of ways of being that are organized around a need to be in charge within the relationships. They have developed a range of controlling behaviours in order to do this. These behaviours can be very diverse: compliance, coercion, caregiving, self-reliance, entertaining; these are all different ways of behaving which are serving the same purpose of feeling in control of relationships so that they feel safer and more predictable. Even predictable anger and frustration from a parent, provoked by extreme coercive behaviours, feels safer to the child than waiting and wondering when the next angry outburst will come. Feeling in charge feels so much safer for these children than being open & engaged with the parents – the source of their fear. These children have learnt to behave defensively to ward off the danger that they are anticipating. They are more comfortable being disconnected than in experiencing connection.

This is where traditional parenting runs into problems. Behavioural management has developed to use with children who believe in the love that the parents offer. As explored in Chapter 1, they experience themselves as unconditionally loved and can therefore believe in their parents' good intentions. When they are distressed, perhaps because of the boundaries and consequences provided for their behaviour, they are able to manage this distress because they can let their parents help them with it. This means that these children are open to the limits the parents are providing and responsive to the praise and consequences used to demonstrate approval or disapproval. Over time the children internalize the values that the parents are trying to instil and are able to behave in acceptable ways. These children grow up well adjusted; they remain open to parents' support, even when they are going through the rebellion and risk-taking of adolescence. They become adults who are socially comfortable, can form healthy relationships and are open & engaged in connection with others.

When love feels conditional this all becomes more difficult. Developmental trauma is an extreme of this experience. These children do not believe in the good intentions of others but view these intentions through the lens of their own feelings of worthlessness and shame. They perceive danger in the most normal of boundaries and they respond with defensive behaviours. These children are highly anxious. This means that they are not open to the limits the parents are providing; they respond to consequences and praise with suspicion and distrust. When these children become distressed they cannot turn to parents for support so easily; dysregulation tends to increase as emotional arousal grows without the ability to regulate or soothe this. These difficulties with relationships and with regulation make adolescence a much more dangerous time. Rebellion and risk-taking are managed without turning to the adults for needed support. These children become adults who remain socially uncomfortable. They form adult relationships that continue to be organized around the need to control. They remain closed to social engagement, more comfortable with disconnection than connection.

Traditional behaviour management relies on parents' problem solving, based on understanding the environmental contingencies that make the children's behaviours more or less likely to happen. When a behaviour occurs in the context of certain conditions and is followed by certain consequences it is more likely to happen again. A simple, but familiar, example is a young child walking past the sweets in a supermarket. When the parent doesn't stop to get some the child has a tantrum. The parent, embarrassed, gives the child the sweets so that the tantrum ceases. The trigger for the behaviour (the tantrum) is passing the sweets and the parent provides a consequence for the behaviour which is rewarding – the child gets some sweets. The contingencies of walking past the sweets and being given sweets for a tantrum make it more likely that tantruming behaviour will occur in the future. Parenting advice focuses on managing the shopping by not passing the sweets, thus avoiding the trigger. If the child does throw a tantrum the consequence is that this is ignored and the child does not get the sweets. Instead, the child is rewarded for different behaviours, say helping Dad put the shopping into the basket. Thus, parenting techniques are suggested with the goal of managing the contingencies in order to increase the frequency of behaviours the parent wants the child to display. Put simply, the parent is advised to reward good behaviour and ignore or provide a negative consequence for bad behaviour.

Highly anxious, developmentally traumatized children become even more anxious when parents try to apply these ideas. They do not understand that the consequences and rewards are focused on behaviour while the parent still loves them unconditionally. Instead, these contingencies are viewed as signs of love being conditional. This increases anxiety that parents have discovered that they are not good enough and perhaps are preparing to abandon them. Not being allowed to have sweets indicates that parents are mean, unkind and not available to them. However, rewards also signal anxiety. For example, if the parent offers a reward of sweets the child experiences this as being evaluated by the parent. The parent is signalling I will give you sweets if you behave. This creates anxiety as the child anticipates that she can't live up to expectations. Behavioural management parenting therefore increases anxiety for these children. The parents need to find different ways to support the behaviour that reduce the children's feeling of anxiety.

THERAPEUTIC PARENTING

Children do need behavioural support but this needs to be provided in a parenting environment that attends to children's regulation and ability to connect. Parents need to offer the children the very experiences that they most fear. Only then will they be able to benefit from behavioural support so that they too can internalize the values of their parents and can grow up to form healthy adult relationships. Parents need to find ways to build connections with their children, even though the children are behaviourally and biologically focused on staying disconnected.

A WORD ABOUT CULTURE

I am white British and this book will be infused with the values that I have internalized from my culture. I respect, however, that these may be different within other cultures, and anticipate that each of you will have different cultural experiences and values. I do believe that the power of connection is universal among human beings and that much of what I am writing will be helpful to parents of all cultures. I invite you to reflect on this within your own cultural beliefs and values, so that as you help children to connect with you it is these that you will pass on.

A DDP-INFORMED THERAPEUTIC PARENTING APPROACH

I am now going to describe a parenting approach called Dyadic Developmental Psychotherapy and Practice (DDP), which has been developed specifically to help children who have experienced developmental trauma (Hughes 2009, 2011). This is a therapeutic parenting approach. By this I mean that the parenting of these children provides healing from their trauma as well as behavioural support.

This is not the same as therapy; parents are parenting first and foremost. It is, however, therapeutic. Some children may also need help from a therapist, supported by their parents. Both therapy and parenting can be provided within the approach. Dan Hughes developed this model based on his observations and understanding of early child development (Hughes 2009, 2011). By considering how healthy parent–child relationships develop we are in a better position to understand the experiences that children have missed out on when their early development has occurred with parents who were not able to meet their developmental needs.

DDP-informed parenting helps family members to develop healthy patterns of relating and communicating. In this way they can all feel safe and emotionally connected. As connection starts to become more comfortable for the developmentally traumatized child, her trust in her parents will start to develop. This trust, which in healthy children develops from their earliest of experiences, comes later and takes longer but can develop with this parenting approach. Trust and connection provide a foundation for the children's safe experience of discipline and boundaries. In the next chapter I have included a summary of the DDP principles as they apply to parenting for those who want to understand this in more depth.

DDP-informed parenting is connection with behavioural support as the parent takes on the dual task of building trust and providing boundaries and discipline. When parenting children beyond infancy there isn't an opportunity to build a connection through demonstrations of unconditional love without at the same time providing limits on behaviour, and this presents a particular challenge for parents. The foundation of connection during infancy is not in place, and therefore the structure of behavioural support cannot be built on this foundation. The parents have to build the foundation at the same time that they are adding the structure.

Dan Hughes has described parenting for developmentally traumatized children as connection with correction (sometimes written as connection before correction). I have drawn on this idea within this book using the term connection with correction to acknowledge the importance of emotional connection before, during and after behavioural support. It is important to note that 'correction' used here is referring to parenting which helps children develop prosocial behaviours by providing appropriate boundaries, limits and consequences within the context of highly warm and nurturing environments.

Behavioural support needs to be developmentally appropriate. Children vary in the rate that they mature. They go through developmental stages at slower or faster rates than other children. They can also be at a different stage in emotional development (the ability to understand and manage their emotional life), cognitive development (the ability to think based on their understanding of the world) and social development, which involves using both emotional and cognitive abilities to make and sustain relationships and to understand the self in relationship to others. Developmentally traumatized children often have immature emotional and social development, sometimes alongside more mature cognitive abilities. This means that even if they appear quite streetwise, or older than their years, this is based on a very thin emotional foundation. The children are slow in emotional development because their emotional needs have not been well supported in the past, and they are now less open to the emotional support of their parents. Children become even younger emotionally when stressed, and if the parents become stressed by the impact of this they may find themselves behaving in more immature ways as well!

When parents are providing behavioural support, it is important that this is matched to the developmental stage of the child. The parent needs to provide a level of structure and supervision that is appropriate for this unique child at her stage of emotional development. It is not helpful to expect more of the child than she can manage. When she fails to live up to these expectations she will experience consequences that are likely to reinforce her identity as a naughty child. It is better to give more structure and supervision that reflect developmentally appropriate expectations. The child is then able to succeed and consequences are reduced. The child can then begin to revise her sense of self, and to feel more confident that she is a good child who sometimes gets things wrong.

Central to helping children develop safety in connection is the parenting approach of PACE. This will be explored in depth later, but, in brief, PACE allows the parents to become attuned to their children through a stance of playful parenting, acceptance of the children's inner world, curiosity about the meaning underneath the behaviour and empathy for the children's emotional state. In this way the parents stay emotionally engaged and available to the children, demonstrating their unconditional love while also providing the safety that comes from appropriate boundaries and discipline.

TRAUMA AND ITS RELATION TO PARENTING

When parents are parenting children who have been affected by trauma it is important that they have a good understanding of this trauma and how it can impact on the children's development and day-to-day functioning. When parents are trauma-informed they are able to parent the children in a way that helps them to feel safe and secure so that they can recover from trauma. Sandra Bloom is a psychiatrist interested in the way that trauma can impact on hospital environments for adults experiencing mental health difficulties. She has developed the 'sanctuary model' as a way of ensuring that the therapeutic environment is trauma-informed, including the patients' traumas from childhood. The alternative is environments organized by the trauma of the patients, environments that do not facilitate recovery from trauma and a return to mental wellbeing (Bloom 2013).

We can think about Sandra Bloom's ideas in relation to parenting, where the difference between trauma-informed and trauma-organized can also be observed. Ordinary parenting, which does not take account of the traumas and attachment difficulties stemming from early experience, can easily become trauma-organized. The parent is affected by the difficulties that the child is having in trusting and entering relationships. The parent responds to the miscuing of the child's attachment needs and tries to manage behavioural challenges without attending to the levels of shame that the child is experiencing. This can result in parents becoming defensive in their parenting as they respond to the defences displayed by the children. As parents become more trauma-informed they can parent the children therapeutically. The parent stays open & engaged with the child, and is able to return to this when he notices himself becoming more defensive. 'Parents who can resist the natural tendency to respond defensively to a child's defensiveness and can recover effectively from inevitable moments of losing empathy with a mistrusting child are the trust builders these children need to have' (Baylin and Hughes 2016, p.73).

When you are living with and trying to parent a child who is becoming defensive to your most gentle of parenting it becomes difficult to stay open & engaged with the child. Think back to the traffic lights diagram in Figure 5.1. This diagram applies to the parents as much as to the child. The child's defensive responses pull the parent into his own defensive parenting in turn. The parent is not feeling safe with the child, which puts his social monitoring system on high alert and the parent starts to become angry and frustrated and may withdraw from the child. In other words, defensiveness breeds defensiveness. However, if the parent can find a way to stay open & engaged, or to notice his reaction and return to this open & engaged stance, the child will not be able to stay defensive. Being open & engaged also breeds being open & engaged. This is central to DDP-informed parenting.

The traffic lights are an example of one visual image that can help parents to understand what is happening in the moment. Another useful analogy rests on the image of a river flowing between two banks to represent integration, as suggested by Dan Siegel (2010). This is depicted in Figure 6.1. Siegel suggests that:

> Integration is the linkage of different parts of something. When we integrate within a relationship, for example, we honor differences between ourselves and the other person. Then we promote linkage through compassionate understanding and communication. In the brain, integration happens when we honor the differences between our higher and lower regions and then link them, or between our left and right sides, and then link them. (Siegel 2014, p.55)

Figure 6.1 The river of integration (Siegel 2010)

This integration allows us to have a sense of harmony, able to be flexible and adaptive towards ourselves and others. This is represented by the flow of the river. Being open & engaged, for example, puts us into the free-flowing river. In this way we can adapt to what the child needs as we respond flexibly and helpfully. We notice and make sense of what the child is doing, and this understanding guides us to provide her with what is needed. Notice that in this state the parent is taking the time to understand the child rather than moving to try to change the child's experience. Thus the parent is able to behave in coherent ways, having energy to change and adapt alongside stability. This flexibility allows parents not to rush too quickly into trying to reassure the child or to solve the problem the child is presenting.

Once the parent understands the child's experience and communicates this understanding then reassurance becomes a way of letting the child know that the parent gets it and that he has hope that they can get through this together. The parent is not trying to change the child's experience. From this position parent and child can jointly find a way forward, if this is appropriate to the situation.

Philip has taken Karen to the cinema while Dawn stays at home with Teagan. Philip has been looking forward to this, a special time for father and daughter. He is disappointed therefore that half way through the film Karen urgently asks if they can leave. He tries to persuade her to stay but quickly realizes that this is not going to happen. They leave the cinema and Philip suggests that they go into the local cafe for a drink. As Philip is putting in their drinks order he notices how frustrated he is feeling. He does not like missing the end of a film, even a children's one. He smiles to himself as he remembers the frustration he felt as a child on the relatively frequent times they had to leave the cinema because of his younger brother's health difficulties. This brief reflection allows him to manage his feelings of frustration and therefore to be open & engaged towards Karen. He asks her what the problem was. Karen is reluctant to say; she just didn't like the film. Philip acknowledges that this can happen sometimes but expresses his surprise that this was sufficient for her to want to leave. Karen then acknowledges that she was frightened by one of the characters. She then expresses her anger with herself for being so silly. Philip is kind and patient. He acknowledges that the character was scary, and tells her that he does not like films that scare him. Karen is surprised by this and wonders if he has ever left the cinema before a film has finished. Philip shares with her a failed date with a girlfriend because they had different ideas about films; Karen is soon laughing at the idea of her dad with a girlfriend and is glad that he met her mum!

Philip is clearly swimming strongly in the river of integration within this example. This enables him to stay open & engaged to his daughter and he gets some special father and daughter time after all.

When parents move from this integrated state, they will be more defensive. Philip has had his share of these when parenting his children; things do not always go so smoothly! When parents move out of the river and onto the banks their behaviour towards their children can be quite different. The banks of the river represent the times when parents have lost flexibility and are less able to adapt to what their children need. The two banks represent rigidity and chaos respectively.

On the bank of rigidity, the parent might become very focused on achieving a task. He becomes stuck on this task, and can see only one way of achieving this. Siegel equates rigidity with being boring and predictable. This is a rational response, but without the creativity that emotional engagement would bring. The parent might try to sort out a problem by becoming stuck on wanting the child to think and feel differently. The parent might become critical and judgemental towards the child.

Jane is looking after Ian while Rachel is away. This is the first time she has been left solely in charge of Ian and she is feeling anxious. She doesn't want to let Rachel down. She has planned an exciting time for Ian with a trip to the local funfair and a meal out. This starts off well, but Ian is unusually indecisive about which rides he wants to go on. Jane therefore chooses one for them; she selects the gentlest of family rides. As they approach it Ian hesitates and then stops. Jane urges him on telling him that he will be fine, the ride is very gentle. Ian manages the ride with this persuasion and enjoys the candyfloss that follows. On the way home Ian asks Jane if they could have a takeaway that evening instead of going out. Jane is thrown by this as she has selected Ian's favourite restaurant and has invited a friend and her son to come along with them. She doesn't want to let the friend down. She lets Ian know that a change of plans isn't an option. The evening does not go well. Ian is unco-operative and soon falls out with the other child. They all end up abandoning the meal and Jane is relieved when she gets a tired and grumpy boy to bed.

Jane is a sensitive parent to Ian but on this occasion her level of stress led to her losing sight of this. She failed to take into account Ian's increased stress in her desire to demonstrate her parenting skill to Rachel. As Ian demonstrates that he doesn't have the emotional resources to manage Rachel's absence and the treats Jane has planned for him, his behaviour causes Jane further stress. Failing to be aware of her own or her son's escalating anxiety, Jane becomes more determined to do the day that she has planned. It is only when she is talking it over with Rachel on the phone that evening that she realizes how rigid she had become. Rachel is sympathetic; after all, she has had her own share of parenting stress. They plan together a less stressful second day, and Jane is reminded to acknowledge with Ian how much they are both missing Rachel this weekend. The rest of the weekend goes smoothly and Rachel is greeted on her return by two smiling faces.

Chaos is on the other bank. Siegel suggests that chaos occurs when things are out of control, overwhelming and unpredictable. In this state we might expect to see much more emotionality in the parent's responses towards the child. The parent feels strongly and expresses these feelings with little thought. The parent might feel angry or hopeless and these strong feelings influence the responses made towards the child.

It is early days following Marian's separation from Robert. Harry is more demanding than ever, disturbed as he is by Robert's departure. Marian is trying to stay understanding but is feeling her own range of difficult emotions about the loss of her husband. On this particular day James is unwell and she is sitting with him. She has put the television on for Harry hoping that this will keep him occupied for a while. It is a vain hope; Harry is concerned about the attention that his brother is getting. He calls up frequently, demanding drinks, snacks, a different film – anything to get his mum's attention onto himself. When Harry starts to provoke James, Marian's patience finally snaps. She angrily tells him that if he doesn't behave he will be going to bed early and he can forget about supper; only her greatest resolve stops her adding that he can go the same way as his father and give her some peace. Of course, Harry's anxiety is increased and he redoubles his efforts to take charge and demand Marian's attention. Now she has a dilemma, as she knows an early bed without supper is not really an option. Her chaotic, emotional response to her son, understandable though this is, has increased the stress for all of them.

Movement between the river and the banks can be led by the children or the parents. Either way, as one of them becomes rigid or chaotic in their responses to the other it is likely that the other will join them on the same bank. This closes down the intersubjective relationship as each becomes lost in the intense feelings they are trying to manage.

The difference between open & engaged and defensive becomes very important as we go on to explore the parenting attitude of PACE. This attitude ensures that the river is free flowing. When the parent moves to either of the banks he is defensive. He loses the attitude of PACE and instead becomes punitive, evaluative or judgemental. The relationship is less connected and the child's mistrust increases. When the parent stays open & engaged, the river flows. He is able to maintain the attitude of PACE, or repair the relationship when this attitude is temporarily lost, and so the connection is strengthened and the child's trust increases.

Therapeutic parenting is parenting which is trauma-informed rather than trauma-organized. In understanding the trauma of the child, and the child's defensive responses, the parent becomes able to stay open & engaged when the child's responses are pulling him into becoming defensive.

Therapeutic parenting helps children to trust in the parent and to become comfortable with reciprocal intersubjective relationships, being open to influence as well as influencing. Parents will have to regulate powerful feelings of shame in the child and meet hidden as well as expressed attachment needs. All of this occurs alongside parenting that provides consistent and developmentally appropriate boundaries and discipline.

SKILLS NEEDED TO PARENT CHILDREN WHO FEAR CONNECTION

Connecting with children rests on parents' ability to make sense of their children's emotional experience and to respond to this. Their responses need to accept and have empathy for this experience.

Let's focus on this internal experience for a moment. What we think and feel is our internal experience and it is important to hold on to the fact that our internal experience is separate from our external behaviour. What we think and feel is neither right nor wrong, it just is. How we demonstrate what we are thinking and feeling through behaviour might be acceptable or unacceptable, but not the emotional experience leading to this.

Karen is just two weeks old and Dawn is struggling with lack of sleep. Philip is back at work after an all too brief time off. Dawn therefore offers to do the night shift. Karen is unsettled, however, and she has been crying and fretting for much of the night. Alongside fantasies of lying in her bed Dawn is dismayed to notice herself also fantasizing about ways to shut up her small infant, some more unpleasant than others. Dawn decides enough is enough; she wakes Philip and asks him to take over for a little while so that she can get some sleep. Fortunately, Dawn falls asleep at once and is saved the frustration of witnessing Karen fall asleep on her father's shoulder!

The thoughts and feelings that Dawn has are neither right nor wrong, but they do act as a signal that she needs to look after herself in order to take care of her infant. A parent who is less aware of her growing feelings might not take care of herself. The feelings grow out of sight until the parent snaps and behaves in a way that is frightening to the child. He might shake or throw the child, for example. If parents are aware of their internal experience and understand the importance of taking care of themselves, their behaviour will be safe and appropriate as well.

Young children do not understand their internal experience as adults do. They need time with parents making sense of this for them in order to begin to notice and understand it themselves. They will have big thoughts and feelings, but only with sensitive, responsive parenting will they learn to recognize these and accept them for what they are. Their behaviour will be a reflection of how good they are at noticing and regulating their internal experience, and turning to others for support with this.

Connection allows us to help children with this. By noticing, understanding and connecting with the internal experience of the child we can co-regulate this emotion. This can reduce the behavioural challenges that the child presents, but even more importantly it will build her trust with her parent. As trust builds the child will, over time, learn how to regulate her emotion and will behave in line with the internalized values she has gained from her parent.

Alongside this the parent is helping the child to learn that her experience makes sense, and that it can be named and talked about. By reflecting with the child on what she is experiencing the parent is co-constructing her experience. The child has a narrative to help her understand what she is experiencing, and to put this understanding into words. In other words, a parent and child can together find a story that makes sense to them both. This story both deepens the child's understanding of what she is experiencing and also helps her to regulate this experience.

There are two key skills that parents need in order to facilitate emotional connection. These are:

- the ability to be mind-minded towards self and children

- the ability to stay regulated so that they can maintain an attitude of PACE.

In this and the next chapter we will explore these two abilities in more depth.

THE ABILITY TO BE MIND-MINDED

As previously discussed, in order to connect with the child, parents need to be able to understand the child's internal experience – what the child feels, thinks, believes, desires, fears and wishes for. It is this that the parent will accept in order to support emotional connection. Doing this rests on a skill which we begin to learn when we are at the pre-school age – the ability to mentalize. In particular, parents need to be able to know the mind of another, or as psychologist Elizabeth Meins coined it, to be mind-minded (Meins 1997).

Another psychologist, Peter Fonagy, has written about the ability of mentalization (Fonagy *et al.* 2002). This relies on having good 'Theory of Mind', or the ability to understand that you and others have minds, with their internal world of thoughts, feelings, beliefs and desires. Theory of Mind is something which typically develops between the age of three and four years. It is a maturing ability, which also relies on the relationships that a child is experiencing. Theory of Mind and the ability to mentalize combine into what Fonagy describes as our reflective functioning. Children who have parents who are not interested in what they are internally experiencing are likely to be slower developing a Theory of Mind, they have weak mentalization abilities and therefore a reduced reflective functioning.

Theory of Mind helps us to understand other people because we can understand what they may be thinking and feeling. This makes their behaviour more predictable to us. Karen notices her mother is crying. She therefore predicts that her mother is having an emotional experience; she is upset. She looks around and sees that their pet cat has knocked a vase onto the floor. She guesses that the broken vase has upset her mother. With this understanding Karen can show some empathy to her mother. Without understanding it is difficult to empathize. Karen has learnt to connect to her mother's internal experience. Without some experience first of her parents connecting with her emotional experience it is likely that Karen would find this much harder to make sense of. It is because others connect and have acceptance for children's internal experiences that they are able to reciprocate and do this for others in turn.

Therefore, in order to connect with children, the parent first has to be able to make sense of the internal experience of the child. He has to make sense of what is happening through clues in the child's behaviour. This curiosity lets him figure out what the child might be thinking or feeling. He then accepts this experience, knowing that it is neither right nor wrong, it just is. With acceptance he can show empathy for the child's experience. The child feels understood and not judged for this experience. This connection also helps her to regulate her emotional experience. Through connection the parent is co-regulating with the child and emotion can reach a tolerable level. Only now will the child be able to reflect on her behaviour. Now is the time for behavioural support.

Lottie struggles to manage her strong feelings, and at first finds it really disconcerting when Belinda makes sense of her experience for her. Lottie cannot engage in any curiosity with Belinda, but after a while becomes used to Belinda's conversations with their parrot. What initially seemed like mad behaviours of her foster carer have become more normal and even give Lottie a sense of containment; she is emotionally regulating more quickly. Even the parrot has learnt to say, 'I wonder' although not always at the most appropriate of times! It is therefore something of a breakthrough one day when Lottie is disgruntled and anxious and Belinda asks her if there is anything she can help her with. Lottie shrugs her shoulders and continues taking her frustration out on her mobile phone. Belinda comments to the parrot that she thinks Lottie has something on her mind and she wonders what it is. Lottie puts down her phone and comes and stands close to Belinda; she even responds when Belinda puts her arm around her. Belinda, reflecting on Lottie's frustration with her phone, wonders if Lottie is expecting someone to phone. Lottie acknowledges that she is disappointed that a school friend has not called after promising to do so. Belinda comments that Lottie must be feeling quite cross with her friend; how horrible it is waiting for a call that doesn't come! Lottie agrees and adds, 'I feel sad; it feels like she doesn't like me after all. I thought I finally had a friend!' Belinda wants to smile, as this is the first time Lottie has noticed a feeling of sadness all by herself. She restrains herself, however, and remains empathic towards the horrible feelings of being let down by friends. Next day, at school, Lottie finds out that her friend had been caught up in a family crisis; maybe the friendship could happen after all!

With this continual experience from the parent, the child is discovering her own mind. The child is learning to organize her experience and this will eventually help her put into words what she is experiencing. This further increases the child's capacity for regulation that has begun to develop within the relationship with an attuned, sensitive parent. Notice how relationship, regulation and reflection are all closely linked.

Regulation and reflection will be much weaker if the children do not have experience and trust in a relationship that is unconditional in its capacity to connect with their early experience. Without regulation and reflection, the child will find it hard to manage emotional experience and not get overwhelmed. This applies to positive emotion – think of an overexcited toddler for example – as well as to negative emotion. If a child can't soothe herself and she can't tell others what she is experiencing, then it is likely to become evident through behaviour. The child might dysregulate, demonstrating challenging behaviour at the verbal or physical level. Some children who have experienced very angry parents when they have displayed these types of behaviours in the past might dissociate, switching off and shutting down.

Lottie's behaviour was very challenging before she was able to let Belinda help her to regulate and make sense of what she was experiencing. She shouted, slammed doors, destroyed property, and on a few occasions had struck out at Belinda. The worst of these behaviours is now largely behind them, although when Lottie is especially stressed Belinda will notice them creeping back in again. At these times Belinda pays attention to increasing all the things that she knows help Lottie to regulate, hot chocolate drinks being a particular favourite for both of them. Understanding that these behaviours are linked to emotional experience is helping Belinda not to get too stressed in turn. She can then stay available to Lottie, providing emotional regulation and being ready to chat to her about her worries when Lottie indicates that she is ready for this.

CONCLUSION

In this chapter, the focus has been on how to parent children therapeutically in order to increase their sense of security. This helps the children to experience and feel safe with emotional connection, and makes behavioural support more palatable. The model that is informing this approach to parenting is Dyadic Developmental Psychotherapy and Practice (DDP), as developed by Dan Hughes. This model focuses the parent on 'connection with correction'. The parent strives to provide an emotional connection with his child. This then allows the child to manage behavioural support with reduced feelings of shame, and less fear that she is not good enough. To achieve this emotional connection parents will need good reflective functioning. In particular, they will need to be mind-minded so that they can make sense of their children's internal world.

Chapter 7

PARENTING WITH PACE

In the last chapter, we explored the importance of emotional connection within therapeutic parenting. Parenting to emotionally connect with children relies on the capacity to remain emotionally regulated alongside the ability to be mind-minded, to make sense of the internal world of the child. When in an emotionally regulated state, parents can use this understanding to help them connect to the children. This is where PACE comes in. This is a parenting attitude of playfulness, acceptance, curiosity and empathy.

THE ABILITY TO MAINTAIN AN ATTITUDE OF PACE

PACE is at the core of therapeutic parenting. This parenting approach facilitates a connection between child and parent which is not possible with a narrower focus on managing the behaviour. Behavioural support is important but if it is not done within an atmosphere of PACE it will reinforce the child's sense of shame and his belief that parents will not continue to love and care for him. The connection that PACE brings builds the trust and security in the relationship that has previously been missing from the child's experience of being parented. With this connection the child will cope better with the normal boundaries and discipline that parents need to provide for their children.

PACE was suggested by Dan Hughes as a way of helping the adult remain emotionally engaged and available to the child (Golding and Hughes 2012). PACE helps parents to demonstrate to the children that they are available and sensitive to their needs. The parent becomes attuned to the child through a stance of acceptance, curiosity and empathy. Playfulness at appropriate times provides an opportunity to increase the fun and joy in the relationship. PACE combined with unconditional love for the child means that the parent is meeting the emotional needs of the child to be loved, nurtured, protected and understood.

Parents will strive to adopt an attitude of PACE, to maintain this attitude even when they are beginning to feel challenged by their children and thus defensive towards them, and to return to the attitude at those inevitable times when it is lost under stress. The ability to do this is strengthened when parents have good ability to stay emotionally regulated themselves. Emotional regulation strengthens PACE whereas dysregulation weakens it. In the final part of this book I explore self-care, social support and self-understanding. These all help to strengthen parents' capacity to stay emotionally regulated when under stress.

PACE rests on the mind-minded ability of parents to become attuned to the children's inner experience. An attuned response to children helps them to feel connected to the adults. They are more likely to be able to regulate and reflect and this can, over time, have a positive impact on their behaviour. Putting feelings into words reduces the use of behaviour to express these feelings.

Notice that PACE is an attitude, a way of being. It is not a behavioural strategy designed to change the child. The parent tries to maintain this attitude, however the child responds. If the child is not able to enter a conversation about this, the parent can simply use PACE on behalf of the child. The attitude as a backdrop to the relationship will provide the child with a greater sense of being unconditionally accepted, however he responds. Thus, if the parents are generally curious and understanding about the child's inner world, acceptance and empathy will come through in the way they are with him. The child, in turn, will experience being understood without pressure to change what he is thinking and feeling.

In this way, the parent does not use PACE to get children to talk, to open up, or to behave differently. The parent is changing her responses towards the child, without expectation that the child will change as well. PACE is a way of being to help children feel more secure. At its best, PACE is a habitual way of engaging with the child, not a technique to turn on and off as needed.

Karen is having a hard time at school. Dawn and Philip suspect she is struggling with some bullying by the other girls but she does not want to talk about it. They are approaching the end of primary school and, as can be the case, some of the children are trying to grow up fast as secondary school looms. It is too easy to tease Karen for being a 'teacher's pet' as a way of managing their own anxiety about forthcoming changes. When Karen is rude to her mother during dinner and then storms off with some rather theatrical door slamming, Dawn calmly puts Karen's dinner in the oven to keep warm. They finish their dinner while allowing Karen to have a bit of time to herself. Philip then goes up to see how she is doing. She is lying on her bed with her head in her pillow. Philip sits down next to her and quietly comments on how changing school can make everyone a bit cranky. Karen cuddles into him and Philip strokes her hair, letting her know that he is there to talk about it if she wants to. Karen tells him it's okay, she can deal with it, but she just wishes the other girls didn't have to take out their 'adolescent angst' on her. Philip laughs as Karen uses her fingers to accentuate the phrase, and wonders how she got to be so grown up and sensible. 'Not so sensible', says Karen wryly remembering her rudeness and how she had stormed out during dinner. Philip lets her know that dinner has been kept for her, and that Mum will be happy with an apology. Karen returns to the table a bit sheepishly; she gives Mum a hug and says sorry. Dawn hugs her back and suggests she eats up her dinner as Teagan has her eye on it. After all, macaroni cheese is quite a favourite with Teagan.

Karen isn't especially keen to talk about how she is feeling with her father, but just knowing he understands is enough for her on this occasion. Sometimes, when children like Karen are verbal and at a developmental stage where they are able to join in the curiosity about their inner world, they might listen to the parent and join in with some exploration of their experience. It is important that the parent matches the child's mood so that the child can feel understood. Thus, if the child is sad the parent will talk quietly and slowly. If the child is angry the parent will talk without anger but with more vitality and intensity. With this understanding the child might feel ready and able to talk with the parent about what has been going on for him.

With the love and care that Rachel and Jane are giving to Ian he is getting better at letting them help him with his feelings. He is more comfortable sharing his emotional life with them and has discovered that they are not overwhelmed by his worries. As Ian approaches the change to secondary school he, like Karen, is experiencing additional stress. Rachel and Jane have noticed that he is moody and less interested in meeting his friends after school. Rachel wonders about this with him. At first Ian is angry with her and doesn't want to talk about it. He yells at her to leave him alone. Rachel responds with a similar energy, but without getting cross:

Rachel: Ian, you are feeling really cross with me. I guess something is really bugging you. You don't have to talk about it but I'm wondering whether I can help.

Ian: (Now a bit calmer) Just leave it, okay. It's nothing.

Rachel: I'll leave it if you want me to, but I can see something is worrying you, and I've noticed you are staying in a lot at the moment. I'm wondering why you aren't doing things with your mates, as there must be stuff happening this near to the end of term.

Ian: Oh, they are just boring; it's just kid's stuff they want to do. I'd rather read.

Rachel: I'm surprised about that. I thought you enjoyed going over to Mandeep's and I know his mum invited you for tea.

Ian: I didn't want to go, and anyway, his house smells funny.

Rachel: Ian, I can see you have some worries at the moment and clearly you are struggling with your friends but I don't like to hear you say things like that. I want you to be kind to other people and respect their different cultures. You know that Mandeep and his family eat different foods from us and I am sure our house smells just as strange with some of the things we cook. Now, why don't you help me understand what is bothering you?

Ian: I didn't mean to be horrible, it's just I think I need to leave Mandeep alone for a while. We're not such good friends at the moment.

Rachel: I am sorry to hear that; you have been friends for so long.

Ian: Yer, well, things change.

Rachel: That's true, sometimes we do drift away from friendships, but this seems quite sudden. Any idea why it has changed?

Ian: I think Mandeep is trying to get in with Jake and that lot. He is going to be at the same school with them next year. That seems to be more important than me at the moment.

Rachel: That sounds kind of tough. I would feel quite hurt if a friend did that to me.

Ian: It's cool. I think it's important he has friends at his school. I hear that there are some mean kids there who might pick on him if he is on his own.

Rachel: Wow, Ian, you have really thought this through, haven't you? But where does this leave you? There aren't too many boys going up to the school with you, are there?

Ian: No, I guess I might get picked on too.

Rachel: Has this been worrying you for a while?

Ian: Yes, but I thought you would think I was being silly. I know how keen on the school you are.

Rachel: I am pleased you have got a place at that school, but I do understand, the change is going to be hard. A new school is daunting for anyone and it's hard when your friends are going elsewhere. I can understand that you would be worried about that. Anything I can do to help?

Ian: No, it will be all right. I am worried, but I'm glad you don't think I'm being silly. I guess I will just have to get there and try and make some new friends.

Rachel: Well any problems, you let me know. It's a big change and lots will be different next year. I think the school have a holiday camp, I wonder if I could enrol you. Perhaps you will meet up with some other new boys there. It might make it easier at the beginning of term.

Ian: (Looking brighter) Yes please! I think they do archery. I've always wanted to have a go at that.

Rachel: Sounds like a plan.

Ian: Thanks Mum. Do you know, I might give Mandeep a ring. I love his mum's cooking!

Ian had some big worries about changes coming up. The end of term was feeling stressful and he was trying to make sense of friendships and how to manage these. At times of stress Ian can easily revert to avoidance, trying to manage his worries on his own. He is initially angry when Rachel tries to help but as she matches his affect, which expresses his experience of anger towards Rachel he calms quickly and is able to think with her about what has been going on. This connection is recent for Ian, and he still doubts that his worries will be acceptable. However, as Rachel stays with PACE, Ian allows himself to be vulnerable and disclose what is bothering him. He is open to Rachel's understanding and comfort, and from this basis can even think with her about whether there is something that might help. Ian is moving towards secure attachment with the sensitive and responsive care that Rachel and Jane are providing.

If the child is not able to listen and join in, perhaps because of immaturity or because of the level of shame he is experiencing, the parent continues to hold the attitude. This is the case for Harry. He is much further away from security than Ian, developmentally immature and easily moves into shame. It is hoped that over time Marian will be able to help regulate the shame that Harry is experiencing so that he becomes more open to her support. This is likely to be a long road, however. Harry has very little stress tolerance, and little things can feel very big for him. This is a strain on Marian, who can struggle to maintain her own regulation at times. She is getting some good support, however, and with this is working hard to provide Harry with a PACE-led home. Harry is still quite resistant to this and is not yet mature enough to share in any exploration of his emotional world. Marian persists in doing this for him. When Harry is fighting with his brother, Marian will separate them while gently commenting that Harry finds it hard to share her with James. Perhaps he doesn't believe she can love them both. When Harry is being controlling and difficult, Marian will comment that Harry is feeling a big need to be in charge. Perhaps he is feeling extra anxious just now. However, she is his parent and will choose how much computer time he has. She understands that these limits are hard for him and will support him to manage them. Harry is becoming a bit more used to this exposure of his inner life. He doesn't rage at her about this as he used to do. It is a start, although there are days when Marian despairs at how far they still have to go.

Children, like Harry, are being introduced to the intersubjective relationship through this attitude of PACE. This is a relationship that they will have sought as infants but the response of their parents was frightening. They have since turned their back on relationships. These children will not always welcome PACE with open arms. The parent needs to be PACE-ful on the child's behalf until he is ready to engage in the relationship. There is an affective and a reflective part of providing PACE.

The affective is the way we experience our emotional states. Affect is the expression of emotion. To connect with children, parents have to match this affect, without getting caught up in the emotion themselves. Imagine being with a friend who is feeling sad. You will be no help to him if you are overwhelmed by his sadness too, neither will it help if you are happy and jolly. The friend will be helped if you can communicate that you understand his sadness and have empathy for it. Words alone will not do this; the affective experience of your friend needs also to be matched. This is communicated through matching tone of voice, intensity and rhythm, and the non-verbal elements of relationships, alongside empathy, which is communicated both verbally and non-verbally.

When parents introduce children to safe intersubjective relationships this is what they are doing. They are helping the child to feel understood because they are recognising the child's mood and matching the intensity and rhythm of this. A quiet voice and slow rhythm will connect with a sad child. When a child is angry connection is made when the parent uses a more intense voice and faster rhythm which again matches the intensity and rhythm of the child. Positive emotional states are also matched. The parent shares and enjoys the child's curiosity, excitement and animation. The child's positive emotional states are amplified as the parent shares the delight and joy the child is experiencing. Affect matching helps the child to know that his parent gets it. She understands what he is experiencing.

The reflective is communicated through words. Putting words to an experience will increase understanding of that experience as well as helping the child to regulate in the face of the experience. Putting words to an experience also helps the child to feel accepted. He is not being judged for his experience but is being understood. A story emerges from this reflection, which is shared between the two of them.

Karen and Ian are both accepting this attitude from their parents. They are learning to explore the story behind their behaviours, and through this exploration discovering that their inner world makes sense and is acceptable to their parents. This increases the connection begun non-verbally.

Children like Harry will struggle with the experience of being this deeply understood. This feels alien and frightening to them. They may fear being exposed and being found wanting; they worry that the parent might discover that they do not accept the child after all. Love will be conditional again. The child might try to avoid this intersubjective experience. They will not share their parent's attention which is focused on the child's experience; they try to distract, to focus the parent elsewhere. The relationship is not intersubjective because each has a different intention – the parent to understand, the child not to be understood. In the same way that a horse led to water will not drink if it does not feel safe, the child offered a relationship will resist this until he experiences some safety and trust in this relationship. PACE takes time and patience.

Children may resist the relationship when the parent is trying to make sense of what is a very difficult experience for them. An easier starting place might be with the more relaxed playful moments that come and go during the course of a day. When parent and child can share a fun or enjoyable experience, the child may be more open to the intersubjective connection between them. Co-regulation of affect and co-construction of experience can still happen, but because it is focused on less shame-based parts of the child it may be easier for the child to tolerate. Playful and loving moments can provide an oasis in a day that feels like a walk through a desert – hard, tiring and with little end in sight. Holding on and treasuring the playful, fun and loving times can carry the parent and child a long way through the desert.

I have been describing PACE as a whole, which is how it is best understood. Here I will summarize each of the components to help you understand it fully. This is a bit like telling you how to drive by describing all the different actions you will need to take. The ability to drive might disappear as you think about each separately but you will then combine these together again. The whole will emerge as the parts recede into the background.

P = Playfulness

The first part of the PACE attitude is playfulness. Parents will help children to develop security in part by helping children to be playful. This is not about providing appropriate toys and activities, important though these are. For playfulness to build security it needs to develop the relationship. The parent helps the child to experience joy in the relationship. Experience is amplified when it is shared in a playful way. It dramatizes that the child is special and lovable. Fun and play are protective; a child can't experience shame while being happy and joyful. Play provides optimism that things can be different. The child discovers his strengths and uniqueness; he experiences having a positive impact on another within a reciprocal relationship. This builds trust as the child enjoys feeling connected. Relationship-building playfulness is an important part of the parenting that the children need.

A = Acceptance

Perhaps the hardest part of using PACE is being able to accept without evaluating the child's inner experience of thoughts, feelings, belief, wishes and desires. Parents need to be aware of the inner life of their child, understanding it without trying to change it. When this inner experience is distressing or difficult for us it is understandable that we move to evaluation, trying to reassure or talk the child into feeling something different. The child will experience this as not being good enough for the parent, and shame increases. Instead, the parent needs to embrace mistrust as well as trust from the child, accepting that the child will move backwards and forwards between these. The child experiences the parent as interested in him, rather than as wanting to change him. In this way shame will reduce and the child will experience unconditional love – you love me in all my parts. We want this experience to be different so that it is more comfortable for the child and the parent; however, security comes from having a parent who accepts the child's internal experience without evaluation. Sitting with the uncomfortable is part of providing a secure base.

C = Curiosity

Parenting that builds relationships is parenting that is also curious and reflective. Through an attitude of not knowing and a desire for discovering who the child truly is the parent can understand the child more fully. If the parent is not curious, he is more likely to make rapid judgements about the child and this is more likely to lead to non-reflective action. This in turn can shut down the relationship. Curiosity is an act of discovery that can lead to responsive, non-judgemental care.

E = Empathy

Curiosity leads to a different understanding and thus a deeper acceptance of the child and his experience. The child experiences this increased understanding and acceptance through empathy. Empathy builds secure attachment. The child feels more secure when inner experience is understood, accepted and empathized with.

The use of PACE to connect intersubjectively is only possible if the adult can stay open & engaged, based on good emotional regulation. When young people become closed, defensive and hopeless it can be easy for the adult to join them in this closed, non-engaged state. The adults also become defensive through their experience of feeling irritated, frustrated, hopeless and so on. All of these responses will close down the intersubjective relationship. When the adult loses the attitude of PACE and instead becomes punitive, evaluative or judgemental, the relationship is less connected and the child's mistrust increases. When the parent stays open & engaged by maintaining the attitude of PACE, the connection is strengthened and the child's trust increases.

Parents, like all of us, are human, with fragilities and vulnerabilities. No parent will be able to stay open & engaged all the time. Breaks or ruptures in the relationship are a normal part of experience. Both parent and child have to find a way of managing these. Learning that a relationship can rupture but can then be repaired is a powerful learning experience for a child. This helps the building of resilience; after all, the child will need to manage many relationships in the future, including all the conflict that goes along with these. For a child with only fragile trust and little sense of safety, ruptures are hard to cope with. Shame can quickly increase, leading to behaviours that can further disrupt the relationship.

There will be ruptures, they are inevitable; the parent's job is to take responsibility for repair. Sometimes this involves the parent apologizing to the child – if the parent genuinely feels that she got something wrong it is helpful to acknowledge this. Over and above this, however, repair is about letting the child know that the relationship is still strong.

This also means that the repair is not about the child's behaviour; that can be supported later. It is about the relationship. By repairing the relationship, the parent is communicating that the child is loved unconditionally and the parent will continue to support the child in all the ways he needs. This will include supporting the child to manage any consequences because of the behaviour. This demonstrates that whatever has gone wrong the child is worth bothering with.

PACE AS A WAY OF BEING

PACE can be an emotional compass for the parents, helping them to remain open & engaged to themselves as well as to their children. When parents are feeling frustrated, despairing or a sense of failure it is important that they are PACE-ful towards themselves. In this way they can find a sense of equilibrium again, with support from others if helpful, and then calmly return to PACE for the child.

In this way PACE becomes a way of being rather than a technique. The parent wants to be with and to understand the child without an immediate motive to change him. PACE allows the parent to get alongside the child and to support and share the experience the child is having. The parent must trust that change will come out of the process as the connection between parent and child becomes stronger.

Using PACE to try and change the child will weaken this connection. When a child experiences the parent as trying to change him he is more likely to be oppositional and non-compliant. The child is helped when the parent has no immediate agenda beyond empathically connecting with her child through understanding and acceptance. When the child perceives the parent as wanting to know him he is more likely to be engaged in the relationship, and behavioural change might indeed follow when this is not the focus. If it doesn't, the parent continues to accept the child and the emotional difficulty he is struggling with, holding on to hope that this will become easier over time.

There are verbal and non-verbal elements to PACE. The verbal element is the content, what the parent wants to understand. The non-verbal elements carries what the parent is feeling. Sometimes a parent may be 'talking' PACE but her non-verbal communication is conveying something else, perhaps frustration or disappointment in the child. When a parent notices this discrepancy between the verbal and non-verbal, she might reflect on this. Perhaps she is not fully accepting her child's experience and this is why she is experiencing some frustration or disappointment. Maybe she is using PACE in the hope that the child will change rather than being PACE-ful without expectation of the child. This lack of acceptance is likely to be picked up by the child who will become more defensive in response. He might become angry or withdrawn as a consequence. When this happens the parent needs time and compassion for herself as she works at understanding the child more deeply. As she accepts her own struggles with this she is likely to find a deeper acceptance for her child. Now PACE will be conveyed in a way that verbal and non-verbal responses match. The non-verbal components reflect a way of self-expression that is unique, deepens and makes the communication more trusted and, most importantly, is received authentically by the child.

It might be helpful to think about how the elements of PACE link together, so that it is appreciated as a whole rather than a series of elements. Notice that there is no starting point – it is a circular process of combining the elements into a whole.

Notice how ACE will always be present, starting with any of these elements, and P will come in and out as appropriate.

It can also be helpful to think about how curiosity can deepen acceptance and empathy. The parent responds to the child's mental state with light acceptance and empathy: 'You are having a hard day today' or 'You are enjoying yourself today.' The parent's curiosity about the child's experience can then increase her understanding, leading to a deeper acceptance and empathy response. 'It is so hard when it feels like I don't love you enough to give

you the sweets' or 'You are loving the way that sand feels as it trickles through your fingers.'

INTRODUCING PACE TO CHILDREN

Children will respond to PACE in different ways. Some children respond positively straightaway and the parents experience a stronger connection with them. Other children might resist the feeling of closeness that PACE brings. It may feel too strange to them, not fitting their sense of who they are. Empathy, in particular, can expose the child to being known in a way that is unsettling. Older children might comment on how the parent is reading their mind. The parents will need to approach these children more slowly; lighter PACE can gradually deepen over time, allowing the children to get used to being known and to feel safe in this experience.

At the annual DDP conference in 2016, Jon Baylin described PACE as surprising the brain. The child has adapted to a world where negative reactions and rejection are anticipated. When the parent does not respond in this way, the child experiences something which is surprising and unexpected. Novelty allows new learning and adaptation to occur.

It is helpful to think about how parents naturally have a PACE-like attitude to their infants and young children. They accept the child and what the child experiences and try to make sense of this experience so that they can nurture and soothe, or stimulate and play with their child. They have no expectation of the child, they just strive to be with him in a way that supports and connects. As the child matures the parent begins to make this more explicit, telling the toddler what he is experiencing so that the toddler can come to understand himself more deeply. Only with the older child does the parent ask the child how he is feeling. Now the child can join the parent in wondering about his mental states; it becomes natural to be curious and to express what is being felt.

When introducing PACE to developmentally traumatized children it can be helpful to keep this developmental sequence in mind. The parent notices where the children are with making sense of internal experience. Do they need the parent to be with them as with an infant, to help them to know what they are experiencing as with a toddler, or can they wonder with the child as with an older child? As the parents developmentally match the children they will be able to connect with them in a way that the children are ready for. Over time the children will learn to reflect on their experience and will be comfortable to experience it. At times of stress this fledgling ability to connect will reduce again and the parent can return to sitting with acceptance for the child without any pressure for the child to talk about what he is experiencing.

PACE BEFORE DISCIPLINE

When PACE is used as a technique in the hope that the child will change his behaviour then the parent is not experiencing acceptance. The parent might, for example, decide to use empathy, rather than have a genuine curiosity from which empathy naturally arises. 'I know this is hard for you but…' The parent is trying to use PACE in order to bring about change. Used in this way, PACE is likely to lead to resistance. Children will react to this with shame, as they experience not being good enough for the parents and experience love as conditional. This only strengthens the behaviour that the parent hoped would change.

When the parent sits alongside the child, understanding and accepting his experience, empathy will naturally emerge. The child experiences a sense of being good enough for the parent and this in turn can lead to feelings of guilt and genuine remorse. The child wants to make amends and does not need to be coerced.

Rather than 'This is so hard, but…', with true acceptance of the child's experience PACE can lead to behaviour change, but this is not something that is forced by the parent. The essence of PACE is being able to be with the other without expectation of change.

Of course, PACE does not mean that parents will tolerate behaviour that is unacceptable to them. Discipline is still needed. PACE continues to be held as an attitude alongside this discipline. PACE helps to continue an emotional connection while the discipline will support the child's behaviour, helping the child to behave in a way that is more comfortable for him as well as everyone else. This helps the child to experience unconditional love even though discipline is present.

Through the connection that PACE brings, the child will experience shame being regulated. Now the child can experience guilt and want to make amends. The connection with the parent provides the continuing support needed to help the child to do this. Consequences become collaborative rather than imposed by the parents, and the ongoing PACE before, during and after discipline allows the child to continue to feel understood, accepted and unconditionally loved. It also allows any relationship ruptures caused by the discipline to be repaired.

CONCLUSION

In order to therapeutically parent children who have experienced developmental traumas parents need to have an attitude of PACE towards their children. Playfulness within the relationship helps the child to experience safety in the relationship and the joy that this can bring. Acceptance conveys that the child's internal world is understood and not evaluated. Curiosity helps to find this understanding, discovering the story that is the child. This understanding is conveyed to the child with empathy. PACE is experienced by the children as emotional connection. It might feel strange and worrying to begin with but over time the children's experience of PACE will help them to feel safer and more secure.

What follows is a longer example of PACE being used. Following a difficult exchange between Belinda and Lottie, Belinda takes responsibility for putting things right.

BELINDA AND LOTTIE: PARENTING WITH PACE

Lottie is now 14 years old. The last year has proved stressful as she is managing the demands of secondary school and coping with adolescent changes. Being emotionally younger than her peers, she struggles with friendships. Her organizational difficulties are also getting her into trouble at school as she is struggling to be in the right place at the right time with the right things. In the last six months Belinda's niece, Elizabeth, has come to live with them while her mother recovers from some health difficulties. On this particular day Belinda is feeling stressed herself – probably not the best time to address an untidy bedroom with Lottie! However, her patience has snapped, as she once again has had to go in and retrieve the dirty laundry and crockery that have accumulated despite repeated requests to Lottie to bring these down.

Belinda: Lottie, I need to talk to you about your bedroom.

Lottie: I know, I will sort it out I promise.

Belinda: That isn't good enough. You have repeatedly promised me but still not done it. If I hadn't gone in today to get your laundry and crockery you would have had no clean clothes and we would have had no cups when we wanted a cup of tea.

Lottie: You went into my bedroom! You know I don't want you to mess with my things.

Belinda: Well, what am I meant to do? I have asked you several times.

Lottie: Just don't mess with my stuff, right!

Belinda: I would happily respect that if you can bring me down your laundry and the crockery, but you don't.

Lottie: You are always having a go at me. I try, but it's never good enough for you. 'Miss Prissy' always gets it right. It's not fair.

Belinda: Her name is Elizabeth, and you know what a hard time she is having right now. I thought you of all people would understand.

Lottie: I hate you! You don't care about me at all. I hate you. (Lottie runs up to her room)

Belinda is left feeling cross and frustrated. She is aware that she didn't handle this very well. She makes herself a cup of tea and gives herself some time. As she has been practising in her mindfulness classes, she notices all the emotions she is feeling right now. She tries to accept and not judge herself, but a part of her is still feeling guilty and she is aware that she is being hard on herself. She decides she will call her friend later that evening. She is also a foster carer, and it will be good to talk things through with her. Taking a deep breath, she gets up and makes Lottie a cup of drinking chocolate and puts some biscuits on a plate. She calls up to Lottie.

Lottie: What do you want?

Belinda: I want to apologize. I didn't handle things very well and I have left you feeling bad. Come and sit with me and have your drink.

Lottie: (Shrugs, but sits down and reaches for her drink)

Belinda: Lottie, I am sorry. I know you find it hard. I am guessing you are feeling bad yourself about this. I think you would like to be tidier but this is hard for you.

Lottie: (Head is down, and hair covers her face, but she nods in agreement)

Belinda: I am guessing you are feeling mad at me right now?

Lottie: (Shrugs)

Belinda: (Smiling) I will take that as a yes then.

Lottie: (Shrugs again, but this time gives a little look at Belinda before her head goes down again)

Belinda: Sometimes I forget how hard you find it to organize things like laundry. I am wondering if I am expecting a bit too much?

Lottie: (Head still down and mumbling) No, I should be able to do it.

Belinda: You are feeling cross with yourself then?

Lottie: (Nods head)

Belinda: What do you think when I have a go at you about your bedroom?

Lottie: (Shrugs)

Belinda: I am wondering, maybe you think I am being mean to you?

Lottie: (Shakes head to say no)

Belinda: You don't? So, did you think, oh no, I forgot again!

Lottie: (Looks up and agrees)

Belinda: How does that make you feel when you realize you had forgotten and now I was cross with you?

Lottie: I was angry!

Belinda: (With empathy in her voice) So, when I told you that I wanted to talk about your bedroom you remembered that you hadn't brought the things down. And then you were cross because you had meant to and now I was having a go at you. No wonder you got mad. You want to get things right, but it seems like you never do. And then I got the stuff from your room myself, which perhaps made it worse that you hadn't done it. No wonder you got angry with me. It must have felt like I didn't trust you at all!

Lottie: You can't trust me, because I don't sort it!

Belinda: Oh Lottie, I didn't know you felt that way. You are such a good kid, but this is hard for you. Organization is so difficult.

Lottie: I'm not a good kid. I never get it right!

Belinda: Is that how it feels, like you never remember, and then I'm cross with you because I have forgotten that this is hard for you? And you have probably had the teachers on your back today as well?

Lottie: (Nods) I forgot my gym kit!

Belinda: (Feels frustration rising again, and stops herself pointing out that she had put it on the side for her so she wouldn't forget it!) So it has been a hard day, with all of us on at you?

Lottie: No different to usual.

Belinda: That makes me feel sad. This is just usual for you. You forget things and then we all have a go at you. You know you have forgotten again, and you feel so cross with yourself, and then you really don't feel good. No wonder you get mad at us. I would get mad too if I kept being criticized for things that I find hard to do. I'm also thinking about how tidy Elizabeth is. That must be hard too?

Lottie: (Head goes down again and she shrugs)

Belinda: I hadn't realized quite how hard it has been for you since Elizabeth came. I am trying to support you both but I wonder what that feels like for you?

Lottie: (Shrugs)

Belinda: That hard, eh? Okay, I am guessing it makes you feel bad that there are some things you don't do as well as her?

Lottie: I don't do anything as well as her!

Belinda: Nothing at all? Oh goodness, you are feeling bad about this. So, you see Elizabeth being tidy, and me spending time with her, and perhaps some other stuff and all of this makes you worried that you aren't the same, and you aren't as good as her. You don't notice the things

Elizabeth gets wrong, but you certainly notice when she does things right.

Lottie: What does she get wrong?

Belinda: (Smiles) Well she certainly got in a pickle the other night, do you remember? She was teasing the cat and I asked her to stop. She went right on doing it. I felt pretty cross with her right then.

Lottie: Oh, I had forgotten that.

Belinda: I think you are so worried that you aren't getting things right that sometimes it is hard to remember what you do well. Then you get really down on yourself.

Lottie: I don't want to leave here. I like living with you.

Belinda: Oh, Lottie. We like having you too. Do you really think you might have to leave? This is really big, isn't it? Is Elizabeth being here making you more worried? Like I might choose between you?

Lottie: (Nods)

Belinda: I hadn't realized how you felt. What horrible worries. I guess after all this time I thought you would be feeling secure here. I realize now I'm wrong. You have moved too many times before to really feel secure, and when I get cross with you it must feel like your bags are already packed.

Lottie: (Looks at Belinda and nods)

Belinda: I am sorry that you feel that way. I want you to know that you will always be part of our family, but I can see now how hard that is for you.

Lottie: (Looks sad and tearful)

Belinda knows that Lottie does not like to be hugged so she just gently touches her hand. They sit like this for a while while Belinda lets her know that she will help her. It won't always feel this hard. She then decides to gently think with her about the issue of her organization difficulties.

Belinda: I need to find a way of helping you to organize your bedroom that doesn't leave you feeling so bad. I will have a think about this. Let me know if you have any ideas about how I can do this. I think we need to have another chat with your teachers too. If we can find the right way to support you it will make life easier for you. And I do need to spend time with Elizabeth right now, but I tell you what, Lottie, we will keep finding time to talk and do things together. In fact, do you want to help me with tea tonight? We could have risotto and I know you enjoy making that?

Lottie: (Smiles) Yes, I would like that. I just need to go up to my room. There is a cup there that you missed!

Chapter 8

PACE: FREQUENTLY ASKED QUESTIONS

In this chapter, we will consider a range of common questions which parents ask when discovering and exploring PACE.

Why do I need to use PACE in my parenting? I parented my other children as I was raised and they have turned out all right. It can be very confusing and sometimes unhelpful to encounter different advice about how to parent children. It may leave parents wondering if what they have done previously was okay, or resentful that they are getting the message that their usual parenting style is not good enough. Secure children will do well with the parents' well-intentioned parenting of them, however this is done. PACE, however, is an attitude that can strengthen any relationship. We all want to be understood and accepted for who we are. When a child experiences safety in relationships she will develop resilience. A PACE attitude from a parent will increase wellbeing even when the child is not needing to heal from trauma and a fear of relationships.

A traumatized child can only start to heal when she begins to feel a level of safety within the relationship, safety that is taken for granted by the more secure child. PACE is an essential part of the parenting experience that can give this sense of safety. The relationship needs to be experienced by the child as more important to the parent than attending to her behaviour; only in this way can the child start to develop trust and thus become open to relationship and the comfort and joy that this can offer. With this trust, she will accept necessary restrictions on her behaviour. Without trust she is likely to be non-compliant and oppositional when restrictions are applied. A traumatized child therefore needs something extra from the parenting she is receiving, meaning that traditional parenting is not sufficient.

I am using PACE but my child is not changing.

It is understandable that parents have a strong motivation to see their child change. They want their child to be successful, happy and healthy and they know that challenges in behaviour can threaten this. Parents can have big feelings of frustration, failure, hopelessness and even anger when they find that their attempts with the child are not leading to positive changes. However, to achieve a happy, healthy and successful life, children will need to be able to trust, connect, enter intersubjective relationships and not experience high levels of shame. A narrow goal of behaviour change, even if it can be realized quickly, is not likely to achieve this for the child. Parenting by the long route is needed to help the child with 'connection' as well as 'correction'. PACE will help the parent to stay regulated, connected and open & engaged with the child. This ultimately will help the child to change in positive directions. This is not a quick fix but a journey that the parent is going on with the child.

I am trying to use PACE, but it is so difficult. What can I do?

PACE is hard, but worth the effort as you notice your child growing in security with you. Some parents use PACE very intuitively; it comes naturally to them. Many of us, however, have to really work at it. With commitment and practice we can improve our ability to maintain the attitude of PACE. The dual capacities for emotional regulation and mentalization will support the use of PACE. If the parent has weak capacity for emotional regulation and struggles to be mind-minded towards his child, he will be weak in PACE. The effort to use PACE will, however, help him to strengthen these capacities. We all have to start somewhere. If a parent makes the effort to adopt an attitude of PACE he will find that he grows in his ability to regulate and mentalize.

Good self-care, social support and self-understanding will also help a parent to strengthen his emotional regulation and capacity for mentalization. Attending to a parent's own needs will strengthen his attitude of PACE. The final part of this book provides guidance for parents in looking after themselves.

When I use PACE my child gets angry and tells me to stop it.

It is very difficult when a parent is working hard to help the child but this is being thrown back in his face. It can lead to concerns that the parent is failing or being unhelpful.

PACE is an attitude that connects emotionally with the child. Children with developmental traumas have learnt to defend against such connections because of the pain and fear that they have experienced when they have been emotionally open to parents in the past. PACE can therefore evoke the child's vulnerability, and the child resists this, anticipating more pain and fear. For example, she does not experience safety in feeling sad and being open to comfort. The anger is a way of defending against this emotional vulnerability. As the child develops safety over time she will begin to feel greater trust in the parents and allow herself to be vulnerable, confident in their support at these times. If the parent can maintain the attitude of PACE and accept the child's feelings of anger the child will, over time, feel less angry and be more open to emotional connection.

At these times, it is also worth being curious about the child's regulation at the point at which the parent is expressing empathy and curiosity towards the child. It might be that the parents need to find ways to help the child feel calmer and more soothed. This can be different for each child. The parent will need to reflect on what works for this child; staying close but giving the child some space, giving the child a hug or perhaps something more active like a walk, food or a drink? When the child is more regulated she may then be open to some gentle PACE or some wondering aloud near to her.

I am trying to have a PACE attitude but my child seems to be getting more distressed.

This can feel like a step backwards. However, as was explored in Chapter 1, children who have experienced a lack of comfort early in life adapt by blocking the experience of social pain; this is pain that arises from within a relationship. When a child begins to find safety in a relationship with a parent she does not need this adaptation any more. It is safe for the child to experience pain and sadness because she now trusts a parent who can offer comfort. The child will begin to allow herself to be more vulnerable, to experience pain and distress that she had previously blocked and to turn to the parent for comfort with these experiences. The child will be more emotionally distressed because she trusts the parent to help her with this. She no longer needs to suppress this distress behind anger and oppositionality. Commonly, the first tentative explorations into distress are brief and the parent might notice an oscillation between vulnerability and anger as the child moves towards and then retreats from these experiences.

The parent might want and hope that the child can be happy, but it is also important that he can stay open to emotional distress. When parents experience distress in their child as a sign of failure or as PACE not working, they will become defensive. This is a sign to the children that their trust was misplaced. When this happens the parent needs to attend to the relationship again, providing a repair to the rupture any defensiveness might have caused. Without such a repair the child is likely to suppress the emotional distress again and revert to previous adaptations, anticipating that the parents will not be available or comforting.

I think that my child is responding to my PACE attitude but then she will do something which just spoils it and it feels as if we are back at the beginning again.

To feel you are making progress and then to see it moving backwards can make any parent doubt what he is doing. However, progress is rarely straightforward; ups and downs are likely to be common. Just think about when you are developing a new skill – progress can feel very inconsistent. It is with practice that the new skill becomes habitual. Any new learning requires new neural pathways to be formed within the brain. As the skill is practised these pathways strengthen, or in neurological terms, become myelinated. Consistency only comes with practice. An analogy might help to understand this. Imagine taking a daily walk through a field. If you walk across the field in the same way a number of times a path will begin to form. At first this path will be unstable; if you walk a different way for a few days the grass will grow back and the emerging path will disappear. The more that you take the same path, however, the more stable it becomes.

However, it can be harder to cope with the ups and downs than when no progress is being made. When the child is doing well the parent can relax and start to enjoy the relationship he is offering to the child, and which is now being received. The child then feels a need to retreat from the warm feelings that comfort and joy in a relationship can bring. She is still uncertain that she deserves this and fears that she might lose what she is starting to like. She does something to create distance again. This might be a way of testing the parent; is this a part of me that will drive you away? Alternatively, she might be ensuring that she can still manage without the thing that she believes she doesn't deserve. At these times, it is easy for the parent to lose confidence. He might doubt that any progress observed was real. He might despair, unsure that he can go through it all again. This can be experienced as a 'dopamine crash'. The warmth and connection that was present in the relationship with the child leads to increased dopamine, allowing the parent to feel good about this. The disruption to the relationship as the child retreats again can lead to a crash, as dopamine rapidly reduces. This can feel worse than not experiencing the dopamine reward at all. It is hard to continue offering PACE with the discouragement and pain that this can bring. Knowing about this possibility, however, can help the parent to remain steady, enjoying the ups and supporting the child through the downs.

My child seems to manage me being curious but hates it when I am empathic.

Sometimes parents can use empathy as a technique without feeling it. Feelings of frustration, anger, or a sense of failure can make genuine empathy difficult. At these times, rather than trying to force empathy, the parent might try to be more curious and accepting of his child's experience. This will increase understanding leading to deep feelings of empathy for the child, which can be communicated with genuine feeling. Parents may try to 'fake it until they make it' but this will not be helpful for expressing PACE, which needs to come from the core of the self. This might be a time when parents need helpful people in their life who can use PACE with them and their experience of the child. As the parent feels connected and emotionally supported by others he will be able to 'make it' without any need for fakery.

Another possibility is that the child is struggling with the intensity of the relationship provided with PACE. Children who have high levels of mistrust may be helped to experience empathy more indirectly initially. Allow them to hear the empathy without having to respond to it. Talk to another person, a family pet, a soft toy. When the child is ready to respond, she will let the parent know.

When direct empathy is provided, think about how you convey it. When we communicate empathy we tend to be quite animated and musical in our communication. We use intonation and rhythm in speech to convey what we are feeling. This is called prosody. Children who struggle with empathy will need less prosody in the voice. This means being more matter of fact in our speech. Prosody can increase as the child becomes more tolerant of empathy, but for a while she might need this lighter empathy.

For my child, empathy is helpful but curiosity just isn't accepted. She calls me a freak and a witch.

When a child appears unsettled about curiosity it is worth reflecting on the child's early experience of others making sense of her feelings and thinking. If the child is not likely to have experienced much of this, it can be disturbing when a parent appears to know what she is thinking and feeling. The parent needs to think about how to express acceptance for the strangeness and perhaps fear of this that the child is experiencing. Bigger empathy and lighter curiosity might be helpful until the child becomes used to others talking about her inner experience. Express curiosity less often and more tentatively.

The child might also be helped by hearing family members wonder about each other's inner experience. Let her witness this without the intensity of having to hear it about herself. Watching TV programmes and films together can also be a way of noticing what others might be thinking and feeling.

When I ask my child what she is feeling she just shouts at me that she doesn't know.

The parent might be helped by thinking about how he is talking with the child. Is he expecting the child to know, without acceptance that the child might not know? Is he losing the story-telling in his well-meaning effort to question the child? In these cases, children can experience the pressure of being expected to have answers, and they fear that they can't meet the expectations for them to know about their internal experience. The parent could try wondering with the child without the expectation that she should have the answer. The child might then become curious herself. If not, the parent can accept this and wonder on her behalf.

It is also important to be mindful about the child's emotional maturity and early experience. With immaturity and a lack of early experience of others making sense of internal experience, the child is unlikely to be able to respond to curiosity about her internal experience. In this case, the child may need to be told what she might be experiencing without expectation that she will be able to express this herself.

When I am playful with my child she just gets over-excited, or spoils it in some way and it all ends in tears.

The parent might reflect on how he is being playful and whether he is mindful enough about regulation as well. Is he expecting too much from the child? Is he over-arousing? For example, tickling can be too intense for some children. Is he planning activities that are too much for the child? Large days out can be too exciting and challenging, and trigger worries for the child that she does not deserve these.

PACE is much more about joy in a relationship than activities. Small, playful moments are equally as important as sustained experiences, if not more so. In fact, children can experience a strong need to put distance back into the relationship after a long period of connection. Small moments, however, can be accepted without anxiety.

I can't always find ways to be playful with my child. Sometimes it doesn't feel right to be playful.

Sometimes parents want to be playful in every interaction, or even think that they need to start with playfulness each time. Playfulness, however, is not always present – it comes in and out. A background of ACE is always helpful but the P comes and goes as suits the moment.

I just can't be PACE-ful all the time. When I get cross or start nagging I feel so disappointed with myself.

Parents have strong motivations to do the best they can for their children. It can be hard not living up to their own expectations of being open and available to their children. It is all right to lose PACE sometimes. This is just being human. Some parents find this hard to accept, and consequently put a lot of pressure on themselves. It is natural to move from open & engaged to defensive. When parents can recognize how normal this is, they can have compassion for themselves. This will help them to become open to the child again.

It is also helpful to remember that however difficult things have been the parent is always able to repair. This means letting the child know that she is still unconditionally loved. The parent does not need to apologize, unless he genuinely feels that this is required. The parent does need to help the child know that the relationship is more important than anything else that has occurred between them. Relationship repair provides the parent with something he can do to restore the relationship even after the most difficult of times.

PACE just isn't working.

When parents stress that PACE is 'not working' they can be experiencing a mixture of feelings. A sense of failure, disappointment that this isn't the answer they were looking for and hopelessness that nothing seems to make a difference. While PACE is a very helpful way of introducing connection to a child, it is not an answer to the many challenges that the child will often continue to present. The focus of PACE is on the relationship and the child's feelings of shame, fear of connection and need for regulation. It is this focus that will help the child to increase feelings of security over time.

If the focus has become too centred on the behaviour, then it is likely that the parent is experiencing less acceptance for the child. The motivation to change the child is getting in the way of understanding and having empathy for where the child is right now. The well-meaning desire to help the child to feel happier, less troubled and better behaved means that it is hard to accept where she is right now. When acceptance reduces, it can make curiosity more intrusive and empathy more misattuned, as it is not matched to how the child is feeling.

How can I use PACE with two or more children?

It is difficult to provide advice on this, especially if there are fewer parents than there are children and so all the children cannot be attended to at the same time. Sibling rivalry can be very intense for children who have developmental trauma because of the fears of abandonment that the children experience. Parents will need to deal with any immediate threats to safety for the children and then decide which child to focus on while helping the other child to know that she is not forgotten.

Typically, a parent will support the most dysregulated child first but this can leave the less dysregulated child who is equally struggling unsupported, perhaps reinforcing the self-reliance that she has learnt to help her survive. The parent needs to find a way to let all children know that they are being thought about while also focusing on the child who needs immediate regulation.

Although it is emotionally exhausting, the parent also needs to ensure that the other child(ren) get some supportive time with the parent as well, even if this is later in the day.

What about when we are in a public place and my child is having a meltdown?

This is a difficult situation and fear of judgement by others can move parents away from being open & engaged. They become defensive towards the child because of the disapproval they are experiencing from others. This can prolong the meltdown.

The focus needs to be on the child, while the responses and disapproval of others are ignored. With strangers, it can be helpful to remember that the parent is not likely to see them again. With familiar people, the parents equally need to block out their judgement but then will decide whether this is a person that they feel they could have on their side. Is it worth investing in helping them to understand the struggles the child is having?

Family members can be equally unhelpful as they try and give good advice or outright criticism. Again, a decision needs to be made about how much to invest in trying to help them understand.

The parents' resilience and confidence in what they are doing will be helpful, and so it is important to have people in their social network who do get it and support them in what they are trying to do. This can maintain resilience in the face of less helpful people.

My child has learning difficulties; will PACE still be helpful for her?

All children, whatever their ability or disability, will benefit from parents who want to connect emotionally with them.

The parent needs to have realistic expectations of what he might achieve. If he is looking for PACE to somehow fix the child then he is likely to be disappointed. PACE can build connection and security but it will be a slower process. The child is likely to find life more stressful and therefore progress can feel as if it is going backwards at times. The child is dealing with a double blow of trauma and disability and so the journey will be longer.

Good support for the parent is an essential part of caring for a child with disability. The parent will also be helped by an understanding school. With good support around them parents will be able to stay with the attitude of PACE and to notice improvements, however small.

Chapter 9

A GUIDE TO DDP-INFORMED PARENTING

This chapter provides an overview of the principles within the DDP model and how these can be applied when parenting developmentally traumatized children. In the last two chapters the focus has been on the use of PACE. This is the main parenting attitude used within DDP-informed parenting. Here I provide further exploration of how PACE can be offered to children through the relationship that parents offer.

The relationship can be:

- *intersubjective* – Past experience has led the children to fear the intersubjective relationships they need to feel safe, to trust and to have healthy emotional and social development. Children use controlling behaviours as a way of avoiding reciprocal interactions. They influence but are not open to influence. The parent connects with the child in order to help him to feel safe in a relationship within which he is open to influence

- *PACE-ful* – The parent holds an attitude of PACE in order to offer an unconditional relationship which is expressed through playfulness, acceptance, curiosity and empathy. The parent maintains curiosity in the inner life of the child and accepts this without judgement or evaluation. This acceptance is communicated with empathy for the struggles this experience can bring. PACE also offers the child fun and joy within the relationship, moments of healthy relationship and respite from the day-to-day struggles

- *open & engaged* – An open & engaged parent uses PACE to connect intersubjectively. Often the children respond by being closed, and defensive. The parents try to avoid joining them in this closed, non-engaged state when they become defensive, irritated or frustrated. These responses will close down the relationship. Of course, the parent will at times lose the attitude of PACE and will become evaluative or judgemental. At these times the parent can avoid the relationship being damaged through relationship repair as described below.

The relationship helps the child to:

- *feel safe and secure* – The parents notice the children's verbal and non-verbal communications and whether these signal that the child is feeling safe or not. Safety can be increased by accepting and acknowledging the child's experience with PACE, and providing co-regulation as needed

- *co-regulate affect* – The children feel emotion, which is expressed through their affect. The parents match the vitality, intensity and rhythm of the affect without feeling the emotion themselves. They can then respond with empathy, verbally and non-verbally. This helps the child to emotionally regulate, contributing to his sense of safety and allowing him to become more open to the parent and the PACE attitude

- *co-construct meaning of experience* – The parents help the children to make sense of both present and past experience. When the child responds to PACE and his attention is held by the parents' attentive stance there is an opportunity to put words to experience. This increased understanding can provide the child with flexibility to respond to events verbally and not just through behaviour.

The parent can help the child by:

- *discovering the narrative or story* – Instead of trying to change the children through reasoning, lecturing or reassuring, the parents engage them in understanding what is happening. In other words, they discover and tell the story of the moment as it is occurring in the present and is influenced by the past. The immediate aim is not to change the child but to be genuinely interested in understanding his experience

- *using affective-reflective dialogue* – As in any good story the parent talks with the child in a way which is affective (expressing emotion) and reflective (providing the content through the narrative). Empathy within PACE provides the affective part of this communication while curiosity helps with reflection. Together the child can experience the parent's acceptance for him and his emotional experience

- *using follow-lead-follow* – To connect with a child, the parent needs to start where he is at, so that the child experiences being understood. Now the parent can lead him into deeper understanding. The child will respond to this and the parent can follow again. In this way the parent sets a rhythm to the telling which allows the story to emerge

- *talking with, about and for* – This way of communicating is emotionally intense, especially for children who have found ways to exist without connection in their past. The parent helps the child to tolerate this without becoming overwhelmed by it. This can be helped by not always talking directly to the child. At times it can be helpful to talk about him. This can be a wondering out loud or perhaps sharing a thought with another person. The child may quietly listen, but if he joins the conversation again the parent can resume talking with him. It is important not to be critical of the child at these times. 'Talking about' is a way of helping the child to know that the parent understands his experience. Sometimes, however, the parent might want to help the child to feel understood more deeply and directly. 'Talking for' can powerfully convey this. The parent talks with the child's voice about how he is feeling, when the child is unable, or needs help, to put this into words for himself

- *attending to verbal and non-verbal communication* – Every communication is non-verbal, and some are also verbal. Noticing discrepancies between verbal and non-verbal signals can help the parent understand the experience of the child. When verbal and non-verbal signals again match, the communication becomes deeper and more open

- *being aware of relationship repair* – The parents will notice ruptures in their relationship with the child. The parent may have become defensive, or the child may have misunderstood. It is important that the more mature parent takes responsibility for repair at these times. Repair means helping the child to know that the connection between himself and the parent is still strong, that he is loved unconditionally. It brings the relationship back into a state of attunement. Authentic apology can be part of relationship repair, but only when it is heartfelt. Repair is a reattunement, and sometimes apology is part of this but not always. As the child experiences connection he may experience remorse and want to make amends. At these times the parent can support the child, helping him to repair the relationship with anyone hurt by what has happened.

Chapter 10

SUPPORTING BEHAVIOUR

Earlier in this part of the book, I discussed the importance of emotional connection and building trust in this connection for children who are developmentally traumatized. This means parents paying more attention to connection than is usual, rather than assuming that this foundation of the relationship is already there as a backdrop for the behavioural support that all children need. In this chapter I develop this further, deepening my exploration of how to provide behavioural support for children who do not trust in the unconditional love that they are being offered.

EXPLORING BEHAVIOURAL SUPPORT

Traditional behaviour management provides many strategies that are helpful for parents when raising their children. These have a focus on the behaviours that children are displaying and provide ways of reinforcing the desired behaviours and reducing the less desirable ones. The importance of having a positive relationship with the child is emphasized, but there is an assumption that the child already wants this. If parents pay attention to ensuring that there are positive times with their children, then they will respond to the parenting strategies. Essentially it is assumed that the children want and are seeking approval from their parents based on the relationship they have already developed. They may push against the boundaries and try out a range of desirable and undesirable behaviours but over time they will be guided by their parents, in whom they have implicit trust.

Most of these assumptions do not hold true for children who have experienced developmental trauma. The essence of this trauma is that the relationship that the child needs and yearns for is also the source of hurt and loss. The children are in a dilemma whether to approach or withdraw from the thing that they instinctively search for but which is the source of pain. The behaviours that they develop are rooted in this basic conflict and the controlling solution that helps them to adapt to this conflicted world. These children are more likely to seek a way to be in charge with their parents than to seek a positive relationship with them.

I remember watching a pre-adolescent child being interviewed in a television programme some years ago. He lived with his mother and step-father. Theirs was a relationship of domestic violence, and the partner's violence to his mother would often spill over towards the child. His mother would be angry with the boy when this happened, trying to instil in him behaviour that would reduce the likelihood of these occurrences. This boy was increasingly out of control, with behaviours that were as challenging as they were negative. The child was asked, 'Why do you do this? It only makes life difficult for you.' The child responded that he wanted attention from his parents. He preferred positive attention, but negative attention was better than none. The sadness and pain in the child's eyes as he told the reporter this said it all. This young boy did not have the relationship he needed with his parents. Love felt conditional: 'I will be loved if I behave.' Unfortunately he couldn't behave well all the time, no child can. This child was constantly getting the message that he was not trying hard enough, that he was not good enough. He did not have implicit trust that his parents would be there for him, guiding him and supporting him as he needed it. He needed a relationship with his parents but he had to do without their approval. He therefore took charge, ensuring that he got their attention. This would have to be enough.

Traditional behaviour management strategies can be helpful when children experience being unconditionally loved, and have trust that their parents only have good intentions towards them. This is the case for Karen and her sister Teagan. They each have their own way of testing the limits and boundaries that their parents provide. Karen will sulk and become quieter, while Teagan is more likely to protest loudly and her toddler tantrums can be spectacular, but each of them is open to their parents' comfort. As they mature they feel safer because these boundaries are there and they are internalizing the values and standards of their parents. They each have complete trust that their parents love them unconditionally and they will make everything all right when it feels as if the relationship has gone wrong. This secure base is standing them in good stead as they journey through their adolescent years. They are testing their limits and experimenting with independence, confident that their parents' arms will always be there waiting for them when they need it.

This is much more problematic for children who have had experience of conditional love, especially when they have also experienced the loss of parents. This combination can lead to core fears of not being good enough and anticipation that current parents will be lost too. Children who have experience of these types of trauma, like Harry and Lottie, will view behavioural boundaries and discipline as being indicators that the current parent recognizes their badness. They imagine that the parents will not be there for them when needed most; at worst they believe that the parents will soon get rid of them. In short, they fear abandonment. Because of these fears, Lottie and Harry experience high levels of stress. This quickly overwhelms their already fragile regulation abilities and they therefore dysregulate quickly, often through displays of anger and temper. These triggers are sometimes hard to see, but they usually centre around interpretations that their parents disapprove of them and do not want to be with them. When Belinda jokes with Lottie that she will be the 'death of her' following a particularly challenging day, Lottie ensures that she has her bag packed ready for this imminent event. When Marian is preoccupied with her sister's latest calamity, Harry becomes more controlling, opposing her every request. When she tries to provide a consequence, he becomes angry with her. She wonders why he needs to be in charge so badly at the moment. Harry, without pausing for thought, tells her it's best so that he will manage when she kicks him out.

The trigger can be as subtle as a slight change of facial expression or a parent not meeting a request quickly enough, or it can be as obvious as a parent giving attention to another child or needing to attend to a task that requires the child to play alone for a while. The children do not want to behave this way, although it can seem that they do as they scream at the parents that they hate them or pick up a knife and threaten them. They have become flooded by anxiety and are emotionally overwhelmed. As this is displayed through challenging behaviours, the children experience themselves as not good enough, increasing their anxiety still further. Alongside this their sense of shame, which is ever present, increases further. Now, when it seems furthest away, the children need the relationship with their parents most. This is a relationship that can help the child to regulate and eventually to move from communicating through behaviour to reflection, being able to put feelings into words.

Relationship

It is at the challenging times that the children need connection most. This is the big ask for parents: to find ways to connect with their children at the times that they most want to put some distance between them. When Harry has been rude and oppositional before storming up to his room, Marian would like to leave him there. She knows he needs her, but also that he will resist this need with every ounce of his being. She also knows that if left alone there will be another wrecked bedroom to deal with. Neither leaving him nor going to him will provide a quick solution. In order to connect with Harry, Marian will need to manage his anger towards her. He will shout abuse at her, throw things and on occasion has picked up a knife or scissors and brandished these at her. If Marian can hold on through this, keeping them both safe while maintaining an open relationship with him, his rage will eventually subside. Now Marian can comfort him and he will be able to receive her empathy for how hard he finds things. Finally, he will let her support him, as long as Marian has the emotional energy to do this by this point. In the background is James, anxious at the rage he can hear his brother displaying, fearful that Marian will be hurt, and in need of his own comfort. Both Marian and James can experience trauma in the face of Harry's outbursts. Marian needs to look after herself as well as her two sons. She holds on to some faith that if she can keep providing Harry with a relationship at these times he will eventually manage these situations more easily, and will let her help him more quickly.

Even children who seem to do better left alone for a while need to know that the door remains open. They need to have parents who are ready and waiting to connect as soon as the child can tolerate this. Dawn and Philip have learnt that Karen needs some time alone when she is upset by their discipline. They judge the moment when she is ready to connect with them, maintaining a close presence until this point.

It is this openness to the relationship that parents hold, even at these most difficult times, that will, over time, build trust and the security of knowing that they are acceptable to their parents, that they are unconditionally loved. As we will explore in the third part of this book, parents need to have PACE for themselves and relationships that they can turn to in order to maintain their resilience in the face of these big challenges. Looking after yourself is an essential part of looking after your child.

Regulation

While children like Harry display behaviours that can feel very targeted, manipulative and intentional, many of these behaviours stem from dysregulated emotion. Harry's emotional arousal has risen to a level where it is threatening to overwhelm him. Alongside this, levels of shame are increasing. Not being able to use parental support at these times, the child does the only other thing he can do – he uses the shield against shame (see Figure 3.1). His behaviour becomes dysregulated as his emotion becomes overwhelming but he turns this outwards, attacking others.

Notice also the child who dissociates rather than dysregulates; because these children are less challenging to others their struggles with emotion can be missed. This is often James's response to emotional arousal. He withdraws, becomes switched off, perhaps more compliant as he too tries to manage without parental support. James did not have the traumatic start that Harry did, but he has been traumatized in his own way by the movements of placement and then the loss of Robert. His needs have been somewhat overlooked over the years, as Harry has taken so much time and energy. This has not been intentional, but it has been hard to keep James in mind when Harry is filling all the space. The impact of Harry's anger and aggression on James has also been intense. For a long time, James feared that they would both have to move if Harry kept behaving in this way. He tried even harder to behave and to be compliant in an attempt to ward off this danger. As James enters adolescence his distress is displayed more clearly through self-harming behaviours. When Harry is having a struggle, Marian has learnt that she has to be vigilant to James, as it is at these times that he is most likely to cut himself. Children like James need relational and regulation support as much as children who externalize their distress and target others.

Parents need to attend to the regulation of the emotional experience that these children are immersed in. Emotional connection allows the parent to help the child to regulate. There is no point trying to help the child reflect, with the aim of changing the behaviour, when dysregulation is driving it. This just sets the child up to fail and increases the sense of shame and inadequacy. The emphasis on the regulation of the child's internal experience means that this approach to parenting is regulatory based rather than behaviour based. Behaviour is still supported, but this behavioural support is successful because it is based on the child being helped to regulate. The child is offered emotional connection with the parent alongside the behavioural support. This is what Dan Hughes captures in his expression 'connection with correction'.

Reflection

Connection can continue to be enhanced at the point that the child is ready to think about what has happened. A more mature child is developmentally able to reflect on her behaviour, but needs help with regulation first. A younger or more immature child will need the parent to do this on her behalf. Just as parents do with toddlers, the parent lets the child know that he understands and can make sense of the child's behaviour. The younger or less mature child is told the story of what just happened.

When Marian initially tries talking directly to Harry about his experience he becomes overwhelmed with shame. Marian finds that Harry responds well to stories about Fred, an invented boy that Marian uses to help Harry to reflect on what he has just experienced. As time goes on she is able to put Fred to one side, as Harry becomes more open to reflection. As long as he can do something at the same time, Harry can now listen while she talks through an episode, being sure to name the feelings that Harry was experiencing. Marian keeps colouring books and crayons to hand for these occasions. Time spent talking through what just happened is beginning to benefit him, but even at 15 years old he still struggles to wonder about his experience with her.

For an older or more mature child the story can be created together. The child is regulated and has experienced the parent as supportive towards her. She is now able to sit with her parent and think about her experience. Lottie has become used to Belinda suggesting that they sit down and figure out what just happened. Lottie might initially resist this, but will then be open to some exploration and can give Belinda clues as to what has been bothering her. They put the story together between them.

Using PACE and having a story-telling attitude at this point can further strengthen the connection between parent and child. This does mean starting with the child's experience and making sense of this before helping the child to consider the viewpoint of anyone else involved. Curiosity and understanding are communicated to the child as internal experience is explored and accepted. Empathy flows naturally as the child's thoughts and feelings are more deeply understood.

This is a slowing down in parenting. The temptation, once a child is calm again, is to focus on the consequences of what has happened. 'See how you hurt me', 'Notice how upset X is.' This is well intentioned. The parent wants to help the child understand the consequences of her behaviour in order to make amends and, it is hoped, to reduce this happening in the future. These well-meant intentions go awry, however, when the child's shame increases – levels of stress build and dysregulation threatens once more. Staying with the child's own experience for longer both strengthens the connection between parent and child while providing further regulatory support. Now the child is ready to reflect on the consequences of her behaviour. Instead of shame she can experience guilt and remorse. The parent is on hand to help her with this, supporting her efforts to make amends.

One of the strengths of this approach is that the consequences for the behaviour can also be part of the building of the relationship. Instead of parent-imposed sanctions, the consequences can be collaboratively worked out between them. This means figuring out what the child can do to make amends, and consequences logically follow the behaviour that caused the upset. It also means figuring out what the parent can do to support the child with this. The parent might reflect on whether there is anything he could do differently to support the child in the future. Perhaps the child needed more supervision, less freedom, more support to manage friendships, and so on.

When Ian is nine years old, Rachel and Jane decide to let him go out to play with the local boys. They feel that they can trust him to behave and to come back on time. They want to encourage him to broaden his friendship group. They do not consider how emotionally immature he can be alongside his peers. They are distressed, therefore, to discover that the boys have been taunting their elderly neighbour, Mr Baker. When Jane talks to Mr Baker about this he admits that Ian has been particularly rude to him. They sit down with Ian to talk to him about this. They let him know that they are aware that this has been happening and wonder what was going on for Ian when he was doing this. At first Ian denies it, but they gently persist, telling Ian that they know he has been rude to Mr Baker, and again wondering what he was thinking when he was doing this. Ian tearfully acknowledges that yes, he was rude, and tells them that he was responding to a dare. They wonder why he took up this dare, as they know he usually gets on well with Mr Baker. Ian is able to tell them that he was worried that the boys would not let him play with them if he did not respond to their challenge. Rachel and Jane express empathy for these worries, understanding that this would be a strong motivation for his rudeness. As they demonstrate this acceptance, Ian is able to express his worry that Mr Baker might not like him now. Maybe he won't let him walk his dog for him, an activity that Ian has especially enjoyed helping with. They agree that this is a possibility and wonder with him how he might make amends. Ian wonders if he could write a note of apology. They all agree that this would be a good idea. Rachel and Jane then acknowledge that they have expected too much of Ian. It is difficult for him to manage these relationships with the other boys. Perhaps he needs a bit more support with this. They suggest he invites one of them to play with him in their garden; perhaps they could build a den using the tree at the bottom. Ian thinks this is a great idea and chooses the boy he will ask. Rachel and Jane are pleased to note it is one of the quieter boys.

REGULATION-BASED PARENTING WITH PACE

When you are using regulation-based parenting you will need to be mindful of the arousal level of the child. As stress increases, arousal also increases and this will change what the child is open to. Bruce Perry suggests that there are five arousal states to be considered, each of which changes the way the child behaves. Each state is governed by a different part of the brain, with the lower arousal states being able to use higher brain regions which are open to thinking. As arousal increases, lower brain regions take over leading to increasingly more instinctive behaviour (Perry 2006):

1. *Calm.* Arousal is low. The child is rational and is open to reflection. In this state a verbal child is likely to be able to join in with PACE, being open to playfulness and curiosity as well as the connection that acceptance and empathy bring.

2. *Aroused.* As emotional arousal increases the child will appear younger and more concrete in her ability to think. She might still be open to PACE but is less likely to engage with curiosity. Her reflection has reduced.

3. *Alarmed.* The child is getting increasingly emotional and this is reflected in her behaviour and increasingly immature functioning. Dysregulation is increased. The child now needs you to be curious on her behalf so that you can communicate genuine acceptance and empathy (A and E). She will not be able to reflect with you.

4. *Fearful.* The child is now very reactive as she responds to the increasing arousal experienced in increasingly immature ways. A and E might still reach her if you keep it clear and simple with a high level of acceptance for her experience.

5. *Terrified.* The child is now displaying a full fight or flight response. There is little more that you can do but hang on and keep both of you safe. PACE, via A and E, is aimed at reducing the panic. Convey acceptance in your voice but the words are less likely to reach her until the terror subsides and she starts to go down the arousal continuum again. This is a time for a high level of nurture, aided by the PACE you are holding on to. This will reduce arousal further. Arousal will subside with time, and the child, emotionally spent, will be open to PACE again.

It might be helpful to think of this as a volcano, as in Figure 10.1. PACE can be effective in reducing arousal during the build-up. During the eruption the child needs to be kept safe but will be open to PACE as it subsides. Keep to A and E to avoid further eruptions, only involving the child in playfulness and curiosity as you move away from the eruption.

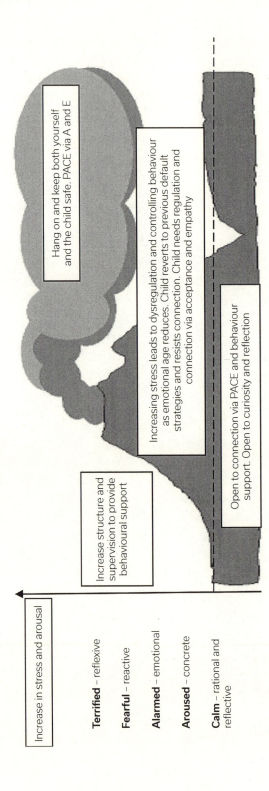

Figure 10.1 The volcano of arousal

This is challenging. You will need lots of PACE and compassion for yourself, supported by others who can hold PACE for you. This can help you to notice the impact the child is having on you (curiosity), and provide support for you with acceptance and empathy. This will then help you to hold on to curiosity for the child. As you understand what she is experiencing, and the thoughts and feelings she is likely to be going through, this will be displayed through your acceptance and empathy for her. The child will feel held by you as she experiences your genuine compassion for her.

In order to do this, you will be working hard to keep a lot of thoughts and feelings at bay: frustration and anger with the child, a sense of failure within you. Give yourself time and space to process this after the episode. Talk to people you trust about this, and choose people who can be curious and playful with you and who will give you the acceptance and empathy you need. If you try and keep these feelings out of sight they are likely to come back and disturb you when you least expect it. A word or look from your child can lead you to erupt in anger and frustration. You are left wondering how you could have dealt with the bigger behaviour so well only to blow it for much lesser behaviour!

WHERE DO TRADITIONAL BEHAVIOUR MANAGEMENT STRATEGIES FIT IN?

Behavioural support strategies can still be helpful, although they may need some adaptation for this group of children.

The relationship

Some of the traditional strategies can help with the building of the relationship. Playfulness is part of PACE and positive time together is part of most behavioural parenting advice. Playfulness looks for moments of fun and joy, which can build towards finding positive activities and time together. Simple is often better – a trip to the park, feeding the ducks, splashing in puddles. Remember secondary intersubjectivity? Children can enjoy the time with parents as together they explore the world around them.

More ambitious activities need to be taken more slowly and with careful preparation. This is because traumatized children are more comfortable with the familiar than the novel. If they are going to do something new, a trip to the seaside or going to a theme park for example, they will need to be prepared for what to expect. A simple story about the activity can help. The parent writes or tells the story of the day so that when the day happens it already feels familiar.

A second difficulty is that the child might not feel she deserves the activity. This can increase her stress and anxiety as she anticipates it all going wrong. If it is successful the child remains anxious, often spoiling it when back home, as she reminds the parent that she did not really deserve this.

The child might also struggle with the return to normal, and the parent's attention no longer focused on her. This can trigger the fears of not really being liked or approved of.

If the child still has fragile regulation abilities the additional arousal which comes with the excitement of something new might be hard to manage. Even positive arousal is difficult to regulate when regulation has not been fully developed. The child may be eagerly looking forward to the event, but once there just spoils it for herself because the emotion becomes dysregulated and behaviour deteriorates as a consequence.

Positive activities therefore need to be built slowly and begin with the familiar to increase chances of success.

Regulation

Other behaviour management strategies can help with regulation, albeit with some adaptation. 'Time in', for example, is an adaptation of 'Time out', a well-known strategy that is not helpful for traumatized children. Time out is used to remove children from situations in which they are getting rewards for inappropriate behaviour. For developmentally traumatized children this can increase the children's fear of abandonment. The removal from the situation, and the parents, can trigger fears that this time there is no way back and they have been discovered as hopelessly bad. They will not be wanted after this. Margot Sunderland describes a simple adaptation of time out to what she calls 'time in' (Sunderland 2008). The child is removed from a situation that she is struggling with but is brought closer to the parent. The parent is now on hand to co-regulate the child's emotional arousal, increasing regulation and allowing her to return to the situation successfully, perhaps with additional parental support.

It is important to reflect on the context for any parenting strategy that is used. Given the child's earlier experience is this likely to increase or decrease the child's feelings of security? Ignoring negative behaviour, for example, is a simple way of conveying to a secure child that the behaviour will not get her the desired attention. However, for the insecure child it can convey another message entirely. The parent unwittingly conveys you are not worth bothering with as the child fails to distinguish between her behaviour as unacceptable and herself as acceptable. Ignoring can therefore increase shame and dysregulation.

Reflection

One very popular way of increasing the child's sense of accomplishment and therefore their self-esteem is through the use of praise and rewards. Instead of helping the children reflect and learn from their unacceptable behaviours, the focus is on positive behaviours. As these are praised and rewarded, social learning theory predicts that they will increase in frequency. The flaw in this plan for developmentally traumatized children is that praise and rewards ultimately work because the children want and desire parental approval within a relationship where they do have some security, some sense of being loved and wanted. When we take this desire away we see children responding very manipulatively to rewards. They behave as requested until the point that they get the reward and then they revert to previous behaviour. The reward is gained while the relationship was never anticipated anyway. Similarly, praise is viewed as a trick – after all, the parent does not approve of them and so they cannot believe in this praise at face value. Global praise that tries to convince a child that she is a good kid simply does not fit the child's sense of self and so has to be rejected. Telling an insecure child that she is good at singing, for example, is likely to lead to the child refusing to sing.

Of course, we do want to help children to feel good about themselves and to enjoy their accomplishments. We would like their self-esteem to increase. Praise and rewards are an important way of conveying this as long as we go cautiously. Praise needs to come from the heart and be a way of enjoying an accomplishment together. If it is used as a technique the child is likely to reject it, but if it is experienced as genuine joy in the child and what she has achieved then she might be able to share in this. Rewards might be accepted if they are low key and descriptive. Reduce the global statements which the child can't accept and notice the small things. 'I like the way you sang that song; you really kept in tune during that tricky bit towards the end', is easier to accept than, 'How great you are at singing.' The first is a moment in time which the child can enjoy without feeling she has to repeat it. The second creates too many expectations of what she might be able to do in the future. Consider that praise and rewards are evaluative. They represent judgements about the children's worth. This is likely to put them on the defensive. Children can experience approval (praise, rewards) for behaviour that they believe they can't sustain. They become anxious in the face of the parents' pleasure, anticipating times when the parent discovers how bad they really are. Thus shame is triggered. Just think about the pressure on you if you are told you are good at something, especially when you find it hard to believe this. Will you be able to repeat it? Can you maintain this approval?

Think back to the traffic lights diagram in Chapter 5 (Figure 5.1). If parents evaluate the child they are likely to trigger the social monitoring system. An insecure child will perceive danger in this and move into defensive responding. If parents are to help children stay open & engaged with the relationship then they need to proceed cautiously with praise and rewards. A genuine thrill about what a child has achieved is less likely to feel evaluative. Additionally, a cautious, low-key use of praise and rewards that does not conflict with the child's global sense of self, alongside the strengthening of connection and relationship, is more likely to lead to change in self-esteem over the longer term. Children need stories more than they need praise and rewards; they need opportunities to make sense of their experience, rather than having this experience evaluated.

What is most important within behavioural support is that the children experience this as occurring within the context of an unconditional relationship. This is conveyed through the emotional connection the parents make with the children rather than any specific response to behaviour. If the parent focuses too narrowly on behaviour without attention to the relationship several problems can occur.

First, a focus on behaviour instead of relationship will convey that behaviour is most important. This does not build the child's trust in the parent, nor does it help the child to feel secure within the relationship. This additionally increases the chances that the child will experience shame, with all the consequent problems that this can lead to.

Many behavioural strategies rely on consequences to convey approval or disapproval in behaviour. Consequences can feel like the loss of the relationship. The children experience this as a reminder that relationships are conditional. Such conditional relationships can be lost. The child anticipates that the parent will stop loving her in the future, and the consequences trigger this fear. However, consequences that are collaborative because they emerge from the relationship can be helpful to the child. The parent is supporting the child to make amends for behavioural transgressions. The child is worth bothering with, and the child's trust in unconditional love and support is increased. Consequences that are imposed by parents are more problematic.

Finally, behavioural strategies tend to focus on providing predictability and consistency, so that the child learns from the consequences of their behaviour. They rely on the child learning from cause and effect. Predictability and consistency are important for children with developmental traumas, but this is not always something they have learnt to trust in. When children have lived in highly inconsistent and unpredictable environments they have not had the experience needed to learn about cause and effect. They have underdeveloped causal thinking. They therefore need predictability and consistency in order to start to develop this capacity. They are not yet ready to make the shift to learning from cause and effect. When effect (consequence) is disconnected from cause the children will experience the consequences as the parents being mean to them. This will lead to further dysregulation rather than learning from behaviour.

CONCLUSION

Behavioural support is an important part of parenting any children. It is this support that can help them to grow up into secure and well-adjusted adults, able to manage their own behaviour in relation to others. Traditional parenting advice stresses this part of the parenting task, offering ideas for parents to manage behaviours that are challenging and to reinforce behaviours they would like to increase. When children have experienced developmental traumas parenting becomes more complex. Parents need to find ways to build security and safety for their children as well as providing support for their behaviour. Emotional connection can be taken for granted with secure children but must be worked at when children have the insecurities and fears that developmental trauma brings.

— Chapter 11 —

SOME PARENTING PRINCIPLES: 'CONNECTION WITH CORRECTION'

At the centre of the DDP-informed parenting approach is the building of emotional connection with the child. This can then provide a foundation on which behavioural support can build. PACE plus discipline can build security for the insecure child. Here I will present a set of parenting principles that are derived from an understanding of child development and the DDP model.

PRINCIPLE ONE: PACE IS A CONSISTENT FEATURE AND DISCIPLINE IS BROUGHT IN AS NEEDED

It is important that the parent strives to hold on to PACE even when she needs to provide some discipline or limits on the behaviour of the child. The PACE before discipline will have helped the child to feel emotionally connected and unconditionally loved by the parent. It is helpful if the child can experience that this connection is continuing even when the parent is setting limits. The child needs to know that the relationship isn't being lost to him, and that he is still acceptable to the parent even though she is not happy with some aspect of his behaviour. This is a message that is hard for children with developmental trauma to get. Disapproval of their behaviour is experienced as shame for self. PACE with discipline helps to maintain this connection when the child is at his most vulnerable, experiencing shame and fear. The continuing PACE can regulate the experience of shame and help the child to respond more positively to the discipline. PACE following the discipline can add to this, providing the child with a continuing sense of being unconditionally loved. It also provides the parent with an opportunity to repair any ruptures in the relationship that might have occurred because of the need for discipline. This means letting the child know that he is still loved unconditionally and the relationship is still strong despite the need for discipline. This is not about apologizing, unless the parent feels that she did something that she could apologize for. It is more about letting the child know that the relationship is central, and remains even when discipline is needed.

PRINCIPLE TWO: TWO HANDS OF PARENTING

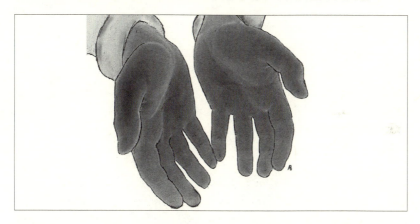

Research has demonstrated the value of so-called authoritative parenting for helping children to grow up into secure and well-adjusted adults (Baumrind 1978). The word 'authoritative' is a bit confusing here. In particular, it can be confused with authoritarian. Authoritarian parenting is low in warmth and nurture and high in punishment. This has been shown to lead to children growing up insecure and poorly adjusted. Authoritative is not the same. It describes a parenting style that is high in warmth and nurture but with clear structure and boundaries provided. This gives the children an experience where development of autonomy is encouraged, matched to their developmental age. This is unlike authoritarian parenting which discourages autonomy – a 'do as

I say' approach; or passive parenting which provides few boundaries – a 'do what you want' approach.

Children need structure and boundaries so that they can exercise their developing autonomy under the supervision and guidance of the parent. The warmth and nurture, alongside acceptance and curiosity, provide the emotional connection while the structure and boundaries matched to the child's development of autonomy provide the 'correction' or behavioural support.

This can be considered as having two hands for parenting:

- *Hand one* provides warmth and nurture and allows children appropriate autonomy matched to their developmental age. In other words, children are supported to make choices and to develop independence but only at a pace that they can cope with. This hand also contains the curiosity, allowing the parent to wonder about and accept the child's internal experience. Hand one supports PACE.

- *Hand two* complements PACE, providing structure and boundaries and the support from the parents that children need to be successful. This can include consequences, but stemming from understanding and used collaboratively with the children.

Two hands of parenting allow for:

- *connection with correction* – while the parent might need to give a consequence for behaviour (discipline, correction) this is likely to be more successful when the child feels understood by the parent (connection). This is not finding an excuse for behaviour – this still needs to be dealt with – but the behaviour is dealt with empathically

- *no correction without understanding* – if the parent responds without understanding, the child will feel less secure and will not build trust in the parent. Again this is not an excuse, but an explanation. The explanation helps the parent to get the consequences right.

PRINCIPLE THREE: THE PARENTING SANDWICH

Misattunements are a normal part of any relationship, and happen between a parent and child. However, for children with developmental trauma these disruptions to the relationship can provide them with the evidence they are seeking that they are not good enough and that they will be abandoned sometime soon. The parent needs to work to try and minimize these experiences. This will mean providing a quick repair to the relationship at these times. In this way these ruptures can present an opportunity to the parent for building trust with the child (Tronick 2007). If a parent can repair the connection with the child soon after the disruption, the child will feel more secure. Thus, parenting a child represents cycles of attunement – misattunement – repair, which strengthen the relationship. One necessary form of rupture occurs when parents need to discipline the child.

Sometimes behavioural support is more about regulatory support, as we have explored. This is not a time for discipline, but a time to help the child bring her level of emotional arousal back to a manageable level. Children being children, however, there will be times when behaviour is pushing a boundary, getting into mischief, trying it on and hoping not to be caught. As with any child, the parents will use discipline to ensure that boundaries are in place and that children do experience clear consequences for their behaviours. Without this the children feel unsafe.

Lax parenting does not lead to good adjustment as the child grows older any more than overly punitive parenting does. Authoritative parenting provides a balance between nurture and discipline. For children with developmental traumas this balance is a delicate one to find. These children are overly sensitive to feeling not good enough and to descending into shame. They also struggle to believe in unconditional love. The children do not relate the consequences to their behaviour and tend to view parents as mean instead.

A useful approach is to model parenting on the early relationships between parents and infants. Infants thrive on emotional attunement, but there are inevitably times when there are ruptures to this attunement, for example if the parent is not able to respond to the infant promptly or misunderstands what he needs. At these times the sensitive parent will repair the relationship, ensuring that a state of attunement is again reached between them. Breaks of attunement that occur because of the need for discipline can be treated the same way. Discipline, in the form of boundaries and consequences, is important, but it can be sandwiched between attunement and relationship repair (see Figure 11.1).

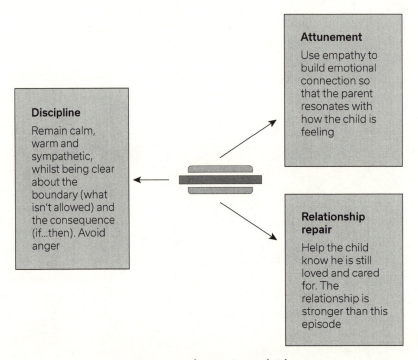

Figure 11.1 The parenting sandwich

PRINCIPLE FOUR: THE ADULT TAKES RESPONSIBILITY FOR THE RELATIONSHIP OFFERED TO THE CHILD

It can be tempting to withdraw from the relationship with the child, especially when he is being very challenging. 'I will come back when you are ready to apologize' can feel like a useful lesson. However, it is a message that the relationship is conditional – you can have a relationship with me only if you behave in a certain way. This will reduce the security a child is feeling. For a child who is already insecure within the relationship this is a body blow, confirming his worst fears that this relationship can be lost too. The child needs to know that the relationship is always open to him, even though at times he also has to manage consequences for his behaviour.

There will be times when parents need to withdraw for other reasons. They may be feeling particularly angry and frustrated such that they cannot stay open & engaged with the child. They need to take care of themselves so that they can continue to support the child as he needs. When in this situation the parent needs to do this in a way that signals that the relationship is still strong and will continue to be open to the child. The parent might, for example, tell the child that she is feeling angry just now and needs to take a break to look after herself. She won't forget the child, and will support him just as soon as she can. In this way the child gets the message that the relationship is still important, but sometimes parents have to take a break for themselves.

All of this is useful advice, but so hard to put into practice. In the heat of parenting it is hard to stay open & engaged. Inevitably the parent's own emotional experience will get in the way at times. Relationship repair, led by the parent, is important following these episodes. This continues to signal the importance of the relationship the parent has with the child.

Taking responsibility for the relationship therefore means:

- *not punishing with the relationship.* Children who are insecure are quick to assume that they are no good and that they are not loved. If the parent withdraws the relationship as a consequence or in anger, then the child is quick to confirm these beliefs. This increases insecurity and moves the child even further away from developing a trusting relationship with the parent. Judgemental disciplinary methods are therefore ineffective (for example, discipline which conveys: 'I am disappointed with you, my relationship with you is conditional on your behaviour')

- *taking breaks when needed.* Parents need to look after themselves. This gives them the strength and resilience to keep going. The parent is looking after the relationship with the child by taking breaks before she reaches breaking point. The child can be helped to understand that the parent is protecting the relationship because it is important to her. The child needs to know that this is not a sign that he is being abandoned

- *taking responsibility, as the adult, for relationship repair.* Parents are only human and it is inevitable that they will get cross or frustrated at times. It is important that these times are followed by relationship repair led by the adult that protects the relationship between them. Parents needn't be afraid to acknowledge that they got it wrong and that they are sorry, if this is how they are feeling. A genuine apology models that mistakes can be acknowledged. Repair following discipline also allows the parents to let the children know that they will continue to be there for them. The parent lets the child know that while she doesn't want the child to feel bad about himself, she does want to support him to manage things differently.

PRINCIPLE FIVE: UNDERSTANDING WITHOUT LECTURES, PREMATURE PROBLEM SOLVING AND RUSHED REASSURANCE

Lectures are the opposite of stories. When we lecture someone we are trying to teach them, provide them with new wisdom. Lectures about behaviour just do not work. Often this is because the children perceive this as a judgement about themselves; that they are a disappointment to the parent and they have let them down. Love feels conditional once again. Stories are an act of discovery together. The parent is working with the child to understand what is going on.

Think about the difference between a parent nagging a child to get on with his homework or wondering with him about why he is struggling. Rarely is homework progressed when parents are on the child's back. When they figure out together why the child is reluctant to do his homework then progress can be made. The child might need some structure and supervision from the parent to help; there may be a problem with understanding which the parent can support by approaching the teacher. This is problem solving at its best, based on a good understanding of what the child is experiencing. Rushing to problem solving before this understanding is achieved can be equally as ineffective as a lecture.

Reassurance is also problematic if it is rushed or used to help the parent to feel better. Quick reassurance signals to the child that his inner experience is not accepted; he should not think or feel that way. This is invalidating of the child and therefore harmful to the relationship.

Often this type of reassurance stems from the difficult feelings of the parents. They are uncomfortable with the emotion the child is displaying and therefore want it to go away. The child proclaims that he is rubbish and will never achieve success. The parent tells the child, of course you are not rubbish, keep practising and you will succeed. The child's feelings are being shut down because the parent is finding them overwhelming.

The parent needs some time to take care of herself, to have empathy for how hard this feels so that she can stay present to the child's experience. The parent is then able to stay longer with ensuring that she understands the child's experience; she can accept this experience, validating the child and then she can follow with some reassurance that holds out hope for the future. 'I know you feel rubbish right now and it feels like practice is not going to help. Those are hard feelings. I am here and am going to support you even though you feel rubbish. I am hopeful that in the future you won't feel like rubbish, but right now I get that you can't believe this.'

Understanding the child therefore means:

- *not lecturing and delaying problem solving.* Children can rarely be talked into or out of behaviour. Remember that behaviour change comes from being understood within relationships so that boundaries are experienced with warmth and empathy. Children might be able to join in with some problem solving – how they might have managed something differently – but they will not engage with this until they really experience parents as understanding them

- *not rushing to reassure.* Reassurance that tries to talk children out of what they are experiencing is not helpful. This is not acceptance. It is effectively saying to the child that you understand what they are thinking and feeling, but they don't need to or shouldn't think or feel this way. Reassurance denies that thinking and feeling is neither right nor wrong, it just is. Reassure to give hope rather than to make yourself feel better.

PRINCIPLE SIX: PROVIDE AN APPROPRIATE LEVEL OF STRUCTURE AND SUPERVISION

Very often parental expectations of children are based on their chronological age. Phrases such as 'Act your age' or 'A nine-year-old should be able to...' show that a parent is judging her child based on what peers of his age can typically do. This does not take into account the child's individual level of maturity. This can lead to increased pressure for the child to manage a level of structure and supervision that is too low for him. Parents need to be mindful of the children's emotional maturity, adjusting their expectations in line with this. This is made more complicated because levels of maturity can fluctuate depending on the level of stress being experienced. We all act younger when under stress and this can be exaggerated in children who are emotionally insecure. Structure and supervision will therefore have to be adjusted in relationship to the child's current level of stress.

A balance has to be found between too much structure and supervision, which does not challenge the child and hampers development, and too little structure and supervision which overwhelms the child with too much expectation of what he can do. Children need sufficient challenge to progress within the supportive relationship of the parent.

Notice that if the consequences are piling up it is a sign that the child needs increased structure and supervision, alongside empathy. If the child is remaining static, not developing in maturity or ability, then maybe too much structure and supervision is not sufficiently challenging him.

A Russian child psychologist called Lev Vygotsky explored this in relation to what he termed the zone of proximal development (Vygotsky 1978). This is a complicated term but essentially means that children will make developmental progress when the parents provide them with some scaffolding. The children can do so much on their own, and a little bit more with parental support. If parents' expectations are within the zone they are holding the right level of expectations and the children are likely to progress. If, however, their expectations are outside this zone the children are less likely to progress because expectations are too low or too high (see Figure 11.2).

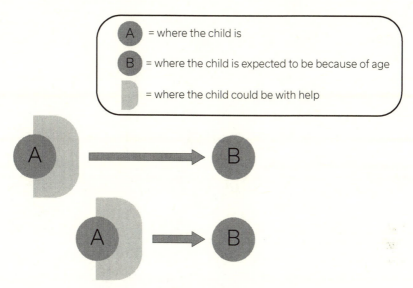

Figure 11.2 The zone of proximal development

PRINCIPLE SEVEN: HELP THE CHILD TO MANAGE SHIFTS BETWEEN PLAYFULNESS AND PARENTAL AUTHORITY

One of the hardest things a mistrusting child can do is accede to the authority of the parent. These children have learnt to control others as a way of maintaining their own safety. Giving up this control is not going to be easy. This means that at times when a parent needs to use her authority for keeping the child safe, providing a boundary and structuring the environment, the child will revert to his own pattern of controlling behaviours. Baylin and Hughes (2016) point out that the shift from what they call 'companionship mode' to 'parental authority mode' can be especially difficult. The child is able to connect with the parent when she is being playful; it is during these times that the difference in power and authority between parent and child is at its smallest. As the parent moves back into being parental (for example, 'It's nearly teatime, let's put this away now'), the child needs to adjust to the parent being back in charge. These relational transitions can lead to very rapid shifts in the child towards anger and meltdown. The parent needs to find a way to stay open and empathic to the child's struggles against letting parents have a benevolent authority over him.

Chapter 12

PARENTING IN THE MOMENT

In the last two chapters I have shared a lot of ideas and perhaps given you some insight into parenting in a way that you are less used to. There is a lot of information to hang on to, and applying this in the moment can be challenging. In this chapter I am therefore aiming to put this together for you: a guide to parenting the insecure child when the luxury of time to think things through is not available. I have therefore called this 'parenting in the moment'. I hope that your reading of the previous chapters helps you to understand why I have put this together in this way. It is a guide, and does not have to be followed rigidly. There are seven stages, but you may find yourself going backwards and forwards between these.

What you will see is that this is parenting by the long route. In more traditional parenting we tend to move straight from stage one to stage six, with stages two to five getting lost on the way. We miss out a lot that is helpful when we take this shortcut. It is the longer route that will allow trauma to be healed and the child to be able to experience safety and build trust with the parents.

'Parenting in the moment' encourages you to maintain an attitude of PACE in your parenting. This doesn't mean talking over everything with your child – that would drive you both crazy! Cultivate an attitude of curiosity about your child – this will increase your understanding, which will increase your acceptance and empathy. Look for moments of playfulness and pick your moments for using PACE with your child, bearing in mind her age, verbal ability and level of emotional arousal.

Parenting in the moment is therefore a set of seven stages that summarize the DDP-informed approach to parenting that is explored within this book. By keeping these stages in mind it is easier to stay open & engaged with the child rather than becoming defensive within your parenting. This in turn helps you to make emotional connections with the child while also providing some behavioural support. When a parent 'connects' alongside 'correcting', the child will experience unconditional love and acceptance along with the safety that empathic boundaries and discipline can provide.

At the end of this chapter I have included a diagrammatic version of these stages. Here I will summarize each one.

STAGE ONE

Notice what is happening. This is the moment when you notice that something is going on that the child might need your support with. It might be an increase in challenging behaviour, it might be the child signalling that she is troubled or worrying about something. You will need to make some immediate decisions. The first is: do I need to step in? You will make a decision about whether your child needs your support right now or whether she is benefiting from managing this by herself. Sometimes watching and waiting can help you to choose the right moment to offer support. At other times it is obvious that you need to get involved. You then need to consider what immediate steps you need to take to ensure everyone's safety. For example, if a child has grabbed a knife and is behaving dangerously with this, you need to take action to remove the knife. Taking these initial actions can give you a breathing space to reflect on where to go next.

STAGE TWO

This may seem surprising but I am going to suggest that you now pause for a moment and notice what you are feeling right now. A quick internal scan can help you to notice the impact the child is having on you. Notice if you are regulated. Can you stay open & engaged or are you in danger of becoming defensive? If you are becoming defensive, do you need a break or can you get back to being open & engaged? If you could do with a break but this is not possible, at the least you can be compassionate to yourself. Obviously, in the midst of challenging behaviour you may not have much time to do this but just taking a moment to notice can help you to stay regulated. It may also be helpful to notice your reactions to reflect on later with more time and with a trusted other person. This will all be part of building your resilience.

STAGE THREE

Now it is time to focus on your child. Notice how aroused she is. Where on the arousal continuum do you think she is? What does this mean for her emotional age right now? What capacity for thinking and reasoning is she likely to be open to? Is she open to some playfulness with you? If not, just use simple A and E (acceptance and empathy) responses. This is light A and E, as you have not yet used your curiosity to figure out what the child is experiencing. Simple statements like, 'I can see you are having a hard time right now', will convey to the child that you are present and available to support her. This thinking will guide you about how to use your relationship with your child at this moment. Should you focus on regulation, or is the child open to reflection? If you think regulation might be helpful you will also need to judge at what sensory, or emotional, level this needs to be. Sometimes children will regulate with your gentle and empathic presence. At other times they may also need some sensory activities to help with this. Food, drink, exercise or calming activities can all help the child into a more regulated state. If you have previously explored what is helpful for your child at a sensory level, you will have some ideas about what might work right now.

STAGE FOUR

At this stage you can fully engage your curiosity and understanding. Figure out what might be going on for your child right now based on your previous experience and with knowledge of her past experience. Wonder about what she is feeling and thinking. What is your best guess about what your child's internal emotional experience is at this moment? Remember that internal experience is neither right nor wrong, it just is. You are not going to judge it, but you will accept it. If your child is open to and able to reflect with you it might be possible to gently wonder with her. Wonder what is going on for her right now and see if she can give you some clues. If this is not possible, use your curiosity on her behalf. Deepen your understanding so that you can help her to know that you get it.

STAGE FIVE

Now you can deepen your A and E because it is based on your curiosity and understanding. Use acceptance and empathy to connect with the child around the best guess of what her emotional experience is. Think about how you can help her to know that you get it. This is a time for focusing on the child's experience. She will not yet be ready to think about her actions and how these have impacted on others. To do this prematurely is likely to trigger shame and further increase her emotional arousal.

STAGE SIX

The 'correction'. At some point, as your child is calm and regulated and when she is able to think about herself, you will judge that the time is right to focus her attention on others whom she may have impacted on. If she is feeling supported and understood by you, any sense of shame will have regulated and she might now be experiencing some feelings of guilt. This is the time that you can support her feelings of remorse and can think with her about how to make amends. Here and in the next stage consequences can be considered collaboratively by the two of you. You will then think about whether you need to do anything further. Are further consequences needed, or is the child on track for making amends? Do we need to do some problem solving? If the child has disclosed a worry or problem to you she may now be open to thinking about what to do about this.

STAGE SEVEN

Now you can think about repairing the relationship. If all has gone well it is likely that there is no rupture to the relationship between you. It is still worth letting your child know that she is loved unconditionally. However, sometimes you will have reacted to things less well as you have tried to support your child. Take responsibility for any mistakes you may have made. Let her know that it may have felt tough but the relationship between you is stronger. Together you have got through it. You can also, following on from the previous stage, help the child to repair any relationships with others who may have been impacted by her behaviour. Often this repair is part of the logical consequence for the child. Many children, who have felt supported through the connection with the parent, will now be experiencing some guilt and remorse and will want to make this repair.

PARENTING IN THE MOMENT AS OPEN & ENGAGED PARENTING

Notice how this parenting helps you to stay open & engaged with your child. Any feelings of defensiveness are noticed and you use curiosity to move out of, or avoid moving into, a defensive attitude. When parents don't take a moment to take care of themselves, and become overly focused on managing the behaviour without ensuring that they have a connection with the child, then defensiveness is likely to follow. The parents will have the best of intentions. They want the child to behave well, not just because that is easier for them but also because they know this will ultimately be more helpful for the child.

When children misbehave, it is easy to become lost in the future, imagining the trouble the children might get into if they can't behave in a societally acceptable way. Concerns about such a future, and an overly defensive parenting approach, tend to move a parent into a more coercive approach with the child. The well-intentioned need to change the child's behaviour overrides any thought about connecting with the emotional experience of the child.

Unfortunately, this move to coercion is experienced by the children as disapproval. This triggers their own feelings of blocked trust and they anticipate loss and abandonment. The children move into a feared future too. Alongside these fears, the children also experience a reinforcement of their experience of not being good enough and their sense of shame increases. As we have previously explored, feelings of shame can be defended against using the shield against shame. The children move into more behaviours which further trigger the parents' anxiety. As the children try to cope with intense feelings of shame, the parents in turn are trying to cope with their own feelings of failure. Often they increase their focus on behaviour. In this situation behaviour management can become increasingly punitive as the parents try even harder to get the children to change their behaviour. Punitive parenting is often a response to big fears that the parent is failing and that the child is going to develop in ways that are unacceptable for her and for society at large. This can increase when parents are feeling judged by others. The child's behaviour becomes a reflection on themselves, and it is an image they do not want to look at.

I am reminded of the incident that got widely reported in the media of the Japanese parents who left their seven-year-old boy on the edge of a bear-infested forest as a lesson to him for some transgression in his behaviour. They drove away, although returned a short while later. Unfortunately, by then the boy had wandered away and was lost. He was found safe and well six days later, but the parents had to face much disapproval of their actions and felt much regret for what had happened. I have no doubt the parents were well intentioned, although misguided. They wanted their boy to behave, as they knew that this would be better for him and would reflect well on themselves. This is a good example of such concerns leading to highly punitive parenting approaches when connection is lost and correction becomes dominant.

CONCLUSION

It is my hope that parenting in the moment can guide parents to more open & engaged parenting within which they can use PACE to connect with their children. This provides a foundation for behavioural support where a healthy balance between connection and correction is found, a balance where any correction that is used serves to strengthen the relationship further because it is collaborative rather than coercive. The following story, based on a real event, illustrates the parenting in the moment sequence in action.

A DIFFICULT DAY AT SCHOOL

It is a hot day in the summer term. The children are all a bit fractious as the end of term approaches. Seven-year-old Benjamin has always found school difficult, and this has increased as the children become more unsettled around him. As his stress increases he is finding it harder and harder to stay regulated. He nearly blew before lunchtime but the teaching assistant managed to step in and provide him with some calm time out of the classroom. Unfortunately, this hasn't lasted. An argument over who has the football leads to Benjamin hitting two of the other boys. It is decided that it would be better for Benjamin to go home than for him to continue to struggle, and his mum is called.

His mum puts down the phone with a sigh. This afternoon was not going to be the afternoon she had planned. She quickly phones the friend she had planned a cup of tea with. She reflects on how she is feeling. She is a bit frustrated that she must fetch Benjamin. Fleetingly she wonders if they could have managed him at school without the need for him to come home. She is okay though, and her empathy for how hard Benjamin is finding school remains high. She thinks about how to help him. She knows that Benjamin is finding school difficult at the moment and she anticipates that his emotional regulation will be very fragile after such a difficult morning. Instead of jumping in her car to collect him she decides to take the time to walk to school. She hopes the walk home will provide some regulatory support to help Benjamin to settle.

When she arrives at school Mum greets Benjamin with a quick hug, acknowledging that it has been a difficult morning. She does not talk about it any further but instead they walk home chatting about what they see. They notice the birds singing and Benjamin is very pleased when he recognizes the blackbird. As they get towards home Mum notices that Benjamin is becoming unsettled again. She guesses that he is anticipating a talk about school. Quietly she tells him that they will have a chat later but for now she just wants him to have a snack and something to drink. She guesses rightly that he has not eaten much of his lunch. After a round of toast and jam and a milkshake drunk through a straw Benjamin is calm again.

Mum: (gently) 'So, school was hard today?'

Benjamin: (head immediately goes down, but he does not run away)

Mum: It's tough being at school when you're feeling hot and tired, isn't it?

Benjamin: (looks up) Yes and it was so noisy. I hated it.

Mum: (nods sympathetically) Yes, it is much harder for you when they are noisy. I wonder why they were noisier today? Mrs Jones said that we were all feeling hot and tired. She told us that it is harder not to argue when you are hot but we should try hard. Do you think that is why you were finding it hard? Were the children all arguing?

Benjamin: (thinks about this) Not all of them, but Justine and Carol got very cross when they were gluing. I think their model broke.

Mum: Well Benjamin, no wonder you were feeling wobbly today. That was a lot to cope with wasn't it?

Benjamin: (hangs his head again and then whispers) I hit Jack and Billy.

Mum: I know, sweetheart. That was when Mrs Jones called me. She isn't cross with you but she thought it would be better for you to be at home this afternoon.

Benjamin: I didn't mean to hit them but they wouldn't let me have a turn with the ball. I had waited ages.

Mum: It sounds like you were trying to be patient, but then you felt very cross with them, didn't you?

Benjamin: Yes, and I tried to get the ball from them...

Benjamin: (hesitates and then whispers) And then I hit them.

Benjamin: (brightens) Mummy, can I make them cards? You know, to say sorry. Can I make a card for Jack and Billy?

Mum: (smiles) Well that sounds like a great plan. I will get the card and pens out and you can make them while I clear up a bit. We must be sure to remember to take them with us when we go to school tomorrow.

Benjamin: (looks pensive, and then looks at Mum with a sense of urgency) No Mum, no, not tomorrow. We must take the cards to school today. I don't want to wait until tomorrow.

Mum: (looks puzzled) Well we could, but what's the hurry? It would be easier to take them with us tomorrow.

Benjamin: No Mum, that won't do. We must go back to school today. You see I don't want Jack and Billy to be upset all night!

Mum: (smiles and ruffles Benjamin's hair) Do you know Benjamin, that sounds like a great plan!

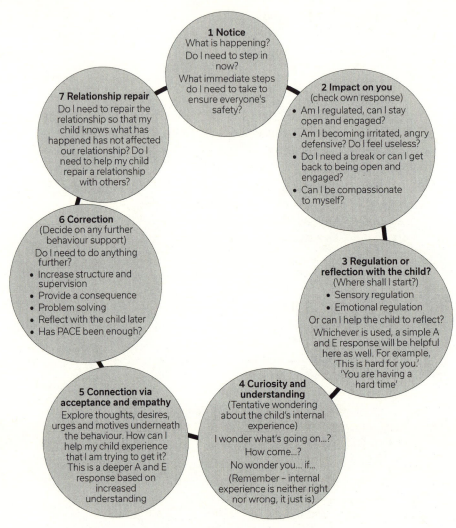

Figure 12.1 Parenting in the moment

This cycle demonstrates a sequence that is helpful to take when parenting a child. By keeping this in mind it is easier to stay open & engaged with the child rather than becoming defensive within parenting. This in turn helps to make an emotional connection with the child while also providing some behavioural support. When a parent connects with correcting, the child will experience unconditional love and acceptance alongside the safety that empathic boundaries and discipline can provide.

— Part 3 —

LOOKING AFTER SELF

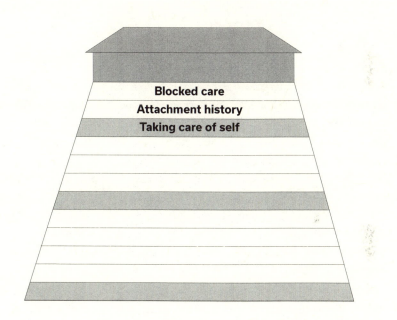

In this final part, the focus shifts from the children to the parents. Taking care of themselves is an important part of parents maintaining the resilience they need for caring for the children. A part of this self-care is to understand their own vulnerabilities and triggers. Understanding what quickly moves parents to a defensive position with the children can help them to remain or return to being open & engaged at these times. Children with developmental traumas can drain the resilience of the strongest of parents. Blocked care is then a real possibility. Recognizing blocked care and gaining support at these times is also an important part of helping parents to remain open to their children.

— Chapter 13 —

UNDERSTANDING ATTACHMENT HISTORY

In this section I am moving from exploring the parenting of the child to a focus on how parents can look after themselves. Much as aeroplane procedures always suggest, helping yourself before helping others is an essential part of parenting children. This is especially so when you are parenting a child who is emotionally troubled. Children who have experienced developmental traumas have a range of difficulties that make parenting challenging. We explored the emotional challenges in Part 1 of this book. Added to this, many of the children have neurodevelopmental issues that contribute to the difficulties they struggle with – difficulties made more challenging because they find it so hard to let parents help them. The combination of emotional and neurodevelopmental difficulties can be an especially tricky pairing, with each contributing to the difficulty presented by the other. The sum of this is that the children will be slow to develop security.

Parenting is a long road to travel. Parents are therefore vulnerable to running out of emotional energy for this parenting task. Staying strong and resilient will be an essential part of successful parenting. This will emerge out of good self-care coupled with a high level of social support. Good self-understanding is an important addition to this mix. This is where this chapter begins. Understanding relationship history can open the door to understanding the impact parenting a child is having on the parent.

EXPLORING PAST RELATIONSHIP HISTORY

Past relationship history can have a big impact on the way a parent relates to her child. Parents may unconsciously parent in the way that they were parented. For example, consider a parent who experienced authoritarian parenting within which her independence was frowned on and she was expected to stay at home and help with household chores. Such a parent may adopt the same parenting style when parenting a child or young person who is trying to establish his own autonomy and develop independence. Alternatively, she may consciously try and parent very differently, perhaps over-compensating for experiences she had in childhood. In this case, the parent may allow the young person too much freedom, failing to provide the boundaries that are needed for this youngster to feel safe.

This becomes even trickier if a child reminds the parent in some way of a past relationship. Parents might find themselves unconsciously reacting to the child in line with their feelings about the past relationship. For example, parents like the one above may struggle when the child is quite needy of them, perhaps restricting what they can do. This might be because of the age of the child or because of difficulties the child has. Parents might feel angry when they can't go out or do things that they want or need to do because of the demands of the child. The unconscious anger towards their own parents' restrictions on them might spill over into their feelings towards this child. Without good self-awareness and understanding, the parenting becomes invaded by previous experiences of being parented.

In Chapter 4, I briefly explored Robert's difficulties trying to parent his son, Harry, who displays highly controlling behaviours. This took him uncomfortably back to his relationship with his own father. A childhood against the backdrop of World War Two, including experience of evacuation, had left Robert's father feeling uncomfortable when not feeling in control himself. He therefore provided a highly controlling parenting environment, which Robert especially resented as he matured into his teens. Robert felt stifled, and this led to many arguments, including his father hitting him when he stepped too far out of line. One memorable day Robert hit back and then went out. When he returned much later his father had locked him out of the home. Robert thought he had left this relationship far behind. Following his parents' divorce, he had very little to do with his father. He therefore did not recognize nor understand why he became anxious when Harry was very controlling towards him. Robert would experience huge rage, and he became very concerned that he might actually hit Harry during one of these episodes. Robert was dismayed, as he valued himself as a patient and kind man, the very opposite of his father. He had always vowed that he would never parent his children as he had been parented, and yet he could feel himself moving in this direction. On top of this the arguments he was having with Marian were uncomfortably like the relationship between his own mother and father before they divorced. Robert might have been helped if someone had explored with him where these strong feelings came from. If he could separate out his feelings towards his father from his understanding of Harry he might have found that he could be more flexible in his parenting, and more supportive towards Marian. Sadly, he instead sought a different option, moving away and out of their lives.

It is not only historical experience of parents that can have this influence. Memories of any past relationships can be triggered by a parent–child relationship, whether it is parents, siblings, extended family, work colleagues or romantic relationships. For example, a parent may have escaped a relationship characterized by domestic abuse, or have left a job because of a bullying boss. If the child starts to become demanding or threatening, this past relationship may come back into the present and the parent experiences fear or anger towards the child that actually belongs in the past with these historic relationships.

This unconscious parenting in response to past relationships is linked to the parents' attachment state of mind. Earlier in this book I explored the attachment patterns of relating that children develop to adapt to the environments they are being raised in. These patterns represent models of relating that are used to guide later relationships that the children encounter. Children will have multiple models based on the range of relationships they have experienced; parents, grandparents and childminders can all exert an influence on the patterns of attachment that the child develops and can draw on in different situations. As the children reach adolescence and beyond these multiple models become cumbersome for the more sophisticated relationships the young person is now managing. A task at this developmental stage is therefore to form a single but more complex model of relating that can be taken forward into adulthood. A simple model such as 'I am lovable, and you will support me' will become more sophisticated: 'I am lovable to some people but less so to others; I can expect support from people I experience closeness with but this is less likely from people I find less easy to get along with.' These models are heavily influenced by attachment experience.

Thus adolescents begin to develop what has been called a state of mind towards attachment experience. The way they learnt to relate to others from childhood, beginning with their attachment relationships, becomes translated into a general state of mind linked to attachment experience. This attachment state of mind influences how adolescents and adults will orient themselves to others in the range of relationships that they develop, including their parenting relationships.

ATTACHMENT STATES OF MIND

As attachment states of mind are influenced by multiple models in childhood, they can be a complex mix of experience. However, it is usual for this to be dominated by one particular style of attachment relating.

Thus if a child has most experience of attachment security, but with some experience of loss that is well supported, it is likely that as an adult her attachment state of mind will be predominantly secure, usually described as autonomous. She might remain vulnerable to further experience of loss, but she is also likely to be confident to seek support for this should it arise.

Perhaps a person, while having a secure childhood, did have a father who valued independence within his son. As an adult this son, while having a generally autonomous state of mind, might lean towards some self-reliance in situations that remind him of his father.

Attachment states of mind are therefore a reflection of the complex range of experiences each of us encounters while growing up. Bearing in mind this complexity I will describe the different attachment states of mind as they are described when thinking about adult attachment.

Autonomous

As mentioned above the secure attachment pattern of childhood becomes an autonomous attachment state of mind. These adults have a balanced view of their childhood. They recognize and value the strengths it has given them but can also acknowledge any difficulties they encountered. They are aware of how this experience has made them the adult they are today. These experiences mean that as parents they can cope well with their children's negative as well as positive emotional states. This makes them sensitive and responsive parents able to stay regulated when their children express distress or dysregulation.

Preoccupied

An ambivalent attachment pattern in childhood becomes a preoccupied attachment state of mind. When parenting a child triggers this state of mind, parents become absorbed or preoccupied with the past relationships. They find it hard to distance themselves from this childhood experience. It's as if they are back there again, and this can result in a high level of emotion, including anger. The feelings they have towards the person in the past become enacted in their parenting of their child. This preoccupation is generally unconscious; the parents experience themselves as responding to the child and not to the left over feelings from their past. Being unaware of this influence, the parents will struggle to alter or adapt their parenting responses to be attuned to the child's needs.

Dismissive

An avoidant attachment pattern in childhood becomes a dismissing attachment state of mind. As adults, memories of childhood can be idealized as the memory of negative experience is blocked or as they deny that this has been of any significance. This is most noticeable when talking about negative experiences. These adults can talk matter of factly about very difficult experiences, appearing to be emotionally unaffected by these memories. They especially value self-reliance and rather frown on people who appear dependent. When parenting the child triggers this state of mind, the parents tend to withdraw from the emotional experience that the child is triggering within them. This is most likely to occur when the child is expressing emotional distress. This distress is minimized as the parent encourages the child to suppress it. Their own emotional avoidance means that they cannot be aware of how the child is currently feeling. This is because they are unconsciously trying to remain unaware of how they felt at the time of their own past experience. Parents will encourage self-reliance in their children as they are more likely to be responsive to them when they are emotionally self-sufficient.

Unresolved

Most difficulty is posed when the parents have unresolved relationship trauma in their past. These traumas can lie buried inside ready to be triggered at unpredictable times; once triggered the parent can become absorbed with the fear or grief associated with this trauma. If the child unwittingly acts as such a trigger, then the parent will not be able to protect or reassure the child. For the child it will be as if the parent isn't there, as her unavailability becomes apparent. Distress in the child can trigger a dysregulated or a dissociated response in the parents as memory of the trauma surfaces. The parent becomes anxious or distressed and this overwhelming emotional experience reduces her availability towards her child. Alternatively, when the parent experiences this trigger she cuts off from what is happening in the moment; lost in the past but unable to make sense of the memories that are overwhelming her she withdraws into a fragmented inner world, becoming unavailable towards the child as a consequence.

Often the memory triggering these responses is implicit; the parent is not consciously aware of it. The parent can become frightened when parenting the child as she fears what the child triggers within her or the loss of control that this can lead to. The unresolved attachment traumas from the past therefore prevent the parents perceiving and meeting the child's need for safety and comfort. This is frightening for the child, and thus traumas are perpetuated.

KNOWING YOUR OWN ATTACHMENT STATE OF MIND

Parents can use their attachment history exploration to notice if they have a tendency to try and avoid feeling things, preferring to rationalize and intellectualize as in the dismissing attachment state of mind. Alternatively, they may find that they are easily overwhelmed by emotional experiences without being able to reflect on them, as in the preoccupied attachment state of mind. In either case the parent will benefit from correcting the balance. Supportive relationships can help her to do this. The dismissing parent can learn to become more open to her emotional experience, while the preoccupied parent can learn to reflect on this experience from a distance, so she is less caught up in her immediate emotions.

Figure 13.1 together with Table 13.1 at the end of this chapter can be used to help you to reflect on your own attachment history. You can mark on the line where you think you fit in relationship to the descriptions of the different attachment states of mind. Remember that this can be different for different relationships.

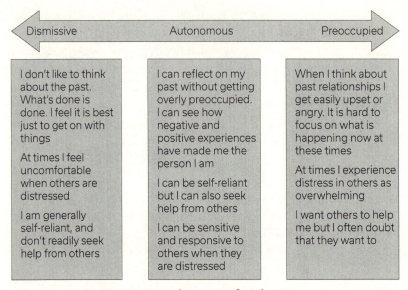

Figure 13.1 Attachment state of mind continuum

THE IMPORTANCE OF SELF-EXPLORATION AS PART OF SELF-CARE

From these descriptions you may notice that when attachment experience is negatively influencing parenting this often happens outside consciousness. The parents may know they are struggling when the child is distressed, but not be able to associate this with their own past experience. As with Robert, the pattern of parenting they fall into is an unconscious one as adaptations or responses they developed in the past are re-enacted in the present.

Things that are unconscious do not need to stay unconscious. The best way of not being hijacked by your own attachment history is to be able to reflect on it and understand it. When we can make the unconscious conscious it no longer has the power to control us and we can behave more flexibly and mindfully as a result. Exploration of past relationship history, including early attachment experience, is therefore an important part of understanding current parenting challenges.

This would have helped Robert and Marian, offering insight about what was going on, and in turn helping Robert to be able to feel good about himself as a parent again. Instead it is likely that he will continue to carry the shame of what happened into his new life without his family.

When it is understood, the past becomes a road map for understanding present triggers and obstacles. Knowing that you are feeling angry with the child because he is reminding you of your father can help you to regulate the angry feelings. They reduce and you can focus on the child responsively again. Being able to reflect on past relationships with compassion for yourself is therefore helpful. These relationships were difficult and understanding how they influenced the adult you have become is important. As you integrate this past experience it will help you to distance yourself from it. In this way, current experience does not keep taking you back to your old struggles.

Such self-exploration can be useful for any parent but is especially useful when parenting children who have experienced developmental trauma. As we explored earlier, these children are often searching for predictability and ways to feel in charge of the adults. Their controlling behaviours are especially satisfied when they discover the parents' buttons and that pushing them leads to a predictable response, which helps the children to feel safer because it is within their control. Anticipating that a parent is going to be angry with you is hard to live with; knowing that you can make the parent angry feels a whole lot safer if only because it is predictable.

Parents will not get very far if they fall into control battles with their children; these children are generally the masters of control, and they usually win! Being able to step aside from the battle by being in control of your own responses can, however, be helpful. Understanding your own triggers is therefore an important part of parenting children who feel a need to control.

MOVING FROM DEFENSIVE TO OPEN & ENGAGED

Understanding yourself better helps you to understand the way a particular child impacts on you. Different children impact on parents in different ways. This is because the unconscious memories they trigger will differ depending on the way that they are relating to the parent.

Some parents will have already explored their attachment history prior to parenting the children. Adopters, for example, will undertake this exploration as part of the preparation to adopt; others may have engaged in this as part of therapy. It would be understandable therefore to wonder if you really need to do this again now that your life is full up with parenting children with their own challenges. My experience with many parents suggests that exploration of attachment and past relationship history alongside active parenting is different. After all, you are no longer trying to predict how this history may impact on you as a parent; you are now experiencing this day to day.

Robert will have explored his relationship with his father during his preparation to adopt. It is likely that he would have acknowledged that this relationship had a big impact on him. He would also have been able to talk about all the ways he ensured that he was different to his father, and he would have predicted that he would be a very different kind of parent to his children. If they had adopted a less controlling child this may well have been true. Robert could not predict how he would respond to Harry's intense need to control, and he ended up being surprised and horrified by this as a consequence.

When you reflect on your history through the lens of current parenting it brings your own vulnerabilities and resilience into view in a very strong and practical way. This can have an immediate impact on your parenting and how you support your child.

As parents notice how their responses to their children are linked to their responses to previous relationships they will be able to consciously change the way they are responding in the present. In particular, they will be able to remain open & engaged with their children rather than becoming defensive with them. Self-reflection does not stop the triggers; they may always be there. After all, your history is yours and cannot be re-written. There is a difference, however, between unconscious triggers that are in charge, making life uncomfortable for you, and conscious triggers which allow you to be flexible in the present. When we are aware of what is happening it puts us back in charge. We can notice and choose not to engage with the trigger. We stay open to the child, letting the impact this is having on us move to the background.

Noticing in the moment but choosing not to be controlled by a trigger can feel very freeing. However, it is an act of repression, pushing the feelings and thoughts that have arisen away. You will also need to allow yourself some time to reflect on these at a later stage. This is more likely to help you to be free of them in the future. Remember that reflecting with a trusted person can be especially helpful to increase your self-understanding. This processing of your experience can increase your resilience to similar future moments with your child.

Alternatively, we might recognize that we are struggling because of a trigger and choose to move away from the child for a while, take care of ourselves and then return in a more open state. Choosing to take a break – letting your child know that this is what you are doing – not only helps you to take care of yourself but also models good self-care to your child.

Sometimes a parent can't physically take a break because there is no one else to care for the child. It is possible, however, to take a break from dealing with the issue at hand. As parents we often feel that if we are not dealing with a behaviour immediately we are somehow failing. Apart from very young children who live in a more immediate world, children will cope with a delay. Acknowledge that you are upset right now, let your child know that while you are not happy with what he has done you do still love him and want to support him. You need time to think about this so that you can help him to make amends for his actions while getting your support for him right. In this way the child is left in no doubt that he has done something wrong, but that he is still loved and cared about. You may need to stay with him to ensure his safety but you do not need to worry about discipline right away.

This might be a time to do something regulating, including the child if he is open to this. It might be a time to let the child have some space while keeping a distant but watchful eye on him. When you are able to become open & engaged again, and if the child is sufficiently regulated, it can then be helpful to reflect together on what happened. Remember to begin with the child's experience and only later expect him to think about the impact on you or anyone else involved, as in the 'parenting in the moment' sequence.

There may be occasions when you have reacted to something from the child that on reflection does not need discipline. Perhaps the child was stressed and dysregulated; he shouted at you and it was this shouting that triggered you to experience anger towards him. You may want to give yourself some space to regulate before you can provide regulatory support for your child. Again this is difficult for a younger child who will need immediate co-regulation to help him. As long as it is safe, an older child can be left for a short while while you take care of yourself. Again, leave the child in no doubt about what is happening: 'I am feeling upset right now. I love you and want to help you but just need a moment to calm myself down.'

Managing these moments when the past meets the present can be some of the trickiest times in parenting. It is so easy to get caught up in your own reactions and not to notice what is going on. Before you know it you are engaged in a shouting match or control battle with your child and the relationship is suffering. Be compassionate to yourself; know that parenting is a hard job and parenting this child has its challenges. You will repair the relationship later and your child will know that even when things go wrong it is recoverable.

With an older young person who is beginning to engage in his own self-reflection you may even want to share something of what you have learnt about yourself. You will only share what you are comfortable with, but knowing that Mum gets cross when she is reminded of how Granddad shouted at her can really help a young person to believe in the unconditional love the parent is offering. It is also providing a real-life demonstration of why it is important to understand your own attachment history, helping yourself and future relationships.

CONCLUSION

This chapter has begun the section on self-care with an exploration of attachment and past relationship history. I have chosen to begin consideration of how parents can take care of themselves with exploring the importance of self-understanding. This is because unconscious knowledge is a dangerous thing; it has unlooked for impacts when we least expect it and this can have an effect both on the relationship with the child but also on how parents feel about themselves. Feelings of failure, despair, hopelessness and a sense that you don't think you can continue often have some of their roots in the attempt to manage the impact of a past relationship while struggling to manage a current one. Understanding your own history and the impact it has had on you, together with your own supportive realtionships, can help you to avoid falling into a state of blocked care. This will be the subject of the next chapter.

Table 13.1 Exploring attachment history

Attachment state of mind	Reflection on childhood experience	Impact on current relationships including parenting
Autonomous *Balanced and valuing* You experienced a secure attachment history or have resolved difficult attachment experience through reflection and understanding, leading to earned security.	You are likely to talk about childhood realistically. You will be able to give a coherent account of difficult experience or loss. You will be aware of the influence of your past on your present.	You are able to regulate, reflect and have empathy for self and others. This makes it relatively easy to be sensitive and responsive towards other people. You are likely to be able to provide comfort. You are likely to remain regulated and be open & engaged when others display distress and need comfort, however this is displayed. If you do become defensive, you will be able to be compassionate towards yourself and move back to being open & engaged.
Dismissing *Minimizing* You experienced an avoidant attachment history which has led to a tendency to distrust emotional expression and to value self-reliance. This has stemmed from experience of not being connected with or soothed when distressed early in life.	When talking about your childhood you are likely to focus on positives rather than negatives, but may struggle to remember actual experiences. You are likely to feel that negative experiences have not made any difference to you. You are likely to value self-reliance and devalue dependence. You are less likely to look to others for support when distressed.	You are likely to find it more difficult to recognize or respond to emotional expression in others and will feel uncomfortable when others are distressed. You can feel disconnected from others and from your own emotions and needs. You will value self-reliance and independence in others. You are more likely to become defensive as you minimize emotional distress in others, encouraging them to get over it and moving quickly to problem solving.

Attachment state of mind	Reflection on childhood experience	Impact on current relationships including parenting
Preoccupied *Maximizing* You experienced an ambivalent-resistant attachment history which has led to a tendency to use emotional expression to keep others engaged with you. This has stemmed from unpredictable experience of feeling safe, soothed and seen by parents, and the experience of being flooded with their anxieties and fears.	When talking about your childhood you are likely to be preoccupied with this experience. It will be harder for you to feel distanced from these past events. You may find yourself feeling easily angry and emotional within current relationships. You may often expect to be let down and you work hard to try and prevent this.	You may get overwhelmed by the needs of others, as you experience anxiety about your ability to comfort them. You try hard to be a good parent, friend or colleague who is valued by others, but self-doubts make it hard to focus on the needs of others. You are likely to experience others as not as interested in you and this can lead to you working harder to get their interest. When others are distressed this can overwhelm you. This leads to defensive responding as you experience anger or frustration. This emotional experience makes it hard to be open & engaged.
Unresolved *For past loss or trauma* You had frightening experiences with parents. This might have included difficult losses or separations. Fear of a parent triggered incompatible needs to move away (flight) and towards (comfort seeking) the parent at the same time.	You are likely to still experience a lot of grief related to past relationship experience. You may find it hard to talk about traumatic events, leading to incoherence when talking about these. It is difficult to balance emotions, have good relationships and think clearly under stress.	You are likely to find that the distress of others can trigger fear and be emotionally overwhelming. Defensiveness will come either from the experience of fear of others, or the fear of loss of control with others.

Chapter 14

SELF-CARE, OTHER CARE AND BLOCKED CARE

This chapter will explore blocked care. Parents can enter this state when parenting the child is very stressful. Risk increases further when there are also other stresses in life. In blocked care, parents struggle to approach or enjoy their child. They are more likely to be defensive than open & engaged. An important protection from and aid for recovery from blocked care is how well parents look after themselves. It is this need for care, from self and others, that we will look at first in this chapter.

SELF-CARE

Self-care, ensuring that parents look after themselves, is a critical part of parenting children with relationship difficulties. Staying open & engaged with someone who is behaving defensively begins here. It is only through self-care that parents can build emotional resilience and enhance their ability to move out of defensive responding.

Self-care involves physical, emotional and spiritual care. Parents need opportunities to build their emotional reserves. If they don't have time and space to recharge their emotional batteries, then they are likely to run out of resilience more quickly. It can be difficult to find time for this. The demands of the children can be very time consuming. Time for self can feel like a luxury, but is actually a necessity. Only with time for self will parents find the energy to have sufficient time to help their child.

OTHER CARE

We all need others to take care of us at times, although the most self-reliant of us might struggle to admit this. The ability to turn to others for support, and the social relationships that surround parents are an important part of how they take care of themselves.

Parents need to have a good level of emotional support – people around them who are not judging them or anxious to fix things. Offering solutions to someone who is sharing difficulties can be frustrating, leaving the parent feeling misunderstood and with a deeper sense of failure. After all, if it was that easy to fix it is likely that the parent would have done this by now. The parent needs a listening ear, without his difficulties being minimized or his parenting being criticized. As he experiences this emotional support he might then want to think about what he could do differently. Now some joint problem solving might be helpful, but led by the parent.

With time for themselves and good social support, parents will find that they are less emotionally overwhelmed by their children. This also provides valuable protection from blocked care, and opportunities to recover from it should the parents have reached this stage. This will be explored further later in this chapter.

LOOKING AFTER YOURSELF AND EMOTIONAL WELLBEING

Dan Siegel and David Rock suggest a 'healthy mind platter' for self-care (Rock and Siegel 2011). They suggest that parents attend to a range of things that will improve their state of emotional wellbeing:

- *Physical health:* aerobic exercise increases heart rate and improves physical health. Opportunities for exercise can also sustain emotional wellbeing.

- *Focus:* periods of focusing on one thing at a time. With so many demands on parents it is rare that only one thing is being attended to. Without making a special effort parents can become worn down by giving multiple attention to multiple tasks. A conscious decision to attend to one thing for a period of time can help parents feel a greater sense of control over all the things requiring their time.

- *Down time:* allowing time in the day when nothing needs to be attended to. This is perhaps the hardest thing to allow yourself to do. It can feel far too indulgent to do nothing when there are so many things demanding attention. A period of doing nothing can, however, be restorative, and when tasks are returned to the parent can be more efficient because of this period of rest.

- *Connecting:* time to connect with others and receive social support. We have already considered the importance of social support. Understanding others around us is an important part of maintaining wellbeing.

- *Sleep:* getting enough good quality sleep. We all know how restorative a good night's sleep is. We have also all experienced the frustration of not getting this sleep. Aiming for good sleep, alongside good settling to sleep habits, is therefore important. Equally, accepting periods where sleep does not come easily can reduce the stress of these times.

- *Play:* time to be spontaneous and have fun. It is surprising how easy it is to forget about worries when focused on enjoyable activities and having fun. The problems don't go away, but time away from these can be very helpful. Problems can feel smaller when the parent has been able to have some time away from them.

- *Time in:* reflecting on the inner world. The final item on the platter is part of developing yourself as a reflective, mind-minded parent. If parents are going to be able to notice and understand the internal world of their children, then they need to be in touch with their own internal experience. Understanding and accepting this allows parents to develop compassion for themselves – an important part of keeping themselves healthy.

It can feel quite daunting when this list is reviewed. It seems a big ask to fit all of these things into the parent's days and weeks. All this and parenting too! However, attention to this can improve mental health and emotional wellbeing, allowing more time and energy for building the relationship with the child. When parents are spending less time combating stress it is surprising how much more time they have for themselves and their children.

A hard message for parents is to put themselves first, to ensure that they give themselves the care that they need and then they will be able to give their child what she needs. In caring for themselves they are ensuring that meeting their child's needs is a high priority.

WHAT IS BLOCKED CARE?

Continually offering a relationship without it being reciprocated can have a profound impact on the parent. Dan Hughes and Jon Baylin have written about this using the term 'blocked care' to describe the difficulties parents can experience when they are not getting enough back from the child (Hughes and Baylin 2012). Blocked care in the parent is closely related to blocked trust in the child.

When in a state of blocked trust children tend to withdraw from the relationship with their parent rather than approach it. They fear relationships and do not experience security in the parenting they receive.

Parents who are used to children trusting them and feel confident in their abilities to offer a safe home and relationship to the child can have the rug pulled from under them when trying to care for a child with blocked trust. Baylin and Hughes (2016) describe how a parent can be blindsided by intense negative reactions to their offers of love and care. This rejection can be intensely painful, a pain which the parent will reasonably try to protect himself from. The child's habitual defence against anyone trying to parent her can feel very personal when the parent becomes the target. The relationship can become lost when both parent and child have retreated behind walls of blocked care and blocked trust.

Marian is parenting the boys alone, without the support of a partner to help her manage the complexity and challenges that they present. She is particularly struggling with Harry. She approaches him with the best of intentions, but rarely do these interactions go well. She finds herself descending into anger and frustration. She knows all the theory; she has been given some good advice and guidance for how to help him and she truly intends to follow this. She approaches him in an open & engaged state, but within minutes she once more finds herself responding defensively. She is beginning to hate herself, and when she is very honest she acknowledges that she hates Harry too. She does not want to be with him; she is finding it hard to be interested in what he might be thinking and feeling; even in rare moments of calm and fun between them she doubts the reality of these. She suspects he is tricking her, lulling her into being off-guard, so that he can attack her again. She drops him off at school with a huge sense of relief; she picks him up from school with a sense of dread sitting deep inside her. She imagines not parenting him any more and then wonders what sort of a monster she has become. How can she want to give up her own son? She knows that Harry had a difficult start in life and when she thinks about this it does make sense that he might find it hard to trust her, but she cannot think about this. She no longer has it in her to feel sorry about Harry's difficult start. She is consumed by feelings of failure and pain, and a part of her wants to attack the source of these horrible feelings. She doesn't; Harry is safe with her. She shouts at him, but when she is close to losing it completely she removes herself. A part of her is doing what she needs to do to keep them both safe but the strain of this is coming at a cost. She is on the verge of a precipice, and if she falls there will only be darkness and despair.

Marian is experiencing blocked care. This is a normal response to a difficult parenting situation but it feels like the end of the road. Marian can feel no satisfaction or success for herself as a parent to Harry and this is making it impossible for her to keep giving Harry what he needs. She feels as if she is failing him, and sees no way forward. Marian is parenting Harry's brother, James, more successfully. It is this that is keeping her on the edge of the precipice rather than falling over. So why is Harry having such a profound impact on her and her ability to parent him? Why does she experience such failure with Harry? Why is she not able to keep on giving him the open & engaged parenting with PACE that she believes in and indeed sees working with James?

To understand this, it is helpful to think about a healthy parent and child relationship. The parent provides care to the child and the child feels safe and secure in this care. The parent provides caregiving and this meets the child's attachment needs. There is a rhythm between the caregiving of the parent and the care-receiving of the child. The child signals a need, the parent meets this need, the child signals satisfaction and soothing. The child develops trust that her parent will be available when needed and the parent develops trust that he will recognize what his child needs and be able to meet this need. In turn, the parent is feeling valued by the child because she responds to the care he is providing.

Harry does not have experience of a secure attachment with former caregivers. He has not learnt that he can signal his need and this will be met in a way that leads to him feeling satisfied and soothed. He has learnt a different lesson. When he signalled need he was met with pain and fear or with nothing. He has an insecure, disorganized attachment history; now he only feels safe being in charge, when he can control the relationship. This means that Harry cannot respond in a reciprocal manner towards Marian – that would mean being open to her influence, giving up control. Neither does he experience security with her that would help him to seek her support and help when he needs this. This means the rhythm between caregiving and care-receiving is lost to them. To Marian, this feels like a rejection – a rejection of what she has to offer, a rejection of what she is trying to offer. Harry cannot respond to Marian despite his love and need for her. To Marian it feels as if he does not love or need her.

This is where another layer of complexity comes in. Marian has experienced rejection before. Marian felt rejected by her mother. She felt not good enough as a daughter. Now she feels not good enough as a mother; it is waking up this previous failure. In addition she has had the pain of the separation from Robert, also waking up this earlier rejection; there is complexity on complexity. It is difficult for Marian to keep offering care to Harry when his response unwittingly wakes up so much pain and sense of failure. Her emotional arousal leads to dysregulation; her social monitoring system signals danger and she moves into defensive responding. Some strength within her stops her descending into full fight or flight and so she can keep the two of them safe, but her capacity to care for Harry is being blocked. There is an uncertain future, and without good support Marian could end up relinquishing her parenting of the boys.

In turn, Harry is experiencing Marian as frightening. When his defensive responding triggers anger and frustration in her, Harry experiences pain and fear. He knows how to manage this though; he learnt this lesson very early in life. Harry remains defensive towards his mother, and redoubles his efforts to stay in charge. Instead of a caregiving and care-receiving synchronous tune playing between them there is discordant defensive responding.

Marian is doing her best but she is low in emotional capacity. Her ability to stay emotionally regulated is being eroded. This means that she cannot provide Harry with the responsive care that he needs, but rejects, long enough for him to develop a more organized and secure attachment pattern in response to his stress.

Marian does have the capacity to reflect; her reflective functioning when not under stress is quite good. This is demonstrated in her care of James. Under stress, however, her capacity for reflection breaks down. She cannot then use this to inhibit her first reaction to the challenges that Harry presents. The failure that this invokes means that it is also difficult for Marian to reflect later about this. Without making sense of what she is experiencing it is hard for her to find new ways to respond to Harry. Even when she knows what she wants to do she cannot do it in the face of the stress posed by Harry's own challenges. Blocked care and blocked trust are preventing both of them from finding new and different ways of being together.

UNDERSTANDING THE BIOLOGY OF BLOCKED CARE

Knowing that blocked care is rooted in biology is a bit of a mixed blessing. On the one hand, understanding that this is a biological process can reduce feelings of shame and the sense of failure that parents often experience. On the other hand, this does mean that it can't be overcome through will power alone. Grit and determination to manage parenting better, as Marian found, simply doesn't work if the environment around the parent isn't conducive to aiding recovery from blocked care. Parents need social support and good self-care if the biological systems are to switch on again so that the parent can sustain the parenting attitude needed to help the child develop increased trust and security.

Dan Hughes provides a biological understanding of blocked care (Hughes, in Alper and Howe 2015). He describes the caregiving systems that need to be active for the parents to provide the caregiving experiences that the child needs. When the child consistently fails to respond with appropriate attachment responses – to be soothed and nurtured – then this is experienced by the parents as rejection. This is experienced as stressful and the parents' own caregiving systems become weak or unstable. Over time and with little back from the child, the functioning of the caregiving systems in the brain is suppressed. This moves the parents into defensive responding and impairs their ability to attune to and connect with their children.

There are five caregiving systems functioning within the brain that allow parents to care sensitively and responsively for their children. I will briefly describe these here; to explore this more deeply see Hughes and Baylin (2012).

Approach

The hormone oxytocin is released in parents to prime them for caring for their children. This facilitates the parents staying open & engaged with their children instead of becoming defensive. The drive to approach and care for the child is activated while the drive to avoid is deactivated. When caring for the child is very difficult, less oxytocin is released and the drive to avoid is more likely to be activated.

Reward

Social engagement with the child leads to the release of dopamine. This sustains the caregiving process as the parent enjoys interacting with and caring for his children. This is a reciprocal process as each enjoys being with the other; the relationship is experienced as pleasurable. Where this reciprocal process does not happen there is less dopamine and thus no feelings of pleasure. This leads to disengagement.

Child reading

The attuned relationship with the child facilitates the parents' deep interest in the child, and a desire to make sense of her experience. The parents can use their powers of empathy and mind-minded abilities to understand the child's feelings and needs. When the attuned relationship fails this empathy and mind-mindedness decline as the parents become defensive and thus are not open & engaged to the child's experience. High levels of stress can reduce reflective functioning, impairing the ability to be mind-minded towards the child. This impacts on the ability to make sense of the child's experience. Parenting can become narrowly focused on changing behaviour, while empathy and compassion are reduced.

Meaning making

Parents are drawn to make meaning of their experience with their children. At its best the parents will construct positive narratives (stories) about their children and about themselves as parents. This links with their past history of attachment and relationships, i.e. we make meanings through the lens of past relationships. When the parent–child relationship is under stress, parents tend to make negative meanings, as memories of past relationship stresses are activated. Under stress, parents are more likely to hold negative narratives about their child or themselves, which increases their defensiveness. They may view their child as 'bad' or 'naughty' and/or themselves as failing.

Executive system

This is the integrative centre of the brain that co-ordinates the functioning of the brain, bringing together all its parts so it can act as a whole. The executive functions allow for integrated brain functioning so that cognitive and emotional parts of the brain work well together. These processes are responsible for guiding, directing and managing cognitive (thinking), emotional and behavioural tasks. Executive functioning allows purposeful, goal-directed and problem-solving behaviours. Parents can regulate their emotions and maintain a caring state of mind towards the child.

This functioning is less dependent on the child's influence on the parents. Executive functioning will reduce under stress but if the parents have developed reasonable executive function they will be able to care for the child safely. However, without the other caregiving systems working well, the joy in this parenting is lost. The parents do the job, but experience no pleasure in it.

If parents have weaker executive functioning, perhaps because of their own history of being parented, this will be more of a struggle. Defensive responding towards children can escalate into parenting that is more frightening and harmful. Physical abuse, highly punitive sanctions or neglect of needs might occur as the parents respond to their dysregulated emotional experience and their fears and beliefs about the children's wrongdoing and/or their own failure. Despite the best of intentions to love and care for the children, the parents are behaving in a way that is harmful. This is not a time for judgement or for giving advice; the parents need support and understanding to help them recover a more moderate and healthy approach to parenting the child.

When not in a state of blocked care, parents can stay open & engaged with their children. Inevitably there will be times where they become defensive but they do not get trapped here. Shifting between open & engaged and defensive responses is a normal part of parenting, depicting the usual give and take of parent–child relationships. Blocked care, however, represents the parent being unable to shift out of a negative state of mind towards the child. The parent remains defensive as a protection against the pain of rejection that he is experiencing from the child (Baylin and Hughes 2016). As blocked trust suppresses the pain of loss, neglect and abuse a child has experienced or anticipates experiencing from parents, blocked care suppresses the pain of rejection a parent is experiencing from the child.

HOW DOES BLOCKED CARE DEVELOP?

Blocked care can develop in a range of ways, as a more generalized influence on parenting or in specific response to a particular child or current circumstances. Four types of blocked care have been described by Dan Hughes and Jon Baylin (2012). These will be briefly summarized here.

Chronic blocked care

This can occur when the parent has experienced very high levels of stress beginning early in life. In this case the ongoing stress means that the care system and the self-regulation system are poorly developed.

Thus the caregiving process is difficult to activate and this, combined with an underdeveloped executive system, makes parenting attuned to the child's needs very difficult. Parents are likely to need a high level of support and therapy to help develop these weaker functioning systems.

Acute blocked care

This can occur when the parent experiences a period of more acute stress that he is finding difficult to cope with. This overwhelms the parent's ability to cope, and caregiving is suppressed. Support at this time is essential so that this temporary state of blocked care does not become more enduring.

Child-specific blocked care

This is the blocked care that Marian was experiencing with Harry. As in this case, it can occur when a child has his own attachment difficulties. The child does not respond in the way the parent is expecting. In particular, the child does not respond in a positive, reciprocal way to the parent's care of him. This violation of expectations leads to more defensive responding from the parent as she feels rejected by and/or angry towards her child. This results in blocked care. Parents can be especially sensitive to this reaction to a child if that child reminds them of someone in their past with whom they had a difficult relationship.

Stage-specific blocked care

Children and adolescents can go through stages of being more argumentative and less open to their parents' caring behaviours. Some parents do well when the child is engaged and receptive to them but really struggle during these stages of more challenging behaviours, especially when they experience this as rejection from their child.

Marguerite and her husband have had a long journey towards adoption. They have had many infertility treatments, during which Marguerite experienced intense feelings of failure as a would-be-parent. Finally, they chose adoption as a more hopeful solution and are delighted to have 18-month-old Harmony placed with them. Harmony, removed at birth from her too young biological mother, makes the transition from her foster placement well. She is appropriately unsettled as she misses the familiar family she has grown into toddlerhood with. She responds to her new parents' efforts to comfort her and gradually she develops some security with them. Harmony does have some emotional immaturities, as all the changes in her short life have taken their toll. It is not until she is nearly three years old therefore that she moves into the phase of toddler tantrums. This takes Marguerite completely by surprise. She has become accustomed to her generally placid and cheerful little girl and isn't sure what to make of this new Harmony. She becomes very anxious around Harmony, an emotional response that Harmony quickly picks up on, becoming more distressed herself. It is only when talking to her adoption social worker that Marguerite notices what she is experiencing. She admits that she has always had a worry that she is not meant to be a parent, that her infertility is in some way proof that she will not be a good mother. Now she realizes that when her daughter is displaying developmentally appropriate tantrums they have greater significance. It is as if her daughter is pointing out her failure as well. Once she understands these fears Marguerite is able to respond to Harmony much more sensitively and the positive parent-child relationship is restored.

Additionally, some stages of a child's development might be more sensitive for the parent, perhaps because of the experiences she had at the same stage of development. When Ian begins to explore his sexuality during adolescence, Rachel initially has a hard time supporting him. She is uncomfortably reminded of her own experiences growing up in a family that did not tolerate her struggles. She denied her own sexuality for a long time because of this. Jane notices that Rachel is becoming very distant from Ian. Together they get through this. As Rachel experiences Jane's empathy for her difficulties, she is able to emerge from blocked care and experience empathy for Ian. This is not the only time that Rachel experiences blocked care, as her own struggles with her mother leave her especially vulnerable. We will hear more of Rachel's story at the end of this chapter.

PROTECTION OR RECOVERY FROM BLOCKED CARE

As explored at the beginning of this chapter, self-care is an essential part of parenting, although it is often neglected as parents put the needs of the children before their own. Parenting, alongside all the other demands on us, is draining of time and resources. Just coping with the day-to-day can be enough; finding time for a social life, recreation and relaxation can feel impossible. Yet without these things emotional resilience will drain away. Stress tends to fill us up until it overflows, impacting on how we feel and how we behave. Self-care builds a valve that we can use to safely release this stress. This increases our emotional resilience, improving our capacity to stay open & engaged with others and reducing the descent into blocked care.

Increasing your emotional health through good self-care will provide some protection from blocked care. Recovery from blocked care might need more intensive support from others. Many of the things I have already considered within this book can also be helpful. Here are a few ideas for further increasing self-care – for protecting against and aiding recovery from blocked care. It is worth emphasizing that support from understanding others is probably the most central part of this self-help.

Know yourself

As I explored in the last chapter, knowing yourself and especially the impact past relationship experience has had on you can be an important part of caring for children who are emotionally troubled because of their experience of developmental trauma. Reflecting on relational history, in particular early attachment experience, can increase self-understanding and make reactions in the present much more understandable. This understanding can help you to strengthen parts of yourself; for example, developing your need for connection if you have a tendency to distance yourself emotionally, or developing your capacity to soothe yourself when others make you anxious.

Develop your capacity for reflection and regulation

Knowing yourself and the impact of your history is a starting point for improving your ability to reflect and regulate, especially at times of stress when this is threatened. It is also helpful to be open to noticing and understanding day-to-day internal experience – your own thoughts and feelings which are neither right nor wrong. As with the children, this experience just is. Knowing these with compassion and without judgement can have a big impact on how far you are able to emotionally regulate when you are threatened by overwhelming emotion. This means being open to and reflecting on this emotional experience, developing the capacity for being mind-minded. Being open to noticing and understanding their own internal experience can increase parents' empathy and compassion towards themselves. This can reduce feelings of failure and hopelessness, allowing parents to stay in touch with the internal experience of their children. When emotion and reflection work well together the parental brain is strengthened, allowing more resilience to stress. As I will explore later, regular mindfulness practice has also been shown to be useful for restoring balance in the brain, strengthening healthy reflection and regulation.

Practise the use of PACE

The attitude of PACE allows the caregiving systems to work well, strengthening these and improving integration between them. At times of stress, if the parents can maintain an attitude of PACE towards themselves, they will be able to avoid becoming defensive and remain open & engaged with the relationship in a PACE-ful way. This in turn strengthens the parents' abilities to emotionally regulate and increases their capacity for reflection. Regulation and reflection both further reduce the likelihood of defensive responding and so an open & engaged attitude to the child is strengthened further. This can have a positive effect on the child, who will also become less defensive and more open to entering an intersubjective relationship with the parent.

This use of PACE requires the parent to embrace the mistrust the child is presenting her with. This has been variously described as hugging a porcupine or a cactus (Baylin and Hughes 2016). As these authors note (pp.90–91):

> We believe that the most powerful intervention for helping mistrusting children learn to trust trustworthy caregivers is to help caregivers embrace the child's mistrust. Rather than trying to redirect the child and eliminate the mistrust, the caregiver who can approach and welcome the child's mistrustfulness, greeting this part of the child with empathy and compassion, can create a window of new learning for the child, an opportunity to experience the crucial difference between past experiences with caregivers and the experience of being with a truly safe caregiver.

Understanding, connecting and being compassionate towards your own internal experience will build resilience and help you to stay open & engaged to others even when experiencing stress.

Seek out good social support

A range of relationships around you can increase resilience and emotional health. It is well known that social isolation is much more likely to be associated with people who are experiencing depression. As social creatures we need people; biologically our brains are designed to link with others. This is why not being able to connect to children can be so damaging to us, leading to blocked care. Social relationships are fuel for our brains.

Social relationships can serve a range of functions. They can offer practical support, helping out with tasks and providing some respite from the children. They can also provide emotional support; having people you can turn to, and talk openly and honestly with, is important for emotional wellbeing. Some people are better at helping practically while others provide a good shoulder to lean on. We feel loved by some people, whereas others are great for getting out and having fun. Different people will provide different things and we need a varied social group around us.

There are people to avoid as well, especially if you are feeling vulnerable. Try to keep away from people who are critical or judgemental of you, or if you need to spend time with such people make sure that you balance this with more people who can offer you unconditional support. The more people you know who have an attitude of PACE towards you the better.

Intersubjective relationships with trusted others can be very protective. These are the people who understand what you are feeling and thinking without judgement or evaluation. They can offer support, but won't be too quick to give advice, and they give you moments of fun and laughter. With people like this around, you will be able to withstand the stress of parenting a challenging child, and be able to stay with your own use of PACE towards that child. These are the people who can provide protection against blocked care and can help you to recover from this when it does arise.

Try therapy

Therapy can also provide support for parents in or at risk of developing blocked care. Therapeutic support offers the parent a non-judgemental, intersubjective relationship with the opportunity to experience PACE from another. This can strengthen emotional regulation while providing the parents with support to reflect on current and past experience and to make sense of how they are responding to this.

MINDFULNESS

One of the most promising interventions for helping parents and practitioners supporting children with developmental traumas is mindfulness. Jon Kabat-Zinn has explored how mindfulness practice can help people with a range of difficulties from depression to living with chronic pain (Kabat-Zinn 2004). In a study by Harnett and Dawe (2012, cited in Alper and Howe 2015), it was found that using mindfulness helped parents to reduce the stress they experienced when parenting their children. Hughes and Baylin (2012) describe how the practice of mindfulness can increase sensitive, attuned parenting. Mindful parental attention helps children to feel cared about and deeply connected with and therefore can improve the relationship between parent and child.

Despite the increasing popularity of mindfulness, which can lead to scepticism and concerns that all that is claimed for it is too good to be true, mindfulness is something to take seriously in our quest to find ways of successfully parenting children who have experienced developmental traumas. Dan Siegel has demonstrated that mindfulness can improve the capacity for compassion and intersubjectivity. This improvement is seen both interpersonally (with others), and intrapersonally (for ourselves) (Siegel 2010). This fits well with the DDP-informed parenting approach, which promotes the intersubjective relationships and the use of empathy and compassion for ourselves and others.

Mindfulness is the ability to deliberately focus attention on feelings, thoughts and experiences in the present moment and in a non-judgemental and accepting way (e.g. Kabat-Zinn 2004). The mindfulness practitioner notices his here-and-now experience without evaluation or efforts to change it. It therefore has a strong resonance with PACE, which helps the parents to notice and understand their child's emotional experience without judgement, evaluation or attempts to change it, and to convey this understanding to the children through the intersubjective relationship. PACE therefore facilitates a mindful approach to parenting.

Building a daily practice of mindfulness into a busy schedule does not have to be as hard as it sounds. When I had a particularly stressful time in my life I found that this was not the easiest time to ensure that I had 20 minutes available each day to do a mindfulness practice, even though I knew it would be beneficial to me. However, I noticed as I took my dogs out how much of this daily dog walk I spent worrying and reflecting on what happened the day before or what might be ahead for me on that day. I was so busy living in the past and future that I had no time to appreciate the present. I decided to approach my regular dog walking mindfully and a whole world opened up to me that I had been ignoring. This simple change to my lifestyle certainly helped reduce the stress I was experiencing.

If you prefer a more structured approach to this there are mindfulness practitioners who can guide you to learn simple practices. Alternatively, there are many resources on the internet. I especially like Dan Siegel's wheel of awareness practice (see www.drdansiegel.com/resources/wheel_of_awareness).

CONCLUSION

Children with developmental traumas have huge struggles to feel safe and secure in their relationships with parents. If they don't feel safe and secure they will grow up into adults who continue to have difficulties with relationships. The children do their best to live in a world without needing these. It takes a lot of strength, resilience and perseverance for parents to take these children gently by the hand and to guide them back into the world of relationships, to help them to discover that safety and security can be found there. There are risks along the way. Blocked care is something that any of us can succumb to, and there is an extra risk associated with parenting children with developmental traumas. This is a biological process that responds to the pain of offering a relationship that is not reciprocated. In this chapter I have explored how to understand blocked care, and prevention and recovery from this. This has brought us up close to the importance of self-care and other care. By putting ourselves first and ensuring that we are cared for we are actually putting the children first. We are ensuring that we have the resilience to go on the long journey with them.

Rachel's story, which follows, explores further the struggles parents can have with blocked care and the recovery that can be made when good relationships are available.

RACHEL'S CHASM: A STORY OF BLOCKED CARE AND THE POWER OF RELATIONSHIP

Rachel has hit a crisis in her life. Her birth son Ian is 15 years old and struggling with the pressures of an academic school. He failed his recent exams, a practice for the real thing towards the end of this term. He is anxious that he will fail these too and, as far as his mother is concerned, he is putting too little effort into his studying. As is typical for Ian at times of stress, he appears to be withdrawing from his mother. Rachel notices him returning to the self-sufficiency learnt early in his life, when she was young and struggling with post-natal depression. Rachel, supported by her partner Jane, has worked hard to respond to Ian at these times, challenging his avoidance by demonstrating their availability. Ian is now able to share his emotional struggles with Rachel and Jane.

This time there is an added difficulty; Rachel's father has been diagnosed with a terminal illness and Rachel is spending her weekends driving over to her former home town to help her mother. While she wants to be there for her father, Rachel dreads these weekends. She has managed a difficult relationship with her mother largely by keeping her distance from her. Now the old tensions have returned and Rachel is experiencing once again the disappointment her mother holds towards her daughter. She failed to provide a father for Ian, and in her mother's eyes failed again when she entered the relationship with Jane. Rachel is moving between the disapproval of her mother and the withdrawal of Ian. This is taking its toll; stress is building for Rachel.

It is raining on Sunday afternoon as Rachel drives home from her parents. The weather matches her mood as she focuses hard on the road. Deep inside she has a growing sense of disgust with herself. Another tense weekend has passed with nothing said between her and her mother. The disapproval grows with each visit as the unspoken remains hidden. Rachel feels like a teenager again as she experiences her mother's silence and watches her ask after Ian and Jane through gritted teeth. Rachel says nothing. She does not have the courage to raise the issues as she cannot face the need to defend herself once more.

Rachel shakes herself and decides not to think about it further. Her thoughts turn to home, but there lie more problems. She needs to get Ian studying harder; if he's not careful he is going to throw away the advantages the school was meant to bring. She wants to sit down and talk to him about it. Jane disagrees, and the rare arguments between them are growing more frequent now. Rachel had some hard words to say to Jane as she left on Friday night, words she regrets and must apologize for when she gets home.

Wherever Rachel looks she is troubled. She puts the radio on hoping music will distract her. As she gets nearer to home Rachel drives more slowly. She realizes with a shock that she doesn't want to get home. She feels no pleasure at the thought of her own house and her own bed. She pictures Ian, hoping to feel some sense of pleasure at the thought of seeing him. All she can picture, however, is his closed bedroom door. She imagines herself opening it, going in and sitting on his bed as she has done many times before. There is a dread in the pit of her stomach. She doesn't want to try and reach him any more. Right now, she is even struggling to care about whether he gets to university or what choices he makes in his life. What has happened to her? She cannot get on with her mother, her partner, her son. Who has she become? Silent tears fall down Rachel's face. She senses a chasm opening up beneath her and feels herself teetering on the edge of falling in. She knows this chasm; it is a familiar enemy. She plummeted to its depths when Ian was born and depression engulfed her.

Rachel experiences a feeling of terror as she feels herself being pulled there again.

Suddenly, Rachel turns her car away from home, just a few miles away. She heads for the beach and parks where she can hear the waves crashing and the seagulls calling. Rachel is lost as she sits there unable to think, unable to act. Her mind silently shuts out everything but the sound of the sea.

This is where Jane finds her two hours later. She opens the car and sits in the passenger seat, moving aside the mobile phone with her missed calls, unnoticed by Rachel. There is no acknowledgement, but when Jane pulls Rachel towards her she feels her body relax. Jane holds her tight and strokes her hair. No words. She knows that Rachel isn't ready for words yet.

Darkness falls and still the two sit together. Now they talk quietly. Rachel tells of her despair and hopelessness; she cannot be a mother for Ian just as she has never been the right daughter for her mother. Jane does not tell her otherwise; she listens and she understands. She was not there for Rachel before, but now she is. She will hold her and keep her from the chasm she is so frightened of. Rachel cries and Jane cries with her. They grieve all that Rachel feels she could not be, until the grief is spent.

Jane knows that Rachel is a good mother; she could have been a good daughter if only her mother could see her for who she was. Jane knows this in her heart. She also knows that Rachel will discover it again too. She doesn't need to tell her; this truth will come to her in time. Intuitively Jane understands this.

And now Rachel is ready to talk. Her first thoughts are for Ian. Jane reassures her that he is fine. She has sent a text letting him know that Rachel is all right. She has found her and will bring her home soon.

Rachel next wonders how Jane found her. Jane laughs, 'That wasn't hard, once I talked to your mother she told me how you were when you left. I knew exactly where you would be. You have always needed the sea when despair touches you.' Rachel expresses surprise that her mother had even noticed. Jane quietly comments that her mother sees and understands more than Rachel has ever realized. 'It will soon be time for the two of you to talk,' says Jane, but that is for another day.

'And Ian? How am I going to reach Ian?' Jane smiles again: 'It's okay Rachel, Ian is fine.'

'But he is withdrawing again. I just can't do it any more. I am going to lose him.'

'Rachel, he is okay. He is worried about you because Grandad is ill. He doesn't want to give you more problems just now. That is why he is trying to manage on his own. He has been talking to me, it is all right.'

'And I have been so horrible to you, how am I going to make it up to you?'

Jane looks at Rachel determinedly. 'You, my dear, are going to teach me to run. You haven't run in ages; it is time you started again.'

'But you hate running!'

'Actually,' Jane acknowledges, 'I have never really tried. It is about time I gave it a go.'

Rachel looks at Jane, a feeling of hope rising within her. 'Whatever would I do without you?' she says.

CONCLUDING COMMENTS

Rachel's story reminds us about the central message within DDP-informed parenting – the power of relationship.

Early relationships cause difficulties for developmentally traumatized and emotionally troubled children, but these are also the route back to safety and security. Children can experience blocked trust, fear of connection, and strong feelings of shame when early parenting does not provide them with what they need. Instead of responsive, available parents, the children experience fear, rejection and silence. They learn to adapt to this experience by miscuing their attachment needs as they try to take care of their own safety.

New and renewed relationships can provide safety where there was fear, availability where there was rejection and connection instead of silence. Children can adapt again to these new experiences, although this does take time and some children will always bear the marks of early experience in the sensitivity of their nervous systems and the fragility of their neurodevelopmental functioning. When parents can provide parenting that emotionally connects with the children, alongside the behavioural support that all children need, then recovery is a possibility. Parenting with PACE provides this parenting.

I do not want to minimize the difficulty of this, and hope the examples of children and families I have used to explore these ideas do convey the challenges that parenting developmentally traumatized and emotionally troubled children can bring. Parents cannot do this alone. They too need relationships around them that they can emotionally connect with and that provide the support that PACE can bring, alongside advice and practical help.

To make an enduring difference to the children's lives we need to establish therapeutic environments within which they and their families can live. This means the health, social care and education professionals surrounding these children all need to understand the trauma that these children have experienced and the importance of relationships to recover from this trauma. When PACE is built into our services we will all benefit.

I will leave the last word to Harry, James and Marian. I have imagined a day in the life of Marian and the difference that comes when PACE is shared by all.

MARIAN FEELS A FAILURE

Take one

Harry is ten years old and Marian is struggling with his self-reliance, rejection of her and need to be in control. Harry is struggling at school both academically and with peer relationships.

Marian puts the phone down with a sigh. It is only 10.15am and she already has a call from the school. She knows from the tone of voice that they think she is a bad parent. They think she doesn't discipline Harry enough. She can already picture the 'walk of shame' as she goes in to collect him later.

She does discipline him, but he takes no notice. Last night when she turned the computer off, after two very clear and firm warnings, what did he do? Laughed in her face and called her a fat cow. When she reminded him that this meant another hour with no computer he just raged at her. How often can she cope with him yelling at her that he hates her and she isn't his real mother? Maybe that is the problem. She isn't his mother, not really. The piece of paper is only a piece of paper. Maybe they shouldn't have adopted him. Maybe he was better off with his 'real' parents. Yes, they drank; yes, they locked him in the bathroom for hours. Is that really worse than this? Last night she had yelled at and then ignored him. Maybe she wasn't really any better. He clearly didn't think so.

Only 10.15am and she still has the phone call to her social worker, Jenny, to make. She knows that she must tell her about last night. When she walked into his bedroom and found that he had taken his brother's computer while he was out, the look of defiance on his face had just made her see red. She knows she should have stayed with the firm, clear consequences. That's what they had told her on the course, but his wilful ignoring of any consequence she gives him makes it feel impossible. She must tell Jenny that last night she yelled at him. Better she hears it from her than from Harry. She knows she came close to hitting him, closer than she has ever been. She won't mention that; the shouting is enough. She reaches for the phone, already hearing the disappointment in Jenny's voice.

Following the phone call, Jenny visits Marian. Jenny is frustrated at having to fit this visit in on a day when she has multiple commitments, including a report that must be finished. She is also concerned about another adoption breakdown. She has had a few recently and her manager has suggested that they look together at how she is supporting her families.

Jenny: Come on Marian, let's have a cup of tea and talk it through. It sounds tough; perhaps we need to think about some different strategies?

Marian: I know you think I'm failing him. Actually I think so too. I feel so bad about yelling at him, but honestly when I saw his brother's computer just lying there on the bed I was so angry.

Jenny: Of course you were. Marian, you are a great mum. You couldn't have done more for him. Yes, we have to think of some alternatives to shouting at him, but this is a set-back not a failure. Come on, between us we can think of a way to get through this.

Marian: And there is school. I have to go and talk to his teacher later. They might as well be wearing 'bad parent' on their top. I don't think I can bear another lecture from them about what Harry needs.

Jenny: He doesn't seem to be settling down at school, does he? Well, it is his support meeting next week. Perhaps that will give us a chance to think about what more support he needs in school.

Marian: Okay, but I'm telling you Jenny, I'm not sure I can take much more of this. I feel such a rubbish mum. Maybe he will be better off back in care. He doesn't seem to want to live here. I don't want to lose James though. If Harry went back into care, would James have to go to?

Jenny: Gosh Marian, I didn't realize it was that bad. Is that course not helping? I thought that it might give you some ideas for managing Harry's behaviour.

Marian: They just don't work. I am trying, honestly, but whatever I do he finds a way around it. Like getting on to a computer last night. He doesn't care about what I think. He just does what he likes. I'm not the mum he needs. He despises me and throws any authority I try and exert back in my face.

Jenny: Okay, but I really don't want to be thinking about breakdown with you. Harry needs a family, and so does James. And we can't split them up, they're brothers after all. I know this is hard Marian, I do understand, but I believe you can do it. Why don't you finish the course, and I'll visit a bit more often? Maybe there will be some more ideas that work better. We can think together about different ways of managing him. Maybe you need a bit of a break as well. Could your parents have the boys now and then to give you a breather?

Later that evening, tea is finished and James is out at Beavers. Marian thinks this is a good time to do something positive with Harry. Following her meeting with Jenny she wants to make another effort to get things back on track. At the back of her mind she is still worried that the children will be removed. At the course they talked about positive play, so she decides to give it a go. She gets out a game she knows he likes. Harry is interested, although suspicious, but it starts off well. When he starts to lose, however, he begins to wobble. He gets silly and starts messing around.

Marian: Come on Harry, you are doing really well. Let's see if you can catch me up.

Harry moves his piece so it is ahead of Marian's piece. He looks at her and laughs.

Marian: Now come on Harry, that isn't playing nicely. Let's put it back where it was. Now shake the dice.

Harry: I did shake the dice. That is where I am now. I'm winning.

Marian: Well if you can't play nicely we will stop. It will be time to fetch James soon anyway.

Harry: That's not fair. I'm winning. I want to play.

Marian: Well if you want to play, shake the dice and move it properly.

Harry gets angry and tips the board over so the pieces go everywhere.

Marian: Okay that's it, let's put it away. Help me pick it up.

Harry ignores Marian. Remembering her conversation with Jenny earlier, Marian takes a deep breath.

Marian: Harry, I didn't realize how important it was for you to win.

Harry: I don't care. I don't want to play with you anyway.

Harry kicks the box where it has been upturned on the floor and walks away. Marian tries hard not to shout. She picks the pieces up and puts the game away. By this time Harry is sitting watching the TV. Marian tells him to turn the TV off. Harry ignores her and remains transfixed on the TV. Marian walks up to him and touches his arm. Harry turns and hits her hard. Marian shouts at him and tells him to go to his room.

Marian: (As Harry walks away she shouts after him) Don't you want to live with us? You won't be able to stay if you hit us you know.

Marian sits down and puts her head in her arms. She wonders again why she is such a failure with Harry.

Take two
Marian puts the phone down with a sigh. It is only 10.15am and she already has a call from the school. The headteacher is sympathetic. She says she understands that Marian is trying her best, and they have seen some improvements. Today is not

a good day, however; perhaps it is time for the teacher, herself and Marian to think together about how to support Harry. They are keen to understand him better and to find some more successful ways to support him.

Marian hears kindness in the headteacher's tone of voice, but she still worries that they think she is a bad parent. Perhaps they think she doesn't discipline Harry enough. She can picture the 'walk of shame' as she goes in to collect him later. Marian is still feeling fragile from the previous evening. She hopes she can get hold of her social worker, Jenny. She wants to tell her about it, and hopes she might have some ideas. She is not sure she will tell her how close she was to hitting Harry though. The shame of that close miss is still burning within her. She reaches for the phone, fearing she will hear disappointment in Jenny's voice.

Jenny doesn't really have time for an extra visit but she knows that Marian is fragile at the moment and therefore decides it can't wait. She is feeling supported by her manager, who has offered to proofread her report for her so that she can fit the visit in.

Jenny: Come on Marian, let's have a cup of tea and talk it through. It sounds tough; tell me about last night.

Marian: I know you think I'm failing him. Actually I think so too. I feel so bad about yelling at him, but honestly when I saw his brother's computer just lying there on the bed I was so angry.

Jenny: So, you had banned the computer, but he just went behind your back and took James's computer from his bedroom? No wonder you were angry with him; he just seems to resist any authority you try to assert, doesn't he? How does that make you feel?

Marian: Well, like a complete and utter failure. It's like he doesn't care about me, or what I think, at all. I really think he would rather be back with his birth parents than living here. And there is school. I have to go and talk to his teacher later. They might as well be wearing 'bad parent' on their top. I don't think I can bear a lecture from them about what Harry needs.

Jenny: Oh Marian, this sounds hard. So, it just feels as if Harry doesn't want to be here, and that the teachers have no faith in you and that even I think you are failing. I know how special adopting the boys was to you, and how important it is to you to be a good parent. When you feel that you are failing with Harry it must really hurt. Well, it makes sense to me that you would be feeling angry with Harry when he doesn't respond well to you. It must feel like he is saying 'bad parent' to your face, and it must be horrible to feel that the teachers and I believe this as well. I know how hard you have been trying with these boys, but right now it is hard for you to imagine that you are a good mum or that we can still believe in you.

Marian: Yes, I just feel rubbish. I was so worried about you coming here today. I just feel like I'm letting everyone down.

Jenny: These are major worries; it's not just Harry and James, is it? You are feeling such a sense of responsibility. It seems to me like you are feeling all alone in this. We are not helping you, just adding another layer of guilt on you.

Marian: Yes, exactly. Everywhere I look I just see disappointment and failure on everyone's faces. I am so worried that you are all going to give up on me and take the boys away. Well if I'm honest, it is James I am worried about losing. If Harry left, I think I would be relieved.

Jenny: Marian, thanks for being so honest with me. I am sorry that I have made you feel this way too. I do have faith in you, but right now I know you can't see this. I want to find a way for both boys to stay with you, but you can't do this all alone. We need to work together. Let's see if we can unpick this a bit more. Can we focus on Harry again? I wonder what you are most angry about when Harry is defiant and rude?

Marian: I do want Harry to stay, honestly. It's just sometimes I feel so useless. I think that's what makes me so angry. I just don't know what else to do.

Jenny: That makes sense to me. I know how much you value being able to sort things out. That is one of your strengths – seeing a problem and finding an answer to it, isn't it?

Marian: Yes, I am always the capable one, people turn to me for solutions, but now, well I don't feel very capable at all.

Jenny: And you can't turn to others at these times? It feels as if you should be able to sort it out?

Marian: Well yes, that is what I have always done. Like with my brothers and sisters – they are always looking to me to sort things out. They always have done.

Jenny: I wonder if this is how you know you are valued – people turning to you for help? I remember, when we explored your own experience of being parented, feeling valued wasn't something you often experienced, was it? It makes sense to me that you would feel such a sense of failure with Harry. It's more than not getting through to Harry, isn't it? It's that people might not believe in you any more.

Marian: Well, I hadn't thought about it like that, but I guess it makes sense. I just feel so angry. Harry looks at me as if to say – see, I don't need you; I can sort it all out for myself. And then I get angry. I thought it was because he wouldn't follow the rules, but maybe it is more about him not wanting me. It is so much easier with James. He will talk to me, and I can help him when he is having a tough time, but with Harry it is another thing entirely.

Jenny: Yes, I see. Harry tries so hard not to need you, but for you being needed is an important part of being a mother. I wonder when Harry is being difficult and defiant is it like he is showing you what a failure you are?

Marian: Exactly, and last night it really got to me. Do you know I was so close to hitting him, when he looked up as if to say: 'See, I don't care what you think, I can get what I want.' I just saw red. I yelled at him and then I had to get away or I know I would have done worse. I went downstairs and just left him for the rest of the evening. I wasn't going to tell you, but it really frightened me.

Jenny: I am so glad you have told me. I know it doesn't feel like it right now but you did really well dealing with him and that big impact he was having on you. You protected both of you by moving away. I was hoping that the course would help you, but it doesn't sound like it is giving you any useful ideas.

Marian: I do try to do what they are saying, but it just doesn't seem to work. I feel like a failure there too!

Jenny: I am sorry for putting your name down for it. It sounds like it isn't right for you or Harry. I think it is just adding to your burden. I tell you what, let me seek some advice and see if there is anything else that can help us. I know this is hard Marian, I do understand, but I believe you can do it. How about if I visit a bit more often? I don't have any answers but I can listen. Harry is triggering such a lot of big feelings for you, maybe if we explore this it will get a little easier. Maybe you need a bit of a break as well. Could your parents have the boys now and then to give you a breather?

Marian: Yes, I think a break now and again would be good but I'm not sure they will manage Harry. Let me think about it a bit more. I do feel better having talked with you. Harry does struggle and I do understand that this is because of his early experience, even though I can't always hold on to this at the time. I think I can accept his rejection of me a little more now, but I know it will be tough. It will be good to be able to talk about this with you and to know you understand.

Later that evening, Marian decides to spend some time with Harry while James is at Beavers. She reaches for a board game, but then remembers some ideas about building relationships through play that she read about in a book. She raids her drawers and finds some straws and cotton wool balls. Harry is suspicious but agrees to play. Marian shows him how to play blow football. Harry loves it and they are soon laughing, but then he realizes that she has won more than him and he starts being silly. He then pushes the ball with his straw to make sure he gets ahead.

Marian: Heh, Harry you want to win so badly.

Harry: I am winning. Mine is getting there first.

Marian: It looks that way. Let's see if you can win without pushing it.

Harry: I didn't push it. I am winning.

Marian: I wonder why it is so important to win?

Harry throws the cotton wool balls down and storms off. Marian wonders what to do now. She calls him back but Harry just glares at her. Marian notices that she is feeling angry again.

She remembers her conversation with Jenny and notices how useless he is making her feel again. Okay, she thinks to herself, this is hard but it is not Harry's fault.

Marian: (Out loud to herself) Harry is finding this game hard. He wants so much to be in charge. Even winning a fun game of cotton wool football is so important for him.

Harry glares at Marian, but he stays in the room. Marian continues.

Marian: I guess Harry feels bad when he doesn't win. I wonder why?

Harry: I'm the best!

Marian: You really want to be the best. I wonder what it feels like when you aren't the best?

Harry: I am the best. Anyway, it was a stupid game. I don't want to play with you.

Marian: Maybe you worry I won't like you if you aren't the best?

Harry: You like James best anyway. I hate him, he's stupid.

Marian: Oh Harry, I didn't know you worried about that. Now I see why winning is so important to you. It feels like I like James best, and if you don't win maybe I won't like you at all. That is a huge worry.

Harry moves closer to Marian.

Harry: Can we play another game?

Marian: Yes, that would be lovely. I know, close your eyes. I am going to hide three cotton wool balls on you. See if you can find them all.

Soon Harry and Marian are giggling together as they take it in turns to hide the cotton wool balls. Marian glances at the clock.

Marian: It's time to go and get James now. I think it might be hard for you. It might feel like I like James more again. That is such a big worry.

Harry: James isn't naughty like me.

Marian: You both have naughty parts, and do you know I love those just as much as the good parts. I know I get cross sometimes, but I will try to remember your big worries.

For once Harry doesn't play up as they walk to the Beaver hut. He holds hands with Marian and tells her about one of his school mates who got into trouble at school that day. Marian knows there will be plenty of difficult times ahead, but she dares to think maybe she can do this after all.

GLOSSARY

ABANDONMENT

Children who do not receive the physical or emotional care that they need experience this as abandonment by their parents. This leads to continuing fears that this abandonment will be repeated in the future by significant people in their life.

AROUSAL STATE

Our arousal state describes how physiologically alert we are. As arousal increases a person moves from calm and reflective to increasingly reactive.

ATTACHMENT THEORY

Psychiatrist John Bowlby developed attachment theory to describe the bond that develops between a child and parent. This bond is a response to the degree to which a parent helps a child to feel safe and secure.

Attachment is dependent on an *attachment behavioural system*. Children have an innate predisposition to display attachment behaviours when they are feeling insecure or distressed in some way. The attachment behavioural system is activated, leading to the child seeking proximity to the attachment figure, protesting separation from that person and therefore seeking to use the caregiver as a secure base. This behavioural system works together with the *exploratory behavioural system*. This is also an innate predisposition, this time to seek novelty and new experience. It focuses attention on exploration and learning. These two behavioural systems are complementary; as one is activated the other deactivates dependent on current circumstances.

The way that parents respond to the cues or signals that children give about their need to attach or explore represents the degree to which they are sensitive or insensitive to these signals. From this experience the children develop attachment patterns:

- *Secure:* the attachment that children develop when a parent is experienced as sensitive and responsive to their emotional needs. The child learns trust in others and appropriate self-reliance.

- *Ambivalent-resistant:* also called anxious attachment. This is the attachment pattern or style of relating that develops when attachment needs are triggered but the child has experienced the parent as inconsistent and unpredictable. The child maximizes the expression of attachment need in order to maintain the availability of the parent.

- *Avoidant:* this is the attachment pattern or style of relating that develops when attachment needs are triggered but the child has experienced the parent as rejecting. The child minimizes the expression of attachment need in order to maintain the availability of the parent.

- *Disorganized controlling:* this is the attachment pattern or style of relating that develops when attachment needs are triggered but the child has experienced the parent as frightened or frightening. The child has trouble organizing his behaviour at times of stress. As they grow older children with these patterns of relating under stress learn to control relationships to force predictability. Controlling relationships develop instead of reciprocal relationships.

Within the insecure patterns, children develop ways of hiding and expressing needs in line with their expectations of their parents. This attachment experience leads to the development of an *internal working model*. This is a cognitive model of the relationship (i.e. a memory or template) that the child has experienced. This model influences how the child will respond to future relationships.

Children develop multiple models of attachment influenced by the range of relationships that they have experienced. The model guides the behaviour that they will display within the different relationships that they go on to encounter.

Through adolescence and into adulthood these attachment patterns based on multiple models transform into an attachment state of mind as the multiple models combine to give the adult a single more complex model to guide behaviour. Four states of mind are described which can be linked to the childhood patterns:

- *Autonomous attachment state of mind* emerges from secure patterns. The individual with this model is likely to have experienced a secure attachment relationship or to have resolved a difficult experience with attachment figures. This experience will help the individual to be a sensitive and responsive parent.

- *Dismissing attachment state of mind* emerges from avoidant patterns. This individual is likely to have learnt to distrust emotional expression and to value self-reliance. As a parent, this experience will make it harder for the individual to recognize the child's attachment needs, will increase discomfort with the child's distress and will lead to a valuing of independence in the child.

- *Preoccupied attachment state of mind* emerges from ambivalent patterns. This individual is likely to have learnt to use expression of emotion coercively to keep others engaged. As a parent, this individual is likely to find the child's needs overwhelming and will quickly feel emotional and angry towards the child.

- *Unresolved attachment state of mind* emerges from disorganized controlling patterns. Past loss and frightening experiences remain a source of trauma. As a parent, the child's distress can trigger memories of this early trauma meaning that the parent is unavailable to the child when needed most.

ATTUNEMENT

An emotional connection between two people in which one person mirrors or matches the rhythm, vitality and affect (externally displayed mood) of the other.

AUTHORITATIVE PARENTING

Parenting that provides children with a high degree of warmth and nurture alongside clear and appropriate boundaries. The children are enabled to develop autonomy (independence) in line with the developmental stage they are at.

AUTONOMY

This represents the degree of personal independence an individual possesses.

BEHAVIOUR MANAGEMENT

Behaviour management (sometimes called behaviour modification) provides a set of strategies for parents to use with the focus on changing the behaviour of the child. The aim is to reduce challenging behaviour and to increase prosocial behaviour — the behaviours we want to see children using. This is achieved through the use of consequences, sanctions, praise and rewards. In this book I use the term *behavioural support* to describe an approach that has a focus on relationships, building connection and helping regulation; the support for the behaviour is then provided in the context of the relationship. This is captured in the expression *connection with correction* (see also social learning theory).

BLOCKED CARE

In a healthy parent–child relationship caregiving in the adult synchronizes with care-seeking in the child. This is supported by five regions in the brain which when working well will help the adult to be a caregiver. These systems are:

1. *Approach:* the parent seeks connection with the child.

2. *Pleasure:* reciprocal process as each enjoys being with the other.

3. *Child reading:* the parent wants to make sense of the child.

4. *Meaning making:* the parent seeks to understand the child. This links with past experience of attachment and relationships. Parents make meaning through the lens of past relationships.

5. *Executive system:* this integrative centre of the brain makes all of this work but is less dependent on the child's influence.

A state of blocked care can result when the child is unable to engage in a reciprocal relationship with the parent. The brain regions (1–4) deactivate leaving only the executive system working.

BLOCKED TRUST

This is a failure in social connection. It develops as a response to frightening and painful relationship experiences with caregivers. The innate need for comfort and companionship is suppressed, leading to chronic defensiveness and a lack of social engagement. The child strives to be self-sufficient, keeping the caregiver at a distance through controlling rather than reciprocal relationships. This adaptation means that the child is not getting the social buffering needed to manage stress and alarm in the world.

In blocked trust five systems in the brain have adapted to living in a harsh social world:

- The *stress system* is chronically activated, easily triggered and hard to switch off.

- The *social switching system* does not move easily between social engagement and self-defence as appraisal of threat and danger during interactions is set very high.

- The *social engagement system* is suppressed.

- The *self-defence* system is activated.

- The experience of *social pain* is blocked.

CONSEQUENCES

Any piece of behaviour is followed by consequences. These consequences will to some extent determine what we do in the future. Consequences therefore can be used to help someone to behave differently. In this book I have called this use of consequences *coercive consequences*, as they are used in an effort to change the behaviour of the other. When the child is supported in a relationship she comes to understand her behaviour and the impact it has had on another. This can lead to feelings of remorse and a desire to make amends. The child seeks a consequence which can help her to repair. The parent can support her with this and thus the consequence becomes part of a collaborative process of planning for and making this repair. Thus in this book I have called these *collaborative consequences*.

CONTROLLING BEHAVIOURS

Controlling behaviours represent a need to feel in charge within the relationship. This is generally because the person fears a relationship which is reciprocal.

She feels vulnerable being open to the influence of the other so she seeks to coercively influence instead.

DEFENSIVE
When we experience physical or psychological threat we instinctively move to defend ourselves through a range of fight or flight behaviours. If these options are not available to us we will move into shut-down responses (dissociation) as a means of survival. These defensive reactions are governed by the nervous system, which can be sensitized to react more quickly for individuals whose earliest experience has been frightening.

DISCIPLINE
Discipline means giving another skills and knowledge through teaching. In childhood, parents use discipline to teach children about their expectations of them and to give them guidelines and principles they can use to live their lives. These are based on the parents' morals and values.

DISSOCIATION
This describes the process by which a person defends against overwhelming stress by cutting off from conscious awareness what is being sensed or felt. At its extreme the person cuts off from contact with others or the world, becoming numb, unfeeling or unaware. Dissociation reduces the ability to make sense of self or others.

DYADIC DEVELOPMENTAL PSYCHOTHERAPY (DDP)
Dyadic Developmental Psychotherapy or DDP was originally developed by Dan Hughes as a therapeutic intervention for families who were fostering or had adopted children with significant developmental trauma and insecurity of attachment. The therapist facilitates the child's relationship with his parents through the development and maintenance of an affective-reflective dialogue which explores all aspects of the child's life: safe and traumatic, present and past. The therapist's and parents' intersubjective experience of the child provides the child with new meanings that can become integrated into his autobiographical narrative, which in turn becomes more coherent. In this way the child experiences healing of past trauma and achieves safety within current relationships. The conversations and interactions (verbal and non-verbal) within the therapy room are all based on PACE and have a quality of story-telling. DDP is therefore an approach within which the child and parents work together with the therapist. The child gains relationship experience, which helps him to grow and heal emotionally as family members develop healthy patterns of relating and communicating.

DDP has a broader application as Dyadic Developmental Practice (see Figure G.1). This provides a set of principles that can support networks and inform and enrich parenting, and can support the child outside the home, for example in residential settings and at school.

DDP is theoretically based on the models of attachment theory and intersubjectivity and is consistent with the needs of children and young people who have experienced developmental trauma.

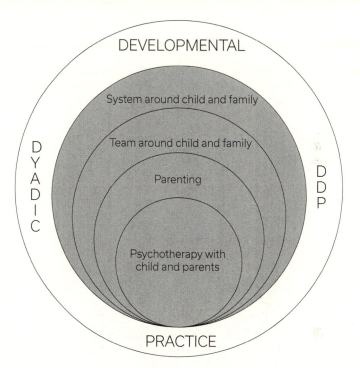

Figure G.1: Model of Dyadic Developmental Practice and its relationship to Dyadic Developmental Psychotherapy

INTERSUBJECTIVITY

In child development intersubjectivity describes the relationship that develops between infant and parent. The infant has an innate ability to co-ordinate her actions with those of her parent so that they are both synchronized. This is a necessary experience for social interactions. Children are able to emotionally connect with others, with their responses contingent on the response of the other. This is a bit like a game of tennis, when a ball is hit backwards and forwards between two players; each player is influenced by the other.

MENTALIZATION

This describes the ability to predict responses based on an understanding of the inner experience of others, for example an understanding that someone is upset by an event might lead to an expectation that the other person will cry. This is dependent on the ability to take the perspective of the other person (*perspective taking*). Mentalizing and perspective taking rest on the ability to think about our own mind and the mind of others, i.e. to have *Theory of Mind*. This in turn leads to a capacity for *reflective function* – the ability to understand why things happen and why people behave as they do.

Mentalization involves the parents holding their children's mind within their own mind and helping the children to experience the parents' mind within theirs.

One aspect of mentalization is the ability to be *mind-minded* – to be able to understand and take into account the mental state of another person, what the person might be thinking, feeling, wishing, believing, desiring and so on. When a parent can understand the internal experience of the child it is easier for her to emotionally connect with him.

MINDFULNESS

This is the process of bringing attention to experiences occurring in the present moment. Attention can be directed to internal experience, for example our internal world of thinking and feeling. Alternatively, it can be directed to external experience, for example to what we are seeing, hearing, smelling, tasting or sensing. When we are mindful we are living fully in the present. It is therefore difficult to be mindful when feeling depressed, as this tends to take our attention to the past, or when anxious, as this tends to focus attention on the future. Regular practice of mindfulness has been found to improve mental health.

NARRATIVE

A narrative is a cohesive story of real or imaginary events. The narrative is at the heart of story-telling. Discovering the story is an important part of DDP, as we make sense of the experience of the other.

PACE

This is the therapeutic attitude that is used within the DDP model to facilitate emotional connection. The attitude of PACE offers an unconditional relationship expressed through *p*layfulness, *a*cceptance, *c*uriosity and *e*mpathy.

REGULATION

This represents an individual's ability to control and modulate her level of emotional arousal. This ability to regulate is influenced by the experience of *emotional co-regulation*. This is the experience children need when parents help them to manage their emotional arousal. *Emotional dysregulation* represents a lack of regulatory ability. This occurs when an individual fails to control and modulate her level of emotional arousal. The emotional experience overwhelms the individual.

RELATIONSHIP REPAIR

This is a psychological term used to describe the process whereby one person in a relationship repairs a rupture that has occurred within the relationship. A parent can re-establish a positive emotional connection between herself and a child (attunement) following a time when the relationship was ruptured because of the behaviour of either the child or the parent.

SELF-ESTEEM

This describes how people perceive themselves and their abilities. It represents their sense of their own worth. High self-esteem suggests that an individual perceives himself positively, while low self-esteem represents a low opinion of self and worth to others.

SHAME

This is a complex emotional state within which a person experiences negative feelings about himself – a feeling of inferiority, not feeling good enough.

SOCIAL ENGAGEMENT

This is the capacity to engage in social relationships, being open to responding to as well as influencing others in the relationship. Biologically we are innately prepared to engage with others, but when we experience fear and trauma such engagement reduces. Within the DDP model the phrase *'open & engaged'* is used to describe a relationship where partners within the relationship are open to social engagement with each other. This is the opposite state to *social defensiveness*, when social engagement is reduced.

SOCIALIZATION

This is a developmental process of helping children to acquire the skills that they will need to engage in social relationships. This includes learning cultural norms and values so that the children are equipped to live within their own communities. This socialization process goes on through childhood and into adulthood, influencing behaviour, beliefs and the way that people make relationships.

SOCIAL LEARNING THEORY

This stems from a branch of psychology called behavioural psychology. Within social learning theory there is a focus on how behaviour is reinforced. The term reinforcement refers to the consequence to behaviour. This consequence can be a *negative reinforcer*. This is experienced as unpleasant. The person behaves in a certain way in order to avoid the negative consequence, for example a parent buys a child some sweets to stop him crying. The sweet-buying behaviour in the parent has been negatively reinforced. Alternatively, it can be a *positive reinforcer*. This refers to a consequence to a behaviour that is experienced as pleasant and thus rewarding. The person behaves in a certain way in order to gain the pleasant consequence, for example the child cries because the crying has been rewarded by sweets. The child's crying behaviour has been positively reinforced. Reinforcement, which is strengthening of behaviour, can be contrasted with *punishment*, which is weakening of behaviour. In behavioural psychology, punishment refers to a consequence to a behaviour that is experienced as unpleasant. The person stops behaving in order to avoid the unpleasant consequence, for example if a child was smacked when crying for sweets the child's crying behaviour would be punished leading to the child stopping crying. As punishment also leads to shame, feelings of low self-worth and doesn't teach the child what behaviour is acceptable it is generally considered to be a poor parenting technique. Parents are advised to reward good behaviour rather than punish bad behaviour. Social learning theory has less focus on relationship and emotional connection and therefore is not attachment focused.

THEORY OF MIND

This is the understanding that other people have their own thoughts, and feelings which can be different from our own. Theory of Mind helps us to understand other people and allows us to see things from their perspective. It typically develops between 3 and 4 years of age.

THERAPEUTIC PARENTING

This is a general term to describe any parenting approach that aims to heal as well as to parent the child. There are lots of different parenting ideas described as therapeutic parenting. In this book a DDP-informed therapeutic parenting approach is described.

TRAUMA

In this context we are reflecting on psychological trauma rather than physical trauma, such as a break to a bone, although they can overlap. Trauma is an experience of an event or events that involves actual or threatened death or serious injury to self or witnessing such an event involving another person. Learning about unexpected or violent death, serious harm or threat of death or injury to family or friends can also represent a trauma. For the event to be traumatizing the response by the individual is of intense fear, helplessness or horror. In other words, it is the experience of the event that determines whether it is a trauma for the individual. An event is traumatic if it is extremely upsetting and at least temporarily overwhelms an individual's internal resources. Such traumas can include extreme emotional abuse, major losses or separations, degradation and humiliation.

Complex trauma occurs when an individual is exposed to multiple traumatic events with an impact on immediate and long-term outcomes (e.g. war, ethnic cleansing).

When complex trauma occurs through childhood with early onset, is chronic and prolonged, occurs from within the family, and impacts on development it is described by some researchers as *developmental trauma*. This is a useful term to describe the experience of children who develop attachment difficulties, blocked trust and fear of relationship. The children can become *trauma-organized* in a pattern of highly controlling behaviours. When parents are *trauma-informed* they can help the children to discover other ways of being.

UNCONDITIONAL LOVE

Unconditional love represents a love that will be given 'no matter what'. When love is only given if certain circumstances exist it is described as conditional: I will love you 'only if' instead of 'no matter what'.

VERBAL AND NON-VERBAL

Verbal represents the use of words to communicate, whereas non-verbal is the way we communicate without words. Communication is generally a mixture of verbal and non-verbal behaviours.

ZONE OF PROXIMAL DEVELOPMENT

Russian psychologist Lev Vygotsky suggested the zone of proximal development to describe how children can achieve more when the adults or older peers provide them with support to do this. He describes the zone of proximal development as 'the distance between the actual developmental level as determined by independent problem solving and the level of potential development as determined through problem solving under adult guidance, or in collaboration with more capable peers' (Vygotsky 1978, p.86). In this book I use this idea as a helpful way for thinking about the structure and supervision that children need to support their emotional development as well as their cognitive development. Expecting too much of children is outside their zone of proximal development, while expecting too little means that the child is not in the zone and doesn't make progress. If the parent provides support within the zone, the child is likely to make emotional progress.

REFERENCES

Ainsworth, M.D.S., Blehar, M.C., Waters, E. and Wall, S. (1978) *Patterns of Attachment: A Psychological Study of the Strange Situation.* Hillsdale, NJ: Erlbaum.

Alper, J. and Howe, D. (2015) *Assessing Adoptive and Foster Parents: Improving Analyses and Understanding of Parenting Capacity.* London: Jessica Kingsley Publishers.

Baumrind, D. (1978) 'Parental disciplinary patterns and social competence in children.' *Youth and Society* 9, 238–276.

Baylin, J. and Hughes, D.A. (2014) 'From Mistrust to Trust: A brain-based therapy model.' *DPPUK Conference Proceedings Birmingham 10–11 Nov 2014.*

Baylin, J. (2016) 'Mistrust to Trust: The Neurobiology of Attachment-Focused Therapy.' Conference presentation, DDP conference, Glasgow, UK.

Baylin, J. and Hughes, D.A. (2016) *The Neurobiology of Attachment-Focused Therapy: Enhancing Connection and Trust in the Treatment of Children and Adolescents* (Norton Series on Interpersonal Neurobiology). New York: W.W. Norton.

Blaffer Hrdy, S. and Sieff, D.F. (2015) 'Chapter 9: The Natural History of Mothers and Infants: An Evolutionary and Anthropological Perspective.' In D.F. Sieff (ed.) *Understanding and Healing Emotional Trauma. Conversations with Pioneering Clinicians and Researchers.* East Sussex: Routledge.

Bloom, S.L. (2013) *Creating Sanctuary. Toward the Evolution of Sane Societies.* New York: Routledge (first published 1997).

Bowlby, J. (1988, 1998) *A Secure Base. Clinical Applications of Attachment Theory.* London: Routledge.

Dozier, M. (2003) 'Attachment-based treatment for vulnerable children.' *Attachment and Human Development* 5, 3, 253–257.

Erikson, E.H. (ed.) (1963) *Youth: Change and Challenge.* New York: Basic Books.

Fonagy, P., Gergely, G., Jurist, E.L. and Target, M. (2002) *Affect Regulation, Mentalization, and the Development of the Self.* New York: Other Press.

Golding, K.S. (2014) *Nurturing Attachments Training Resource. Running Parenting Groups for Adoptive Parents and Foster or Kinship Carers.* London: Jessica Kingsley Publishers.

Golding, K.S. and Hughes, D.A. (2012) *Creating Loving Attachments. Parenting with PACE to Nurture Confidence and Security in the Troubled Child.* London: Jessica Kingsley Publishers.

Hughes, D.A. (2009) *Attachment Focused Parenting.* New York: W.W. Norton.

Hughes, D.A. (2011) *Attachment Focused Family Therapy: The Workbook.* New York: W.W. Norton.

Hughes, D.A. and Baylin, J. (2012) *Brain-Based Parenting: The Neuroscience of Caregiving for Healthy Attachment.* New York: W.W. Norton.

Kabat-Zinn, J. (2004) *Wherever You Go, There You Are: Mindfulness Meditation for Everyday Life.* London: Piatkus; new edition (26 Aug. 2004).

Main, M. and Solomon, J. (1986) 'Discovery of a New, Insecure Disorganized/Disorientated Attachment Pattern.' In T.B. Brazelton and M. Yogman (eds) *Affective Development in Infancy.* Norwood, NJ: Ablex.

Meins, E. (1997) *Security of Attachment and the Social Development of Cognition.* Hove: Psychology Press.

Perry, B.D. (2006) 'Chapter 3: Applying Principles of Neurodevelopment to Clinical Work with Maltreated and Traumatized Children. The Neurosequential Model of Therapeutics.' In N. Boyd Webb (ed.) *Working with Traumatized Youth in Child Welfare.* New York: Guilford Press.

Porges, S. (2011) *The Polyvagal Theory: Neurophysiological Foundations of Emotions, Attachment, Communication, and Self-Regulation.* New York: W.W. Norton.

Porges, S. (2014) 'Social Connection as a Biological Imperative.' Conference presentation, Melbourne: Australian Childhood Foundation.

Rock, D. and Siegel, D.J (2011) *The Healthy Mind Platter.* Available at www.drdansiegel.com/resources/healthy_mind_platter, accessed on 3 May 2017.

Sieff, D.F. (2015) *Understanding and Healing Emotional Trauma: Conversations with Pioneering Clinicians and Researchers.* East Sussex: Routledge.

Siegel, D.J. (2010) *The Mindful Therapist. A Clinician's Guide to Mindsight and Neural Integration.* New York: W.W. Norton.

Siegel, D.J. (2014) *Brainstorm. The Power and Purpose of the Teenage Brain.* Melbourne/London: Scribe.

Sunderland, M. (2008) *The Science of Parenting.* London: Dorling Kindersley.

Trevarthen, C. (2001) 'Intrinsic motives for companionship in understanding: their origin, development, and significance for infant mental health.' *Infant Mental Health Journal* 22, 95–131.

Tronick, E. (2007) *The Neurobehavioural and Social–Emotional Development of Infants and Children.* New York: W.W. Norton.

van der Kolk, B. (2005) 'Developmental trauma disorder. Towards a rational diagnosis for children with complex trauma histories.' *Psychiatric Annals* 5, 401–440.

Vygotsky, L.S. (1978) *Mind in Society: The Development of Higher Psychological Processes.* Cambridge, MA: Harvard University Press.

ADDITIONAL READING

Archer, C. (1997) *First Steps in Parenting the Child Who Hurts: Tiddlers and Toddlers.* London: Jessica Kingsley Publishers.

Archer, C. (1999) *Next Steps in Parenting the Child Who Hurts: Tykes and Teens.* London: Jessica Kingsley Publishers.

Archer, C. and Gordon, C. (2006) *New Families, Old Scripts.* London: Jessica Kingsley Publishers.

Bailey, B. (2000) *I Love You Rituals.* New York: HarperCollins Publishers.

Bombèr, L.M. (2007) *Inside I'm Hurting. Practical Strategies for Supporting Children with Attachment Difficulties in Schools.* London: Worth Publishing.

Bombèr, L.M. (2011) *What About Me? Inclusive Strategies to Support Pupils with Attachment Difficulties Make it Through the School Day.* London: Worth Publishing.

Bombèr, L.M. (2016) *Attachment Aware School Series. Bridging the Gap for Troubled Pupils. Book One: The Key Adult in School; Book Two: The Senior Manager in School; Book Three: The Key Teacher in School; Book Four: The Team Pupil in School; Book Five: The Parent and Carer in School.* London: Worth Publishing.

Bomber, L.M. and Hughes, D.A. (2013) *Settling to Learn. Settling Troubled Pupils to Learn: Why Relationships Matter in School.* London: Worth Publishing.

Cohen, L.J. (2001) *Playful Parenting.* New York: Ballantine Books, Random House Publishing.

Davis, J. (2015) *Preparing for Adoption. Everything Adopting Parents Need to Know About Preparations, Introductions and the First Few Weeks.* London: Jessica Kingsley Publishers.

Donovan, S. (2013) *No Matter What. An Adoptive Family's Story of Hope, Love and Belonging.* London: Jessica Kingsley Publishers.

Donovan, S. (2015) *The Unofficial Guide to Adoptive Parenting. The Small Stuff, the Big Stuff and the Stuff in Between.* London: Jessica Kingsley Publishers.

Elliott, A. (2013) *Why Can't My Child Behave? Empathic Parenting Strategies that Work for Adoptive and Foster Families.* London: Jessica Kingsley Publishers.

Forbes, H.T. (2012) *Help for Billy. A Beyond Consequences Approach to Helping Challenging Children in the Classroom.* Boulder, CO: BCI.

Gerhardt, S. (2004) *Why Love Matters. How Affection Shapes a Baby's Brain.* East Sussex: Brunner Routledge.

Golding, K.S. (2014) *Using Stories to Build Bridges with Traumatized Children. Creative Ideas for Therapy, Life Story Work, Direct Work and Parenting.* London: Jessica Kingsley Publishers.

Howe, D. (2011) *Attachment Across the Lifecourse. A Brief Introduction.* Hampshire: Palgrave Macmillan.

Hughes, D.A. (2012) *It Was That One Moment. Dan Hughes' Poetry and Reflections on a Life of Making Relationships with Children and Young People.* London: Worth Publishing.

Hughes, D.A. (2017) *Building the Bonds of Attachment, Awakening Love in Deeply Troubled Children,* third edition. New York: W.W. Norton.

Karr-Morse, R. and Wiley, M.S. (1997) *Ghosts from the Nursery. Tracing the Roots of Violence.* New York: Atlantic Monthly Press.

Lloyd, S. (2016) *Improving Sensory Processing in Traumatized Children: Practical Ideas to Help Your Child's Movement, Co-ordination and Body Awareness.* London: Jessica Kingsley Publishers.

Music, G. (2011) *Nurturing Natures. Attachment and Children's Emotional, Sociocultural and Brain Development.* London: Psychology Press.

Perry, A. (ed.) (2009) *Teenagers and Attachment. Helping Adolescents Engage with Life and Learning.* London: Worth Publishing.

Siegel, D.J. and Hartzell, M. (2003) *Parenting from the Inside Out.* New York: Tarcher/Putnam.

Silver, M. (2013) *Attachment in Common Sense and Doodles. A Practical Guide.* London: Jessica Kingsley Publishers.

Staff, R. (2016) *Parenting Adopted Teenagers. Advice for the Adolescent Years.* London: Jessica Kingsley Publishers.

Sydney, L., Price, E. and AdoptionPlus (2014) *Facilitating Meaningful Contact in Adoption and Fostering. A Trauma-Informed Approach to Planning, Assessing and Good Practice.* London: Jessica Kingsley Publishers.

Szalavitz, M. and Perry, B.D. (2010) W*hy Empathy is Essential – and Endangered. Born for Love.* New York: HarperCollins Publishers.

Tangney, J. and Dearing, R. (2002) *Shame and Guilt.* New York: Guilford Press.

Taylor, C. (2010) *A Practical Guide to Caring for Children and Teenagers with Attachment Difficulties.* London: Jessica Kingsley Publishers.

INDEX

Italic names refer to case studies